# ‑⊸◠ DEDICATION ◠⊷‑

---

I dedicate this book to the love
of my life and my best friend,
Jill, and our incredible kids:
Bradley, Josiah, Gabriel, Andrew
and Annabelle. You guys are by
far my life's greatest adventure!

**– Pastor Chuck Ammons**

---

# LIFE IN THE OVERFLOW

A NOVEL BY

## CHUCK AMMONS

ISBN
978-0692733677

## CHUCK AMMONS
South Brandon Worship Center
4929 Bell Shoals Road
Valrico, FL 33596
(813) 661-2273
pastorchuckammons@gmail.com

# CONTENTS

# ACKNOWLEDGMENTS

My heart is filled with gratitude to so many people who have helped shape this book and who continually help to shape the man who wrote it.

To my beautiful bride and dearest friend, Jill: Next to Jesus, you are the greatest joy this heart has ever known. Thank you for your unending support, patience, compassion, humor and love for life. I love you more than I could ever express.

To my kids, Bradley, Josiah, Gabriel, Andrew and Annabelle: You make life an incredible adventure. I am overwhelmed with how much I love you. Thank you for wrestling, living room dodgeball and a home filled with laughter. I am so proud of you guys for just being "you" as you take the messy journey to follow Jesus!

To my mom and dad: I learned compassion and hard work from watching you. Thank you for believing in me and for always being in my corner. Mom, thanks for your unique sense of humor, too!

To my spiritual fathers, Len and Chris: You two have shaped my life for the Kingdom of God more than anyone on the planet. Len, thank you for your unwavering patience, selfless leadership, the countless hours you sacrificed to seek my best, and for continually seeing in me what I cannot see in myself. I treasure you as my spiritual father. Chris, what can I say? You are my hero and my best buddy, my mentor and my brother. Through plenty of laughter and tears, you've been there. Thank you for showing me the Father's joy and for constantly fighting for me to experience everything God has in store for me.

To SBWC - Staff, leadership of Floodgates, Overflow and members: Thank you for being our family! It is the greatest honor to serve our King arm and arm with you. To the crazy, abandoned sons and daughters of God who are exemplifying what it means to "sell the field" and run after Jesus: You inspire me. You make me hunger more for Jesus. It is such a joy to take this journey with you!

To Edgar: Thank you for seeing the call to write in me and being so relentless in your encouragement to see this work carried through.

To Philip: I wouldn't know an "Overflow" could exist without you. Thank you for continually walking in a rare blend of humility and fiery passion for the full Kingdom. Love you, man.

To all who listened and encouraged me throughout the book's development: You are amazing!

To Lisa Thompson: I expected to hire an editor. I didn't know I would gain a friend. You are incredible. Thank you for treating this project as your own. The Holy Spirit worked through you to make this work so much stronger. Can't wait for the next project, friend!

To Jeff Damm: I never saw a cape, but I'm pretty sure you're Superman! Thank you for the anointed vision you brought to the design of this book (inside and out). Your tireless and enthusiastic work has birthed something that matches the picture God gave me…and far surpasses it!

Finally, to my Daddy God: I spent a lot of exhausting days not really understanding your heart for me, but you tore the veil and this "messy kid" is slowly starting to see you. Thank you for being everything to me and for calling us to be with you and reign with you. In this dance called life, I step on your toes a lot, but this heart is yours.

# ✍ ENDORSEMENTS ✍

"Life in the Overflow" is a powerful book with an incredible message that everyone needs to read. Chuck is a gifted writer, but more importantly, he has something worth saying. Many people are content to just go through the motions but for those who want more — who want an abundant life or who want to make an impact on this world — Chuck has given some great keys to living a life that overflows with God's love, power and joy.

**Richard Mull**, *Author*
"The Jesus Training Manual" and "The God Speaks Bible"

...........................................................................................

Reading "Life in the Overflow" greatly affirmed what I already knew about my friend, Chuck Ammons — a very talented and well-respected godly leader whose light shines so brightly as a champion of God and the Christian faith! Chuck encourages us in this book to explore the delight in intimacy with Jesus and challenges us to make Jesus the "One Thing" that will endure all in this troubled world. A simple, yet thought-provoking read, this book is for those new to exploring their faith or for those of us along the journey who want a deeper dive and who need to be reminded of the power of stillness, active listening and living for all God has in store for each of us.

**Cindy Sofarelli**, *Associate Director of Donor Relations*
Metropolitan Ministries, Tampa, Florida

...........................................................................................

Chuck Ammons is a genuine lover of God with a huge heart. His life and love for people display his full surrender to the love of our Daddy,

God in a way that refreshes and attracts everyone around him. Chuck has not written a book; he has given us a window into the way he lives — a window into our intended purpose as children of God. I am honored to know this son of God who has given everything over to life in the overflow of God's love!

This book contains revelation straight from the heart of the Father. It will release rivers of living water into your life if you simply take the plunge. So with hands up and eyes wide open, prepare yourself to dive in over your head, falling more in love with Jesus after every page. I humbly recommend "Life in the Overflow" to every believer who wants to know the heart of God in a deep and unquenchable way. You will be released into the abundant life that Jesus came to bring as you read.

**Caleb Hyers**, *Author*
"Living in Dependenceville"

............................................................................................

I love stories about how people suddenly come to live with Jesus, how they explode from a life of running on fumes into the overflowing love of a God who has been pursuing them their entire lives. This is one of those stories, and Chuck's ability to be transparent and open draws us right into his experiences. He shows us that there is nothing greater than peeling back the veil to reveal a God whose love is bigger than we can imagine, One who wants to bring every part of us to life and transform everyone around us. He challenges and stretches us out of our comfort zones while inspiring us with the knowledge that we can! This book is for all of us who are not satisfied with a simple taste of God but who yearn to be so full of him that his love and power flows out of our entire being.

**Jesse Birkey**, *Author*
"Life Resurrected" and "Finding Home," www.jessebirkey.com

............................................................................................

I first met Chuck Ammons through his lovely wife, Jill, who is an amazing teacher and one of my sweetest friends. I just assumed that Chuck was the same. He is all these things but with a twist — he can slide easily into any conversation in one of two ways — intelligent humor and authoritative truth. I'll never forget the first time I met him, and he cracked this random joke in the hall as he helped other dads. For the life of me, I can't remember exactly what he said, but I laughed quietly about it for days. The 'Chuck' in real life is exactly who you will come to know in these pages. His humor, his encouragement to others and his convictions about the power of Christ in your life shines through every word.

About six months ago, I asked Chuck if he would be interested in teaching a high school discipleship class. He asked if he could use his own curriculum. As a principal, of course I wanted to hear what "his curriculum" was! As Jill sat sweetly at my side, Chuck bubbled up with a fountain of wisdom in front of me! Leaning back on his chair, in front of the cotton, lime-green curtains in Jill's third-grade room, he succinctly explained what you will read in these pages as he flowed in the power of the Spirit. I was mesmerized as "Jesus" goosebumps flushed my arms. My spiritual identity lens was challenged by the power of God in that moment as I am convinced Mary's was when she sat at Jesus' feet. I'm pretty sure that Chuck only thought he was explaining how he planned to adapt this book to a class, but the Lord wanted to do more.

As I have read through these pages, I have experienced the power of Christ in my own life with fresh intensity. I want my students who take Chuck's class to experience it as well. I pray that you will experience it. As you read, don't rush. Take time for the Holy Spirit to speak to you. You may experience healing. Scales might fall off the eyes of your heart. Let them! Let the Lord do the work. Like Mary, sit at his feet and listen. I promise it will be worth it!

**Danielle Marolf**, *Founder and Principal*
Wellmont Academy, St. Petersburg, Florida

# ⊸⊸ FOREWORD ⊸⊸

I love quality books and thus am reading all the time. I write many endorsements, prefaces, forewords and the like. When reading a book, we invest our most valuable commodity — our time. Introductions from various people help us undergird the certainty that we are spending our time wisely.

This is an encouraging and powerful read! At first, I deferred the offer to endorse this book to a later time but had second thoughts as I read the index and tasted the early chapters. Interest developed into intrigue, and intrigue sparked observations and "Voila!" the following came forth.

## SHARING NEEDS

The author takes time to share his walk and hunger and, yes, his desperation for something "more," a desire that we all have. His honesty is an invitation for us to join him in a search for the ultimate, the highest, the noblest. After careful reading, I came to the conclusion that "this boy's got it!" From there on, I was all in!

## GIVING WITNESS

In reading a book, one soon learns the difference between talking about a subject and living out the truth of it. The reader "joins the journey" with the author, and reading becomes an adventure as the author reports his discoveries with wide-eyed wonder.

## TELLING STORIES

Personal stories, sometimes intensely humorous, capture our attention.

This book is full of them, and we find ourselves vicariously enjoying them with him! As Chuck's stories turn more serious, we identify with his transparency and realize that we, too, can experience the same.

........................................................................

## PRESENTING PRINCIPLES

These pages demand your attention and guarantee a follow-through. You, the reader, will likely not be able to close the book when finished reading and forget about it. Our "wow!" experience will instead develop into an exciting episode as the author's passion becomes ours.

........................................................................

## A LONG, BENEFICIAL CLOSING

I thought I had finished the book but, Josiah's, Chuck's son's, report was refreshing, and the series of appendices are tremendously helpful. Don't miss any of these! Thanks, Chuck, for a job well done!

**Jack Taylor**, *President*
Dimensions Ministries, Melbourne, Florida

# ⤙ PREFACE ⤚

*""Ok. Here we go. No more putting it off. Today is your day. It is time to put on paper what God has placed in your heart. You have been called to write. It has been confirmed on multiple occasions. You **know** it. So...now what?"*

This internal conversation must have played through the corridors of my mind countless times over the last year and a half, only for me to wind up staring at a blank computer screen for a few awkward minutes before retreating into some other activity — any other activity that occupied my attention and pushed the mental "snooze" button for a few more days. It wasn't as if I needed something more to do. I'm married to the love of my life and a daddy to five unbelievable — and very energetic — kids, which means my home is full of plenty of "joyful noise" and activity. I'm a full-time pastor to some incredible middle school, high school and college students. I feel compelled to run toward more opportunities to preach the gospel, lead people into the presence of God in worship and minister so that people will discover the overwhelmingly beautiful love of our Daddy.

And let's be honest: even if I had all the time in the world, what do I have to share that anyone really wants to read that hasn't already been said, anyway? I'm the kid who, at 6 years old, shoved a crayon into my own nostrils during nap time only to have it melt there in the Florida sun. The same kid who tried to convince the doctor that the crayon became lodged in my nose when another kid threw it from all the way across the room! I'm the guy who only enrolled in college so that I could hang out with my friends and who completed so few assignments that I was asked by more than one professor to drop the class before I failed! I'm the guy who finally got his act together and felt called into ministry only to show up at Bible college without ever reading the Bible. I was simply there as broken and unprepared as I was because the God of grace said so. And in my heart, I have known that I am called to write for the same reason: God said so. I just didn't know what I was supposed to write...until now. I sat day after day, trying to figure it out, asking God and not hearing a clear answer until it finally hit me like a ton of bricks: I'm to write on the one thing that I cannot seem to shut up about, the one thing that I've been ministering in and sharing about for years — my journey from the hamster wheel of performance to making my residence in a place called the Overflow.

I'm to write about how everything in his Book, every miracle and every promise, is *still* true because God hasn't changed. I'm to write to urge you to dream again — to dig up that radical version of you that still exists somewhere, if only as a whisper — the one who believed that God could do *anything* through you, the one who would've charged hell itself with a water pistol, the one that you set aside in the wake of a flood of seemingly unanswered prayers or the constant "'to dos" of everyone else's expectations of all that you were 'supposed' to be. I am to write to tell you that the gospel, the true Gospel, is still bigger than we've experienced, that it's still a matter of power and not just of talk and that it is so much simpler than we've ever imagined. I'm to write to the tired, the frustrated, the weary, the lovers of Jesus who really want to experience "Christ in me, the hope of glory," but who cannot see through the fog how to live there.

You've experienced God in moments of your life like an oasis in the middle of a terribly hot desert. Maybe it was at a summer camp, a mission trip, a revival...but you've "tasted and seen the Lord is good" (Psalm 34:8). In that moment, you've felt his presence and grace. You've been able to breathe as he has lifted the burdens of guilt and stress off your shoulders. In that moment, you've believed again that anything is possible. Maybe you stayed in that place for a day, or even a few weeks, but inevitably, you slowly faded back into the "grind" of daily life and just "settled" for mediocrity while you waited for the next oasis. So life becomes just that: the grind of being faithful until the next waterfall in the desert. Without trying to, your walk with God becomes more about the effort of disciplines, plans and programs to follow, tools to add to the tool belt and manageable steps to be more faithful today than yesterday…but precious little about which to get excited. No adventure. No wonder. Just faithful and manageable. Maybe you've even come to feel that all of that "miraculous Christianity" and "changing the world" stuff is reserved for a select few who are really gifted or influential. I know the feeling because that was me. I was diligent and passionate and had tried everything that I knew. I didn't know if I could ever live under anything else but effort. But that was before this happened — before I found a waterfall in the desert that had a mailbox with my name on it. That was before I came to live in the Overflow.

# CHAPTER 1

# DEATH IN ROOM 120:

*How I left the hamster wheel of performance
to live under a waterfall in the desert.*

I never thought that I could live here. To be completely honest, I never knew "here" existed. For nearly 20 years, I would have defined my life as dedicated to knowing Jesus Christ and living as his disciple. I regularly read my Bible and talked to God...a lot. I knew the feeling of being moved deeply in my soul in worship. I did my best to walk in integrity because I wanted to please him. I had a "testimony" that included places where God had set me free of destructive habits from my past. I tithed and gave generously above that. I had served as a leader and pastor in several churches. I had two degrees from well-respected theological schools and 18 years of ministry experience, for crying out loud! I was the guy who helped other people break down barriers so that they could fully run after God. Of course, I was "walking with God!" How could my life be anything but that? Then, Naples, Florida happened — God showed up and took my theological boxes, my well-crafted spiritual formulas and my popular logical views of what he was up to, and he did the most beautiful and gracious thing that he could ever do: He gloriously **wrecked** them.

## "POWER AND LOVE"

I heard that a "Power and Love" conference was coming with Todd White, Tom Ruotolo, Bob Hazlett and other mighty men of God who were experiencing a life that looked like the New Testament. They were regularly hearing God speak to them and seeing him pour through them to bring healing and miraculous freedom to people everywhere. I heard a fire and an outpouring of God's presence and Kingdom flowed all around them. I believed that it was still possible. I wanted it. But I had to admit that in all of my studies, in all of the books that I'd read, in the countless hours of theorizing, preparing messages and counseling — in all of that, I wasn't living it. Oh, I had "a form of godliness" that was admittedly impressive enough so that others wanted to emulate it. But I experienced precious little of its power! I knew there was more. Deep down, I'd searched for it for years. Every conference, every book, every campaign was the depths of my heart crying out for more. It offended my pride, but I heard that these guys were living something that I hadn't experienced. So, almost impulsively, I registered to attend. I hoped that they would give me some practical training to add to my already bloated "spiritual toolbox" of methods and disciplines that I had come to call 'spirituality.' I had no idea what I was in for!

Todd White was not at all what I expected. This rather imposing man, who even had muscles that looked like they had muscles, stood unashamedly speaking about Jesus. To his very core, he was in love with Jesus. He was bold, yet unafraid to cry for the King who had changed everything. He was unapologetic about what was supposed to be "normal" Christianity yet walked in an arresting humility. He wasn't trying to impress us or make a name for himself. He realized that Jesus had already given him his name. He wasn't trying to hype up people or give them a program or formula to follow. He simply urged us to believe the real gospel. I listened in amazement as I heard this man connect intimacy with his Daddy in heaven to what he called "lifestyle Christianity:" just being with Jesus and taking him everywhere that you go. He shared story after story of not only the power of God flowing through and around him but also of the messy journey of being a kid learning to fall in love with his Daddy. He told us that we'd mess up, and if our eyes were on Jesus, it didn't matter. He shared about the amazing grace that waited for us if we'd just jump "all in."

God had been speaking this very thing to me in my quiet time. I had renamed our youth ministry 'Floodgates' just a few months earlier because I knew that springs of living water were supposed to Overflow from us when we fully experience life with the Holy Spirit. I had just never seen it lived out like this before. In that moment, all of my excuses were gone — and then they did the unthinkable and announced that we would participate in "Love in Action" over the next few days. We were to just go wherever we felt the Lord was calling us and ask God for opportunities to show his love — to do the very type of thing that Todd White had been doing, but to allow God to flow through our individual personalities. Todd White said something like, "Some of you are freaking out because you don't want to miss where God wants you to go. Ask him, but then don't overthink it. Are you hungry? Then go get something to eat! People everywhere need to see the love of God."

It was refreshing to hear that we should naturally flow as sons and daughters of God…but were they serious? I mean, didn't they know the "rules?" People like me came to conferences because we felt insecure and ill-prepared. Weren't we just supposed to be like "really inspired spectators" who hear the anointed speaker's insight so that we could feel better about ourselves? Then later, when the dust has settled, and we have figured out what to do next with this boatload of information, we can apply a little nugget here or there to climb our ladder a little higher. What were they thinking?!? We're not supposed to actually **do** anything at a conference! Where were my tools? My program? Where was my script to follow? They actually wanted me to show up places "unscripted" and just ask God to "give me the words to say!" That was insane!

I was the "leader" for our church group. The others who came from our church were looking to me, but I was now officially in over my head. I had no way of "working" through this one. I needed God to show up. We went on our first few "Love in Action" outings as a group and saw some fruit, but to be honest, I felt like I was just cloning some ideas that I had heard in testimonies, which felt unnatural. When our afternoon session ended, my entire group ditched me! One by one, they felt "called" to go with complete strangers that they had met to get a different perspective — and these weirdos were actually excited about it! I was thrilled for their zeal but had no interest in carpooling with strangers. After all, my mom firmly told me to never do that! So I started walking to my car, shrugging my shoulders in complete defeat when I heard that all-familiar voice that I had come to know as the Holy Spirit tell me: "Just go to your hotel room."

I started to argue: "But God…that's kind of the anti-assignment. The whole idea of this is to be around people, not be a recluse who avoids others so that I can quietly process my thoughts!"

The prompting continued: "Just go to your hotel room." I felt like I was being benched in the third quarter of the championship game, but I obeyed. I walked past the front desk and turned right down the hallway, head down, shoulders slumping. I pulled out the key to my room that faced the parking lot on the first floor: Room 120. I walked in, and the door closed behind me. It was the last time that anyone would ever lay eyes on that guy again.

## CROSSING THE LINE

In the room, I began to apologize and even complain to God. I wanted that life. Why was I so hesitant and afraid? As I talked, I put a worship song on repeat from the conference called, "Come Away." As I sat, I heard this: "I know that you love me, but you're trying to 'incorporate' me into your life. You care too much about what people think." Deep down, I knew it was true. I was only at the conference because I wanted another tool to give me more confidence and add to my already busy life so that I wouldn't make any more of a fool of myself than I needed to. I was very concerned with my reputation, but I didn't have a clue about my identity.

What I really needed was to die. I knew that the world did not need my talent or my charisma or my speaking ability or my wisdom. It needed to see a soul set on fire by the Spirit of the living God — an ordinary guy with a life that couldn't be explained naturally, someone with an all-consuming love for God that overflows into a love for them. Then people could say, "If God can do that for him, he can do it for me." The message cut me to the core.

I repented and asked God to show me who I really am and to show me who he is. My prayer was heartfelt and sincere, but I did not feel anything remarkable. I regularly experienced prayer times like this. Even so, I was encouraged and didn't feel quite as bad. Just before leaving the room, I saw a vision of what looked like a thick line across the carpet, and I felt a prompting, "Are you ready to cross the line, son?" Something rose up within me. Yes, I wanted to be done with carefully guarding my reputation. I was ready to receive my true identity and to give everything to really know God. I lunged across the "line" only to look up and notice that my curtains had been open for anyone in the parking lot to see this whole time! Only God knows how many people that I freaked out that afternoon, but strangely, it didn't matter. I gathered my Bible and notebook, turned off the music and headed for the door.

About three days later, I finally realized that from the moment that I left the threshold of the doorway of Room 120, something had noticeably changed in me. I saw people now. I saw the joy my Father felt for them and was encompassed in the love that he felt for me. As I walked down that same hotel hallway, everything seemed so much brighter now. I felt like a Christian version of the movie "Elf!" I passed by a maid and greeted her with an enthusiasm that screamed: "Hi! Look at you! I love the linens! This place is magical!"

I practically skipped past the front desk with the same goofy grin on my face and over to the adjoining Cracker Barrel, overcome with joy. As I approached the restaurant, I saw two elderly people, a man and woman. He was struggling to place his walker on the sidewalk. I quickly rushed to help and then struck up a conversation. I felt like I was supposed to ask them if they were married, and before I knew it, the words were out of my mouth. She replied that they were brother and sister, and as I helped them toward the door, holding it open, I told them about the special bond God was showing me between them. She went in with a smile on her face, a little beside herself as she observed, "Well, you just don't see that anymore!" Bright eyed, I walked to the hostess booth and happily announced that I would be dining all alone! I pulled out my Bible on the table and began to read. Something was different: I wanted to breathe in God's Word now. It wasn't a "chore" that I felt compelled to complete so that he wouldn't be disappointed in me. I wanted him!

## WAITRESSES AND SALES ASSOCIATES

As my waitress came, she must have wondered about me because by now, I could no longer contain my goofiness. I ordered my meal with so much enthusiasm; you'd think I'd won the lottery. In a way that was so much more eternally fulfilling than any scratch-off ticket, I had. Jesus said that his Kingdom is like finding a treasure buried in a field. From the surface, it looks like nothing special, but when someone finally sees what their everyday eternal reality can be, they sell everything to own the field. I didn't know it yet, but I had sold it all, and Jesus had become my treasure. Every time my waitress graced my table, I extended more "thank yous" than I think she'd ever heard. I found myself moved toward this daughter of God and sincerely wanted to pray for her. I also felt prompted to take a practical step of encouragement and tip her 100 percent of the price of my meal. I don't share that for a "pat on the back" but to demonstrate that I was simply a kid taking his first steps to obey. I told her how grateful I was for the amazing hospitality and care that she poured into her job and asked if I could pray for her. I was still unsettled about praying with her at the table, but it was progress. She shared that she was a double major in college and needed strength. As I left the restaurant, I asked God to astound her with his love and plan for her life along with abundant strength and joy to encounter him deeper. Though I'd just met this waitress, God's care and compassion flowed from my heart, prompting me to ask my King to make her dreams come true. Maybe this "Love in Action" thing wasn't as scary as I initially assumed.

As I approached my car, I saw that I still had a fair amount of time before the conference started again. Then, I heard God say, "Go to Family Christian and buy that Bible you've always wanted!" I started to question the directive as it seemed superfluous. I mean, I was already holding a perfectly good Bible under my arm. Wasn't it poor stewardship to buy another one? Plus I was in a new city, and I wasn't even sure where the nearest Family Christian Store was located. Was my imagination just playing tricks on me? I decided to check. Sure enough, a store was pretty close by. Although God had spoken and told me exactly where to go, like Moses, I hurried to come up with an excuse. Trying to sound holy, I argued with God that I needed to go to "lost" people, not more "church" people.

I will never forget his response: "Son, all people need my love!" In that moment, I realized that much of my "love" for "lost" people was really motivated by the obligation to see them "saved" instead of by a true driving love for them. I even put them in boxes of how lost they were. I could easily connect with a person who simply didn't know the gospel, but what about someone of another religion? Another lifestyle orientation? What about an atheist or a Wiccan? I had categories and rules to follow to engage each of them, but too often I failed to see faces. I wanted people to be saved, and I really did care, but did I really want to know the myriad of different people who daily came across my path? Did I really desire to love them like Jesus does? It required letting go of my judgments and performing a "cease and desist" on treating certain people as outcasts or even as enemies. Furthermore, in all of my obsession with helping people just "believe right," I failed to slow down, stop being the junior Holy Spirit, and listen to my Father with a desire to be his hands and feet and simply love.

God wasn't just blowing up the box I put him in but destroying the boxes where I stuffed others. He was calling me to simply see all people as he sees them — beautiful kids desperately needing to know the hope found only in him. How much simpler is that? Just love everybody, always! Now, I am no way inferring that lost people don't need to be saved. Of course they do.

7

Jesus is the way, the truth and the life. He is the payment for our sin and our only hope. But I wondered how much of my obsession with "encountering the lost," my planning of outings and trips and my urging for more training would be alleviated if I would just truly love everybody who God brought into my path. I needed to stop being in such a hurry so that I could listen to what he wanted to say to them. He is the hope of the entire world and every day, every moment, every person needs to encounter him. My Daddy loves **all** of his kids. I just need to go and manifest his overflowing presence to all people. That day, God started changing my idea of what a "mission field" is from a start-stop assignment focused on "lost" people to a constantly flowing presence to all of humanity.

Although I felt as if I was going just a little bit crazy, I quit protesting and drove to Family Christian. As I walked in the door, I immediately noticed a sales associate who seemed very preoccupied. I sensed that a burden was weighing on her. Immediately, the Holy Spirit spoke, "She's the reason you came!"

I wish that I could say that I ran right to her. Instead, like a little kid, I asked, "Can I still buy my Bible?" He responded that I could, and I sensed his joy. When I went to the counter to pay for it, she waited on me. I asked how I could pray for her, and she answered that she needed direction. I felt that I was supposed to pray right there in the store, but I hesitated because it seemed "churchy" and presumptuous. Besides, who was I? I had just met her. Even so, I didn't buy my own arguments. Instead of following the prompting, I made small talk and awkwardly exited. I was discouraged as I drove away and started to apologize to God for my lack of boldness. As I prayed for this daughter of God, he gave me a specific message for her. "I see you. I hear you. I love you." I glanced at the clock as I was already on the interstate on my way back to the conference. Just then, he prompted me again: "You have the phone number on the receipt. Call and give her that word." Now these instructions seemed more involved and awkward than if I had just prayed for her face-to-face. The beauty of it is that our God glories when his kids learn to dance with him. As Todd White taught,

I failed, but it didn't matter. My eyes and my heart were fully fixed on Jesus. I dialed and not surprisingly, heard her voice. I fumbled over my words. "Uh…this is um, the guy who just bought a Bible."

She interrupted, "Yes, Chuck!"

"Um…yeah. I was praying for you, and I don't know if this, um, resonates, but I feel like a burden of stress is weighing on you, and God, uh…gave me a message for you."

"Ok," she replied as her voice lit up.

I continued, "It's really simple. He just wants you to know that he sees you. Um, and he hears you…and he loves you." It was silent for a second. My internal dialogue kicked in: "See, I told you this was crazy! Now this poor lady thinks that you are some religious nut!"

My monologue was interrupted by a calm and quiet tone: "That was **exactly** what I needed to hear." She expressed great thankfulness for my call and obedience and said that she would specifically be praying for me. I hung up in shock, which quickly overflowed into a celebration of Super Bowl stature! I screamed and pounded on my steering wheel, thanking God for what he was doing in and through me.

## LEARNING TO TRUST WITHOUT OVERTHINKING

We went to the session the next day, and I was understandably more eager about participating in "Love in Action" time. As we left for lunch, I closed my eyes and asked God where he wanted me to go. I heard the name of the restaurant, Applebee's, and two specific girls' names, and I typed them into my phone's notepad. I quickly told my group, "I know where we need to go!" However, my friend, Philip, overheard me mention Applebee's and informed me that they were closed for renovations. I was confused but learning not to let it stress me out.

9

Instead, we went to another restaurant where we blessed our server with a generous tip and asked if we could pray for her. She was appreciative but said that she didn't have any specific requests. The prompting to pray with her wasn't leaving me, but I didn't know how to pray, so I just continued our conversation. I asked her how long she had been serving, and she shared that she had been there for two years, and exhaled a little as she looked down and commented, "I'm just here until I find out what I'm supposed to do with my life." It hit me like a lightning bolt — that was what I was supposed to pray for! I excitedly hit the table with both hands, startling her and the friend with me.

"That's it!" I announced. "That's what I should pray for!" I asked her if it would be ok if I prayed with her right there. She already knew that I was a pastor and wasn't sure how to respond but agreed, and just like that, I began to sincerely pray for her from my heart. I prayed about how much God loved his daughter and how I was confident that he didn't only have a great plan for her, but that he wanted to *reveal* his plan and his love to her. As we finished, her demeanor completely changed.

She looked at me and urgently asked, "Where is your church? What is the name of your church? If I am ever in town, I am coming!" I was shocked by what I saw in her face when she encountered the love of the Kingdom of God. I was becoming convinced that there were so many more people like this precious server who really hungered for the God of the Bible but who had become wary of Christians because they had a hard time seeing Jesus through the religious forests of our rules, quirks and sometimes, our judgments. As I was just beginning to overflow in his love for me and others, I was shocked at how abundant and ripe the harvest field really is.

After our afternoon session, we planned our final meal together, finally settling on Arby's. I thought back to the whole prompting for that note: Applebee's and those two girls' names. I was still a little confused. What was the deal with that? As I drove, I listened to the others share awesome stories from the last two days. I noticed the Arby's sign, and as I got ready to turn, directly across the street was Applebee's…and they were **open**! I flipped around the car, frantically telling them about my note. We discussed what else God might want to say to us. One person heard something about a blonde lady. I sensed something about a pregnant woman, but I was already struggling with what was happening and didn't want to say anything else. We sat in the galley area where all the servers come in and out of the kitchen, giving us a view of every server in the restaurant. Attempting to read each name tag, I probably looked like a creepy stalker. Twenty servers must have been there, but I didn't see the names that I wrote down.

I was so focused on finding these two names, I wasn't loving or encouraging our waitress. When I finally "let go" of trying to figure everything out, I realized that she was blonde. Then, she commented that she was forgetful because of her "prego mind!" As a daddy of five, I began to share about the joy of having kids. She excitedly talked about having this baby with her boyfriend. We asked to pray for her, and she was noticeably moved, saying, "Y'all are gonna make me cry!" She told us that her back had been in pain during the pregnancy. We prayed for healing, and a new revelation of God's love for her. The dad in me felt every word as I asked for her son to discover and live out all of God's plans for him. As we prepared to leave, we asked if she knew anybody with the "mystery names," but she didn't. Nonetheless, we knew that we were on assignment at Applebee's. You can't make this stuff up!

During the final session, I asked God, "Who are those two girls?"

He immediately floored me with his response. "They were two of the most gifted and vibrant leaders you've led in youth ministry." I hadn't put it together before, but he was right. These two youth had unique leadership abilities and personalities and stood out among many during my 18 years of youth ministry. They were very similar to one another…and to this waitress! Now that God had my attention, he showed me that both had

11

struggled deeply with their identity, relationships and purity. I knew that he wanted me to pray for this waitress and both of these precious former youth to know who he is and how wonderfully he sees them. I prayed for their futures, their families and a fresh revelation of himself for all of them with a heart full of love for my God.

## WHY DON'T WE SEE IT HERE?

I prepared for the three-hour trip home after the whirlwind of the last two days, but God had one more exclamation point to add to this new adventure. Bob Hazlett led a powerful final session and at the end, he called out some specific ailments: Fibromyalgia. Multiple sclerosis. Respiratory issues. COPD. Knee problems. He challenged the attendees to be the hands and feet of Jesus and to pray over those who responded. My friends, the crazy men of God who came with me, lunged out of their seats without reservation and dispersed across the auditorium to pray in a beautiful and emotional display. They were walking in their identity. I watched their compassion and authority and was so proud to know them. I was excited to pray as well, but tentatively asked God, "What about me? Where do you want me to go?"

He responded, "You need to pray over a bad back." The phrase was clear and interesting: *"bad back."*

"Ok," I thought. "I will wait until they call people with back problems forward." After all, people often struggle with back ailments, and many other infirmities had been listed. But then, just like that, the service abruptly ended with the simple charge to take some time and minister to those around the room. I didn't understand. After all that God had shown me through the weekend, it seemed silly to ask, but, had I missed it?

I waited a moment or two but didn't hear anything further, so I decided to locate my friends and tell them goodbye since we were traveling separately. Navigating through the clusters of people praying across the auditorium proved difficult, but I smiled at the beautiful chaos. However, I found all of my friends except one. As I tried to locate him, I felt a tap on my shoulder. A lady asked, "Excuse me. Do you happen to have a bad back?" Needless to say, she had my full attention.

"No," I answered, "But I am supposed to pray over someone with a bad back." Her eyes lit up, and she frantically pointed to someone nearby. Between her tears, this sweet woman announced, "That's me!"

She shared that she had discs missing from her back. She had been to multiple doctors and had tried everything. She wasn't even supposed to attend this conference, but her friend invited her. As she talked, I felt overwhelmed in the natural, but I sensed in my spirit: "The same God who is the architect who built her back from nothing has no problem recreating it. A creative miracle is easy for Jesus." I voiced a simple but sincere prayer. Nothing. All of the pain remained.

Still crying, she started to take false responsibility: "I know it is because I must be doubting." As she spoke, I felt strongly prompted to minister the truth about the love of God. I prayed again, as compassion deeply flooded me for her. I longed for this woman to be healed. I even quietly pleaded with God that if I were hindering his working that he would bring someone else to her who better understood healing. Once again, God began leading me in a strange direction. I was learning that he often tells us things that only make sense when we share these impressions. This time, I strongly sensed that I needed to ask her husband what he thought about this. I hoped that I wasn't hearing correctly.

Her husband awkwardly leaned away from us against the front platform, making an imposing figure. He stood with his arms crossed and looked as though he just wanted to hurt somebody. I thought, "Thanks, but no thanks, Lord. I'm willing to give my life for you, but I'd rather not do it tonight." I already felt, as the song says, "deeper than my feet could ever wander,"[1] and now, my God was calling me to ask a man who loved his wife, as she continued to cry, what he thought about my strange prayers and promptings that, to this point, had yielded no outward improvement. I prayed for the rapture, but when I opened my eyes, and we were all still there, I hesitantly obeyed. "Excuse me, sir. You are her husband, right? I, uh…know this might be a little weird, but as I prayed, I kept hearing that I needed to ask you what you're thinking right now."

He stepped forward inquisitively: "What I'm thinking about???"

His wife tried to rescue us: "My back. What you're thinking about my back."

But that wasn't it. "Nope," I answered. "Just what you're thinking. What are you feeling right now?" Yep. I was asking this man's man about his feelings. He stepped forward, uncrossing his arms. I braced for impact.

But then he broke down, speaking tenderly and emotionally: "I just want her to experience what I'm experiencing with God." As he spoke, God showed me places to pray over their marriage. I asked them to join hands and placed mine on top and began to pray with boldness and conviction. I sensed that she was going to wake in the morning with no back pain, but at this moment, God was at work doing so much more than healing her back. I felt that it was exactly what they needed, but my knowledge and programs never could've led me to minister in that direction. It took God speaking to a spiritual toddler who was just crazy enough to listen.

I rushed home and began to tell my wife and kids about all that God had done and the life that was available. I told them how God sees us as his sons and daughters and how he wants that intimacy with us. I shared what happened to me and what I had seen in several hundred other crazy children of God. I shared how the promises of God didn't have an expiration date: that he was **still** the same awe-inspiring, miracle-working, currently speaking, ever-present God that he was in Bible. And I told them that other than just continuing to sit at my Daddy's feet in intimacy, I had no clue of what that looked like. As I finished, I experienced one of those "out of the mouths of babes" moments from my 10-year-old son, Bradley. With too much innocence to recognize the potentially scathing rebuke in his words, he asked, "Dad...how come I hear these great stories of how God moves in these big ways at conferences and retreats you go to, but we never see it here in everyday life?" Ouch! A form of godliness, but no power. Good morals, but no urgent life-changing mission to give up everything for. He didn't mean it as a correction, but I had modeled the goodness of Christ without his power, his hope. I think he realized by the look on my face that his question might have been over the line: "How come we don't see it here?"

He prepared to apologize, but before he could, a smile came across my face, and I told him what would have been impossible to say two days earlier: "We will, son. Oh, we **will**."

##  COME AWAY

Come away with me. Come away with me.

It's never too late. It's not too late. It's not too late for you.

I have a plan for you. I have a plan for you.

It's gonna be wild. It's gonna be great. It's gonna be full of me.

So, open up your heart and let me in.

## QUESTIONS:

1. What emotions did you experience as you read through this chapter? What could you relate to? What did you read in Chuck's story that you want God to release in your life?

2. Chuck shared the key hindrance that kept him from a life of full abandon to God: guarding his reputation. Are there any hindrances, such as fear, pride, lust, jealousy/anger, religious traditions or others, that keep you from following God with full abandon? What are they?

3. What positive words and qualities would you like used to describe your walk with God? Take a few minutes right now and ask the Holy Spirit to make these attributes a reality in your walk with him! If you need some suggestions, look at Galatians 5:22, 23.

## CHAPTER 2

# HOPE
# COMES HOME

After the powerful way that God showed up at the conference, I was excited but honestly feeling a little nervous. I had left a lot of conferences "fired up" to live out the transformation at home that I had experienced only to watch it eventually fizzle without true sustained change. Nonetheless, something about this — something about **me** — felt different. I wasn't trusting in a conference or following a complex blueprint of steps for success. I was simply waking up every morning and taking seriously the charge of Jesus in John 15, one of my favorite passages that was suddenly laden with new meaning:

"I am the vine. You are the branches. Abide in me and you will
bear much fruit. Apart from me, you can do nothing"
John 15:5
(Loose paraphrase by author).

Branches don't have their own life-giving value. Branches — whether isolated or connected — can't hold branch-strategy conferences to figure out ways for producing grapes through their own effort or wisdom.

Branches don't grow grapes. Vines do. Branches are simply the joyous carriers that deliver the fruit because of their connection to the vine. Just as an isolated branch cannot bear fruit but can only eventually dry up and wither away, a connected, healthy branch cannot fail to deliver fruit. All fruit-bearing comes from the vine — the mastermind, the producer and the deliverer. The only responsibility of the branch is to abide in the vine, and if the branch abides, it has to bear fruit!

The Greek word for abide, "meno,"[3] is a beautifully complex word that means to remain, to stay, to endure — to stay in tough times. It means to wait — to choose to stay even when you'd really like things to move at a different pace or direction. Most significantly, "meno" means to dwell somewhere and not depart — the difference between occasionally staying overnight in a hotel for a business trip and the home where you've unpacked all your stuff because you live there. I have often amped up the intensity of my daily walk with Jesus because I encountered a situation where I felt I "really" needed to make a difference for him: a mission trip or breakthrough desperately needed for a loved one or a lost acquaintance with whom I needed to share the gospel. I left my place of comfort to really bear fruit for the Kingdom. I wonder how that looks any different from the businessman who unpacks his bag for an overnight stay and makes the necessary sacrifices because he knows that tomorrow, when his task is done, he can go home. I wonder how many nights I was content to live with self and its merited wisdom only to visit Jesus in the land of fruit-bearing when a crisis overwhelmed me. But now that I'd tasted and seen how amazingly good he is, how could I ever go back?

We are such restless beings — obsessed with progress and the supposed worth it gives us. We exhaust ourselves to accomplish the next objective, to climb the next rung of the ladder, to clear the next hurdle. But what if Jesus doesn't want us to run or to accomplish or to produce? What if that's **his** job, and our job is to live with him so that when he moves, we get to go with him? What if it's supposed to be easy, not burdensome? What if all that he wants is just for us to be a branch and to learn how to live in his presence and stay — no matter what comes, even when he is growing and stretching us out of our comfort zones? Even when he is putting us through the uncomfortable process of pruning away what's dead and what doesn't belong anymore? Even as we learn to not cling to the dead stuff but just to sit at his feet and stay, recognizing that all we are on our own is just a brittle branch, but that we've been invited into a supernatural relationship that courses life through our very veins and allows us to participate in the impossible? We're not called to be vines. We're just branches, and he said that any branch that would stay will bear fruit. It doesn't matter what side of the tracks you grew up on or how far you went in school. It doesn't matter what color your skin is or how many zeroes you have in your salary. It doesn't matter whether you think you're talented or awkward; dynamic or shy; level headed or a "hot mess." You have been invited to live connected to the vine who is the source of all life, and if you say "yes" to his invitation and choose to remain there, you **will** bear fruit!

I am coming to understand, though, that the opposite is also true. We live in an age of greater leadership development and resources than ever before. Never in history have people been able to glean so quickly and so completely from the brightest minds of virtually every field of thought. We have conferences, colleges, tools and training seminars. And we can exhaust ourselves looking for the next key to success. But here's the point: you were made to know God and through him to bear fruit, and while your work and effort can produce a lot of fans and perhaps some applause, it can never bear fruit. Fruit only comes from the vine, and you are just a branch. Dress it up in a suit, make it a great public speaker, let it use really big, impressive words and earn lots of money: it's still just a branch. Our only hope of living a fruitful life comes from the supernatural exchange that occurs when we learn how to live and stay in Jesus' presence.

I didn't have a lot of answers, but in the days after the conference one thing was clear. If I did nothing else, I was going to live in my Father's presence and learn what it meant to truly abide. I remember waking up every morning and just smiling from ear to ear before my eyes even fully opened. It was a new day, and I was grateful to be alive. Tears of joy often welled up in my eyes, spilling over at the most inopportune times. I had never been a crier before. In fact, my wife could count on one hand the number of times that she had seen me break down in tears, but she cannot say that anymore! Once God overwhelms you, his presence comes out, one way or another! I don't apologize for my expression of joyous gratitude that often surfaces in tear-filled emotions. A heart for my Daddy is alive and beating within me.

I began to ask God to make this abiding life a reality for my family. It had taken me 35 years just to begin to see the simplicity of the gospel. Now let me make this clear: when someone walks into the abiding life that Jesus purchased, your age matters very little. All that matters is that you're there! I didn't need to live another second, regretting that my arrival to this place had been delayed by my need to perform. That was my past, and like the Apostle Paul, I was letting go of what was behind me to press on to where my Daddy was presently calling me (Philippians 3:13). That said, I didn't see any reason why my 8- and 10–year-old sons, who had already asked Jesus to be their Savior, couldn't run and play and live in this same place that I had recently discovered. After all, he said that he hid the Kingdom from those who thought they were wise and learned but joyfully revealed it to "little kids." Yep, my sons qualified for that.

One night after dinner, I asked my boys if they wanted to understand and truly "hear" the Holy Spirit speaking to them. They eagerly did. We prayed a simple prayer that lasted no more than 30 seconds.

A few minutes later, my 8-year-old son, Josiah, came to me, looking confused. Scratching his head, he asked, "Dad, do we have a neighbor named Joy?"

I responded, just as confused: "Nope, bud. I don't know anybody named Joy on our street. Why?" He proceeded to tell me that, for the last few minutes, he had been hearing the word "Joy" repeated in his head. That made sense to me. As an incredibly creative and dynamic kid, Josiah has the energy of a tornado, but at the time, he had been struggling a lot with discouragement and a poor self-image. My wife, Jill, and I had been praying that the Lord would show him who he is and lift the burdens he felt off his young shoulders. Now he had asked God to speak to him and continually heard the word, "Joy." It came as no surprise that Jesus wanted to give Josiah joy. Just as I started explaining this to him, God floored me with further revelation — our friend, Nancy, was coming over for a meeting, and I had a special nickname for her because of her overwhelming exuberance for life with Jesus. My son had never heard me say it, but every time that I saw her at church, I grinned from ear to ear and, without fail, called her: "Joy!" She wasn't a neighbor, but "Joy" was indeed a person...one who happened to be on her way over at that very moment. I knew that God had spoken and that he wanted Nancy to pray for Josiah for an impartation of the same joy that she had.

Nancy was delighted to pray and shared that the joy that exuded from her was nothing short of a miraculous move of God in her life...a transformation from burdens and heaviness to the overwhelming reality of the greatness of Jesus' love for her.

Next, I looked for a relevant Bible verse to anchor my son in the days ahead. I glanced over some great verses, but none of them seemed right. I sensed that I was looking for something more specific. The NIV Bible has 242 references to "joy." Josiah again emerged with a puzzled expression and asked, "Um, dad...is there any Bible verse that says 'joy' and 'empower?' " Josiah is 8. He has a lot of words in his vocabulary. "Epic"? Yes. "Poop"? Quite often. But he could not have come up with "empower" on his own. I checked to see what kind of connection I could find.

"May the God of hope fill you with all joy and peace as you trust in him, so that you may overflow with hope by the power of the Holy Spirit" Romans 15:13.

This verse called out to the God of hope so that he would have both joy and peace in such measure that he would **Overflow** with hope — exactly what my downcast son needed. The verse reminded him that joy, peace and hope were not available to him because of his performance or feelings but that they were his by the power of the Holy Spirit.

I started laughing. What else can you do? Though my Bible told me story after story about God personally engaging his creation through personal communication, my past experiences had made it so difficult. How many hours had I spent toiling to be worthy enough to get the simplest direction from God? How many lists had I made of steps that I needed to take to discern what God wanted? And yet, in all of it, here was my 8-year-old son simply praying a 30-second prayer and hearing specifically from God regarding joy, a friend named "Joy" and a key verse to walk out the promise. What a powerful experience for my son!

Josiah started hearing God speak in March of 2015, and the beautiful change taking place within him as he continues to hear the voice of his Daddy touches me whenever I remember it. In fact, just this week, he came to me and announced, "Dad, God's telling me to write a book!"

Like many parents, I was proud, honored and smiled inside thinking, "That is so sweet"…until I read what he had written. It is my son's telling of **this** story and what has been happening since then entirely from his perspective. He hasn't read my account or been helped by anyone other than the Holy Spirit. It is so powerful that I have decided to include his story in his words in Appendix 1 in the back of the book. After you read it, you will be so inspired at the greatness of God who speaks to those with the faith of a child!

## "SEND MORE PEOPLE LIKE US, LORD!"

My 10-year-old son, Bradley, was now about to personally see what God would do. I was starting to understand that every moment around people was an opportunity to display our Father's love to them. While at the local grocery store, I awaited his prompting but wasn't trying to force anything. As we made our purchases, I picked up two extra items, saltines and a bunch of bananas although I didn't know why. At the checkout, I was drawn to our cashier and bagger, two ladies who were both approaching retirement age. I felt led to encourage them and simply obeyed. The important part about loving people is to always focus on them, not on achieving some dramatic "story" to demonstrate how holy or bold we are to those around us.

We left the grocery store, but even so, I felt frustrated as I sensed that we were supposed to do something more. After all, my son had asked for God to work. Encouraging some cashiers was a good start, but God still had more to do. I asked God out loud to show us anyone who he desired for us to encounter. As I pulled up to the exit, I told Bradley that we needed to keep our eyes open. Across the street, I saw a makeshift homeless camp with four pretty rough-looking guys. I had never noticed them before despite shopping at the store for years. Interestingly enough, I only saw them one other time after that, and then they never returned. We had a beautiful and unique window of opportunity. We pulled across the way, and I remembered the extra groceries that we bought.

I parked, and one of the guys, "Joe," headed toward me. I quickly exited and gave him the groceries, asking what else he needed. He admitted that he was wearing the only pair of jeans that he owned. Without hesitation, I responded, "That's easy. I live around the corner from here. I have a lot of clothes that I want to bring you." Emotional, Joe quickly lunged to hug me. Although he was homeless and smelled like it, I didn't care in the least. I embraced him, and as he wiped away tears, he told me how hard life had been. He told me that most people simply judged him, and he could feel it by their looks. He had a hard time getting up most mornings to face another day. He confessed that although he wouldn't ever take his own life, he was ready for God to take him home.

I was moved by his pain and by the incredible love I felt that God had for him. I told Joe that God really loved him - that I could feel it - and I asked if I could pray for him. As I did, Joe sobbed. He hugged me again, clinging to my side as I released God's heart over him. As I finished, I told Joe that I was going to go gather some clothes and more food from my house and would be back soon. He beamed with hope. I got back into the car to tell my son what had happened. However, the windows were down, and Bradley had heard the entire thing.

At home, I grabbed two trash bags and started clearing my closet. Although I realized that these men were homeless and that the clothes wouldn't last long, I still went for quality clothes. The enemy had lied to them about their dignity and worth. They were sons of the King, made in his image, and they needed to be treated accordingly. After I collected pants, shorts, shirts, boxer shorts and socks, I went to the pantry with another bag and grabbed every non-perishable item that I could find: beef jerky, trail mix, cashews…*my* snacks. I didn't care. I was so abundantly blessed and grateful to share what I had with these men. This experience was especially close to my heart because ever since Bradley was young, he has had a tender heart for the homeless. Growing up, he often prayed for "the poor to not be the poor anymore." He had asked Jesus to use him, and Jesus allowed him to minister to the exact burden that gripped his heart.

On our way back, we swung by McDonald's to buy some hot food for them. However, Bradley seemed quiet, even somber. With some prompting, he explained, "Dad, I think it is great that we get to help them today, but tomorrow, they are still going to be homeless, and so many more are like them. I hate it." His words pierced through me. I blessed him for his large heart. Maybe Jesus' picture of childlike abandon holds so many more truths than we realize. I want to love like my son does.

We drove in silence the rest of the way, heartbroken yet hopeful. Finally, we prayed for them. Bradley's prayer for the homeless inspired me. The Kingdom of God doesn't operate like kingdoms of this earth, giving preference to the aged or learned. In the Kingdom of heaven, even the youngest can walk with great influence. I asked Bradley if he would like to pray for our new homeless friends when we arrived. He admitted that it was scary but that he really wanted to pray. I told him that I would lead and back him up.

When we pulled up, Joe wasn't there. I found out that he had left because of a disagreement with another man. Rob, a long-haired muscular brute of a man who looked like he belonged on the MMA fighting circuit, explained the details, telling me that it was Joe's birthday. He was angry about how the other man had spoken to Joe and didn't mince any words. Rob introduced us to another man, Larry. Joe, Rob, and Larry — it sounded like "The Three Stooges!" Somehow, I didn't think Rob would find that as humorous as I did, so I just kept that little nugget to myself. I looked around the homeless camp as Rob talked, noticing beer cans strewn all around, the unavoidable stench and the raw language. But real love is messy. You don't find it in safe places, spending time with people who act and talk like you. You don't find it by looking down on people or judging them. You don't find it by holding them at an arm's length until they prove their worth. Real love only happens when you put yourself in someone else's shoes and choose to draw near with humility, patience and compassion. We came to show real love to these guys despite the mess. Even so, this was a tough place for a 10-year-old to pray.

Since Joe wasn't there, I shared the clothes and the food that we had brought with Rob, who was very appreciative. I then told him that my son had been praying for the homeless since he was able to speak and that he would simply like to pray for them. Rob and Larry agreed and then insisted that we hold hands in a circle. I wasn't about to protest. As we stood there, I watched my son, his small frame eclipsed by Rob's bulk. We closed our eyes, silent for a minute. I started to wonder, "What kind of father exposes his son to this? Have I set up my son to fail?"

Just then, a feeble voice emerged, "God…I thank you that you see these guys, and you…love them. I pray that they would know how much you love them and that you would send other people like us, Lord, who would be kind to them and see how you love them. Amen."

I glanced up at Rob, this large specimen of a man with the mouth of a sailor. He was shaking and crying some of the largest tears that I have seen. He pulled up his shirt to wipe them away, excusing himself as he walked a few steps into the woods, clearly moved by a kid who saw him the way his Creator did. Meanwhile, Larry walked up and hugged Bradley, who didn't pull away. Rob returned, commenting on how much the prayer impacted him. Excitedly, he announced, "Now, it's my turn to pray!" Back in our circle, I listened as Rob prayed the Lord's Prayer with more passion than I have ever heard. Here we were, having "church" in this stinky, beer-can-infested homeless refuge, and now, "cursing Rob" was bringing the message.

If we aren't careful, our religious filters can prevent us from seeing the beautiful image of God in his kids...even those who really color outside the lines. Our judgments keep us from being a voice that shows them "the way of God more adequately" as Paul did with Priscilla and Aquila in Acts 18:26. It also keeps us from receiving what they understand about God or life more clearly than we do. I am convinced that we can learn something from just about anyone if we walk in humility.

Bradley had been bold, and Jesus showed up. Before we left, I felt led to give Rob a hug, stating, "I know it probably isn't manly, but I feel like you don't get this enough." Before he could protest or drop-kick me, I rushed in to hug him as he hugged me back. We had experienced a beautiful encounter of love.

Back at home, I started noticing supernatural invitations to demonstrate the Kingdom in ordinary moments if I'd only slow down, see people and remember that he waits to Overflow out of his kids. I prayed over a neighbor for supernatural healing in the middle of our driveway. I begged an exhausted convenience store employee to let me take out the trash because I saw her the way her Daddy does. I approached a stranger inside a Chipotle because I heard a very specific message about a job that I believed was from the Lord. At our worship gatherings, people were healed right before our eyes.

One night, in our small gathering of about 20 people, I sensed that someone suffered with an injury or pain to their left leg. In a group that size, it sounded crazy, but I obeyed. They waved wildly from the sound booth, explaining that our buddy, Carlos, had been in pain in his left leg all night. I had no idea. As we prayed, the pain left. Then, another young lady came forward with a cast on her left foot due to a bone that was too short. I had no idea she was there. We prayed for supernatural growth, and she reported to our next meeting cast-free — the bone had indeed grown out! People with back pain, neck pain, a clogged artery...we were hearing some pretty cool testimonies of God healing his children. I also started receiving specific visions and direct words for people as I prayed for them. Little did I know that I was next — someone was about to get a very specific word for me.

## AWAKENING A LONG-FORGOTTEN SONG

As a kid, all I wanted to be was a professional football player. My uncles played football at Clemson, and I idolized them as a young teen. My Uncle Richard came to my house regularly, and he taught me the game. We drew up plays in the front yard, and I imagined myself catching the winning pass in the Super Bowl. While my mind was clearly destined for the gridiron, my body looked more like a flat iron! I was shorter than anyone in my class and could not gain weight to save my life. Oh, what I'd give for that metabolism again!

Nonetheless, I decided to suit up for PAL football: The Police Athletic League. Since they had no tryouts, everyone made the team, playing at least one snap in every game. I was so small that the placekicker looked like a linebacker to me, but I was on the team, destined for greatness. I didn't realize it, but I had completely banked my identity as a man on my ability to connect with the pigskin. In my mind, I "had" to excel because that was my only path to true worth. I had a friend on the team who encouraged my dream, and my uncle seemed to support me. My stepdad didn't protest my suiting up, either. Everyone was on board...except my mom. My mom, very much wanting to protect her only son, was a little less delusional... and quite vocal about her thoughts about my football prospects. I think her exact words were, "Those guys are giants. They're gonna kill you!"

I ignored her counsel, determined to be great. Unfortunately, my determination succumbed to their bone-crushing tackles, and I didn't even last three games. I turned in my pads and shrugged my petite, young shoulders in defeat as my mom tried to encourage me with a list of other activities. School band tryouts were coming up, and I saw the drums. Although it wasn't a sport, I could still hit something, so I signed up. Well, it just so happened that music was in me. I excelled quickly in the arts, learning percussion and then piano. I played by ear and started picking up songs without lessons. I continued in drums, making all-county, then all-state and even winning an award for the best male student in my class.

A friend encouraged me to sign up for chorus, where I also excelled, achieving all-state in my first year. In high school, I joined drama, again, making all-state and performing in two productions at our school as the male lead role during my senior year. While I had struggled to build an identity as an athlete, I accidentally found the unique song knit into the fiber of my being when I stumbled upon the arts. I didn't **need** to be great at football. I was great because my Father made me, and I found my uniqueness when I stopped trying to live up to false expectations of success.

When I started playing the piano, I began writing songs as a way to express my heart. They came naturally to me, bringing a lot of joy. In the early days of my walk with God, I wrote many dark songs, mostly because I felt that I was failing and flailing at life with Jesus. I wrote about love, faith, relationships and the loss of my father when I was young. If it was in my heart, it poured out in song. But something happened along the way. I started noticing that I was writing music that didn't sound anything like what I had heard before. And I listened to the lie that it must simply mean that it wasn't that good.

I wrote music from the eighth grade until I finally abandoned it six months or so before I went to Naples. I had probably written 25 complete songs and about 60 or 70 partial songs. Finally, in my mid-30s, I concluded that I must be sub-par and moved on. Shortly after going to Naples, I was leading worship at an awesome, local church. God had told me to go without a team — just me and a keyboard. I had been leading worship for as long as I'd been in the ministry but felt that I could hide behind the safety of a team. This was *just* me, and it was very uncomfortable. As I started singing, God spontaneously gave me unplanned declarations in song. They flowed naturally. Even though I hadn't seen this modeled much, I had heard worshipers like Jason Upton. I heard songs in my spirit and occasionally dropped my guard enough to share them with others. The fear of rejection was real although it was quickly losing its grip on me since Naples.

So there I was, completely alone in an hour-long worship set. I expressed those declarations and at the end of the night, received a spontaneous song. Suddenly, an elderly woman started singing the spontaneous song with me as if we were offering complementary and echoing parts of a song that we'd practiced for months. But I didn't even know her! As I wrapped up the song and ended worship, she made a beeline for me. "You are a prophetic worshiper," she announced with such authority that it nearly knocked me over. She continued, "I've been at this for 35 years, and it takes one to spot one. You are a prophetic worshiper." She asked if she could pray for a greater anointing of what the Holy Spirit had birthed in my soul, and I agreed.

The next morning, I arrived at the church office to start my day when I walked past my best friend's office, who happens to be our worship pastor. He has a guitar hanging on his wall, partially to save space and partially to feel cool and hip. As I glimpsed at his guitar, the Holy Spirit strongly prompted, "I told you to write. Who said that was just books?" I tried to argue but decided to obey. Twenty minutes later, a full song called, "Love Like This," was completed — something different yet hopeful. I then remembered the woman's prayer over me. I sent a recording of the song to some people who I really trust, and they also sensed the musical difference.

Before the next worship service, I completed yet another song and then still another at youth group the following night while the speaker was talking. For a songwriter, this was unconventional for sure. I wasn't even sure it would make sense or flow well. At ministry time, I came up to play what I had heard. As the night concluded, the speaker asked an interesting question. "Is that my song?" I realized that I had received inspiration as soon as she started sharing. She went on to tell me that the message of the song was exactly what God was speaking to her in her quiet time with him. I had no idea. I simply wrote what I heard with a willing heart that allowed my King to encounter people through me.

I am becoming convinced that much of the Kingdom of God is intended to be just like this. After all, he's the vine — the mastermind. He's the Savior who intercedes day and night for his beloved. But the crazy part is this: even though he could do it all on his own, he takes great delight in beckoning us to partner with him.

In the next weeks, more songs flowed forth. I began to share my experiences, and people seemed to come out of the woodwork with similar desires. Many of those shared that they wanted to be used by God in poetry or music or art but had been sidetracked or, like me, believed that they were just no good. But they began rejecting the lies and started to dream again. Friends who had never written songs randomly sent me things that the Lord had laid on their hearts during their devotions, on vacation, in the middle of a college class. As I read their words, the Lord inspired me, and we began to collaborate together. As we wrote, we shared these songs as declarations during our worship gatherings, and God started moving powerfully. In the midst of worship, we received spontaneous songs that ministered to the specific needs of people in the room. People were moved to tears and experiencing breakthrough. They shared that our music held a gentle authority and an anointing of healing. The Holy Spirit was using a familiar medium dating back to the Psalms to communicate with his kids, and it was exhilarating! During the following three months, we wrote 30 complete songs.

I thought that my failure on the football field meant that I was a "disappointing letdown" and that my performance — or lack thereof — somehow determined my worth. But I was just now beginning to realize that God knit a unique song in my soul from my mother's womb that looked different than how he created my uncles. Not better. Just **different**. And as I began to discover it, I was filled with joy, and lives started changing all around me. That's what happens when ordinary sons and daughters of God begin to unlock their destiny. God shows up. Our obsession to achieve worth by looking like everyone else is an age-old scheme of an enemy who is terrified that you might actually discover who you **really** are. I share my story because you need to understand — no, you need to embrace — the following.

God knit a unique song in your soul, too.

It might not have anything to do with music or sports or modeling or public speaking. That point is that you — the real you — have so much more within you than you realize, and it's good! It isn't just a song that God has written for you but a song that God has been deeply longing to write with you! You need to discover it because the world around you has been yearning to hear it. The symphony can never be complete without you. God doesn't just want to bring hope to my town. He wants to bring it to yours, too. Right now. Through you. If God can move through the sincerity of an 8-year-old who just wants to hear his Father's voice — if he can break down broken and hardened homeless men through the boldness of a 10-year-old — if he can awaken a long-forgotten song in a son's heart through an unnamed 70-year-old lady — if he can do all of that in our little city, then he can definitely do it through you in your city!

For the rest of our journey together, I want to help you discover who you really are and prepare you to live your own "Life in the Overflow." Each chapter is intentionally written not only to inspire you but to practically help you identify and remove wrong belief systems that you might have been holding on to for a long time. Ultimately, it is written so that you would embrace what Jesus intended to be "normal Christianity." It isn't for a select few. Every believer is invited to the dance. We've already been given all that we need. "The Overflow" is a real place, and you can live there. Jesus said that he hid the Kingdom from the wise and learned and gave it to young kids: little, wide-eyed, passionate, messy kids who are crazy enough to believe again that the gospel is even better than we've imagined. Little kids who look at his Book and believe that he has never changed and that he still wants to miraculously manifest love everywhere through ordinary people. I encourage you to slow down through the chapters ahead. Your goal isn't to finish the book. It is to know your Daddy. Allow the Holy Spirit to speak to you. Invite him into the journey right now. Be willing to stop in a section and deal with what he's revealing to you for as long as it takes. If it takes two months to mine through a single wrong belief and find freedom, don't worry. You're dancing with Jesus, and he is pleased. This is where the exciting part begins. You've read my story: now, it's time to write yours!

## QUESTIONS:

1.  Read John 15:1-5. God calls you to simply be a "branch" so that your whole life is about abiding with him. Where do you find yourself trying to produce your own fruit — in your personal life, family, career or walk with God? What would it look like for you to cease striving and start abiding?

2.  God stirred Chuck's son, Bradley, with a need in his hometown that was close to his heart. What needs are in your community that strike a particular chord with you? Pray for God to reign in your neighborhood and ask the Holy Spirit to open up opportunities for you to be a light!

3.  Is there a long-forgotten dream in your life that you've pushed to the back burner? Why did you stop pursuing it? What is God saying to you about it now?

## CHAPTER 3

# HITTING ALL OF THE WRONG TARGETS

I have had the rare privilege of serving at the same church since 2003 with some incredible people who I love. In 13 years, we have built a lot of really deep relationships along with some pretty funny memories. For example, my friend, Wayne, one of our deacons, co-led a small group with his wife, Leisha, and me and my wife. He also managed a really large orange grove, including keeping the grove free of anything that would harm the crop. Their biggest threat: wild hogs.

Wayne grew up in the Midwest, a man's man and a hunter. A few men in our small group were cut from the same cloth. Then, there was me, the entertainer. They talked passionately about guns as they'd list off gauges: "We could take the .30-30 or the 30-ought-6."

In a weak attempt at humor, I interrupted with something like, "I personally use the 90210 or the 867-5309." Wayne scheduled a day for the guys from our small group to travel to the grove and help eradicate the wild hog problem. Once we arrived, we armed ourselves, climbed into the back of a pickup truck, reviewed plenty of safety rules that I'm convinced were just for my sake and then kept our eyes open. If we saw a wild hog, we were to unload from the truck and from our guns.

I watched the skill of my friends as they dropped a hog some 25 yards away with a single shot. They didn't seem surprised, but I was wide-eyed and yelled something like, "Wow! You **got** one!" This was clearly my first time shooting anything other than the breeze. Minutes later, I saw one. He was much closer, maybe 10 yards away. I got out, ran through my safety rules, took aim, prepared for the glory of my first kill and fired. I watched as the dust flew up a full 5 yards in front of him. He ran. I fired again. He was still pretty close, but my shot wasn't. I fired another few shots before he disappeared out of sight. Each time, like an old western showdown, you could see the dust kick up in front of him. I'm convinced that the safest thing that hog could have done was to just stay still because I couldn't hit him to save my life. After that, the guys decided that I might be "better suited" to carry something smaller and handed me a pistol. I'd tell you the name of it, but I think that I just kept calling it "The Noisy Cricket."

At the very end of our trip, I had one final chance to redeem myself. Another one of the guys hit a hog at a distance, of course, injuring it so that it couldn't move quickly. We pulled up the truck and were now just 5 yards away. I couldn't miss! Instead, I turned the pistol sideways like I was in "Boyz in the Hood" and started a gang-style monologue that sounded like an early 90s rap group. "Yeah, Boyee!" The guys cracked up, but I was simply stalling because I just couldn't do it. Another guy had to take the shot. It had been a long, successful day, no thanks to yours truly. I was tired. After all, I had been crouched in the truck for hours with my eyes peeled and full of nervous energy. I jumped in and out of that truck more times than I could count. I took off running several times to get in position to shoot a hog, adrenaline rushing through my veins and fired my weapon, hitting several ant colonies, the orange trees we were supposed to be protecting and several great punchlines. I just didn't hit the one thing that I was supposed to hit. If the experience had been to warm me up to the idea of being a "marksman," it failed miserably. More than ever, I was convinced that I did not have a clue what I was doing. I was impressed by my friends, but I was just "not like those guys." I thought that I must not be cut out for this.

I often feel like that's exactly what is happening in the church at large. We are exhausted because we are undertaking and overseeing so much important activity — programs, sermon series, small groups and Bible Studies, outreach events, conferences and a full calendar of events for every life stage. We teach on everything under the sun: love languages, marriage, communication, conflict resolution, money management and personality types. We are doing a lot and hitting a lot of targets, but sometimes at the end of the day, I wonder if we are **really** hitting the one target that we were sent out to hit.

"Go and make disciples of all nations" Matthew 28:19.

Jesus' command to the disciples after the resurrection is so important that we've titled it "The Great Commission," our great mission. We are told to **be** disciples who **make** disciples everywhere. We are charged to live wisely and make the most of every opportunity to be the salt of the earth and the light of the world. As Christ's ambassadors, we plead with people on God's behalf to be reconciled to him. We are aliens and strangers on earth who should live with such hope that people are drawn to glorify and know God by just being with us. The Holy Spirit has empowered us so that we can be his witnesses to the ends of the earth. We are called the beautiful feet of those who bring good news, the very feet we are to clothe with the shoes of the gospel of peace.

The whole story is about God purchasing hope and life and restoration for his captive children. We were designed to be with God, our Father, in a privileged relationship as his beloved children. We were invited to join in his work and reign with our King as his appointed princes and princesses. **Be** with Him. **Reign** with Him. Remember the beginning of the story?

From the very beginning, Adam and Eve — and all of humanity — walked with God. They saw him face to face, and he spoke over them. They found complete joy in his presence, intimate and profound. But it didn't stop there: Adam and Eve also found great joy in partnering with him. The Almighty beckoned them to tend and work the garden. Work came before the fall. It wasn't intended to be a four-letter word but was an invitation to partner with the God of the universe in profound purpose. And he gave them more than just the garden: God's design was for mankind to rule over all of creation:

"Then God said, "Let us make mankind in our image, in our likeness, *so that* they may rule over the fish in the sea and the birds in the sky, over the livestock and all the wild animals, and over all the creatures that move along the ground." So God created mankind in his own image, in the image of God he created them; male and female he created them. God blessed them and said to them, "Be fruitful and increase in number; *fill the earth and subdue it*. Rule over the fish in the sea and the birds in the sky and over every living creature that moves on the ground" Genesis 1:26-28 – Emphasis added.

Did you catch that? God created us "so that" we would reign with him and created us "in his image" so that we would be in relationship with him.

**Be** with him. **Reign** with him.

Have you ever noticed how obsessed we are with success and significance? Go to any bookstore, look at the magazine covers at the checkout stand as you buy your groceries, even watch the commercials on TV, and you will see it: we are inundated with airbrushed pictures and flashy titles urging us and practically strong-arming us to be enough and to accomplish enough in our lifetime. We are consumed by it and worry about it and stress over it: being enough. Accomplishing enough. Like a magician, we try to fool our own hearts with the sleight of hand of countless distractions, hoping that they divert our eyes away from our feelings of inadequacy or deaden the pain of our unmet expectations for long enough to come up with a plan to fix it. Why do we care so much about being loved and doing something great with our lives? Are we really that vain? No. I believe that the answer is simple: the drive is hard-wired into us.

## "CRYING OUT" FOR LOVE

Our core problem isn't that we want to be loved or that we want to be valuable. Every fiber of our being, every single delicate detail of what makes us who we are — spirit, soul and body, all of it — was hand-knit while we were held in the loving embrace of the One who could have called himself anything but chose to identify himself as our Father, our Daddy. So, I repeat: our problem isn't that we want to be loved. Our problem is simply that we keep drinking from polluted wells that dried up long ago and will never quench our thirst. When we look to find our worth from popularity, beauty contests, our physique or our performance, we're just drinking from muddy puddles in the bottom of an abandoned well. As long as comparison is your measuring stick, you will never measure up or be enough. Someone will always outperform you.

But we're missing the point. The cry of our heart to be enough has *already* been met. We don't need to exhaust ourselves chasing it or worry any longer that we will miss it.

"The Spirit you received does not make you slaves, so that you live in fear again; rather, the Spirit you received brought about your adoption to sonship. *And by him we cry, "Abba, Father"* Romans 8:15 –Emphasis added.

The longing within you to be wanted was placed there. Your spirit — the real you — is crying out to be enough. To be understood. To be loved. The "cry" might look vastly different from person to person but don't mistake it: on every continent, in every era, the cry of our heart to be wanted echoes. It's why bullies become bullies and why kids who are bullied are so devastated. It's why we marry and why a broken marriage shatters our hearts. It's why we sacrifice to go to college and why we stubbornly work more hours than are asked of us. It's why we're obsessed with selfies and why we criticize our reflection in the mirror at the same time. We want to be enough, but we fear we are not. We want to do enough but feel the clock of life working against us while our dream of significance seems to drift just out of reach. We are all crying out because we were made for love — to be loved by the Almighty and to love him with everything in return. We cry out because our lives were created to be a song of love that we sing and dance with our Creator and until we find our worth in his arms, we will always be chasing something or someone else.

You are either crying out a song of slavery or one of sonship. The harsh voice of the bully's bravado is, in reality, a dissonant cry of grave insecurity. The cry of the jilted lover is a dirge of rejection. The cry of the middle-aged businessman, sacrificing another weekend for a job that holds no meaning, is the slave song of the hamster wheel, running in place with all that he has in the hopes that he will eventually arrive somewhere worthwhile. A thousand different songs of slavery have rung through every one of our lungs. We've served foolish things and taken desperate measures just to be noticed. But when we come to Jesus, something remarkable happens. He changes our song. Our heart still cries, yes. That's what a living heart was made to do. But now the song is hopeful, alive — a song of emancipation as sons and daughters to our "Daddy!" That's what the word, "Abba," really means: it is our heart screaming in ecstasy that we've found the embrace of the one we belong to: our Daddy! It is the sound of shackles falling off, of grave clothes being cast aside. It is the sound of someone who has slaved their whole life to be loved, learning that they never had to do a single thing to earn it except to simply receive it. You want to be loved because you were made to be.

## YEARNING FOR GREATNESS

I will take it one step further. Not only were we created for love, but we were created for success.

Yes, you heard me right.

We were never supposed to settle for second-rate dreams or be content with mediocrity. It isn't as if God made the heavens and earth and "saw that it was good," and made the animals and "saw that it was good" and then made us and said, "Ahhh, they're adequate, I guess. Not great, but not terrible. They'll pass." No. He made mankind as the exclamation point of creation, and when he finished, he declared that it was "**very** good!" We were made to be great! Our problem isn't that we desire success but what we define as "success" is often a shallow imposter, a hollow target with nothing of substance behind it. Much of our pursuit of success is driven by winning the applause of people, accumulating a massive storehouse of money or possessions to showcase our great importance or surrounding ourselves with an endless buffet of comforts. We live in a consumer culture that preaches self as god and success as sufficiently feeding and appeasing that deity. The problem with our obsession for success is not that we want too much from life but that we are willing to settle for far too little. I love the way C.S. Lewis put it:

> "It would seem that Our Lord finds our desires not too strong, but too weak. We are half-hearted creatures, fooling about with drink and sex and ambition when infinite joy is offered us, like an ignorant child who wants to go on making mud pies in a slum because he cannot imagine what is meant by the offer of a holiday at the sea. We are far too easily pleased."[4]

That's it exactly. We were made to be great — to reign over all of creation with the God of the universe, but the enemy of our souls has blinded us to it and convinced us to settle for the empty allure of image and comfort.

And here's the kicker: the more that we receive all of that "stuff," the less that it actually fills the need of our hearts because greatness can never be found there. Without realizing it, we become like the residents on the ship in the Pixar film, "Wall-e." Their planet was in an hour of desperate need, and they should have rightfully stepped up to bring life back home. But they failed to realize who they were or that they could solve the problem. Instead, there they sat, wasting away the hours of each day, as if they were on a permanent vacation. There they sat, eyes glued to a screen, self-absorbed with entertainment and accumulation. There they sat, totally unaware that they were listening to the wrong voice who fed them lies about "importance." There they sat, constantly feeding their "needs" yet wasting away.

Your life matters so much more than you realize. You were called to be great, and when you received the Holy Spirit, you received more power and purpose than you will ever fully realize this side of heaven. By the glory of the cross, love and greatness are now fully yours for the taking.

## HOPE RESTORED

We might have lost our way in the garden and wandered aimlessly in the wilderness for far too long, but our redeeming God came back for us. Jesus' entrance wasn't simply a rescue mission but a long-awaited invitation for restoration to our original glory and purpose: to *be* with Him and to *reign* with Him!

"Jesus went up on a mountainside and called to him those he wanted, and they came to him. He appointed twelve that they might *be with him* and that he might send them out to preach and to have authority to drive out demons" Mark 3:13-15 – Emphasis added.

At the very outset of Jesus' ministry, he chose 12 disciples who marked the inauguration of the government of a new kingdom. Just as the 12 tribes of Israel were positioned at the center of the first kingdom and covenant, these 12 "ordinary, unschooled men" stood at the defining moments of a new kingdom age. Echoing the call of the garden, on a mountain, Jesus extended the invitation again. Sin kept us from fulfilling our original calling, but now, the One who would demolish our sin and make a spectacle of the enemy was here, extending his hand. If we want to focus on and hit the target, then we must understand that Jesus came to restore our original purpose! We live and move and breathe so that we will **be** with him as children and **reign** with him as princes and princesses.

Everywhere that Jesus went with the disciples, three things regularly took place. They taught people about his Kingdom; people were healed of all kinds of sicknesses and diseases, and people were set free from the oppression of the enemy. This wasn't once or twice, but these stories show up on nearly every page and in every trip to every city — **everywhere**. Why is that? Some say it was a temporary display of the power of the Kingdom, a sort of flare in the sky to grab people's attention and validate Jesus and his message. They say that signs like laying hands on people for healing or receiving miraculous words of knowledge or prophecy for people to be set free — the stuff that fills the stories of Jesus and the pillars of the early church — ended after the last apostle died because we now have the written Word of God that tells us all that we need. I love the Word of God. I used to think that it was duller than watching paint dry, but then, I fell in love with the story and the God of the story. Our Bible is amazing and incredible. And **it** is why I believe that things like the ministry of healing and setting the captives free were never supposed to dry up and go away.

The Bible tells us that the miraculous gifts will continue to exist until "completeness" comes, and we see him face to face in all his glory. They will operate with purpose until we "know fully even as we are fully known" in 1 Corinthians 13:8-12. Some insist that this "completeness" was the authorship of scripture, and thus, when we received the Bible, we didn't *need* God to work in this "hands-on" way anymore. But the word, "completeness," means "consummation, something becoming fully complete and lacking nothing." It is the words, "The End," on the final page of a great novel. "Completeness" is what happens when the guy gets the girl, and they get married and ride off into the sunset. It is the "happily ever after" when the curtains close. And it's coming, oh yes, the glorious day is coming, but this isn't completeness. My Bible isn't completeness. My King parting the clouds and finally putting all things under his feet, sending our enemy to his fiery doom and me looking into the eyes of the One who created my soul for all of eternity — that is completeness. And until that day, he told me that he would keep moving just like he did when he called the 12 to be with him and reign with him by healing the sick and setting the captives free.

To say that we shouldn't expect the miraculous and personal partnership that the disciples experienced with Jesus because the Bible is our completeness is sort of akin to saying, "Daddy doesn't talk much to his kids anymore because he wrote a letter that detailed all that he cared to say." The Bible must be our plumb line to test every prophecy and "hold on to the good" (1 Thessalonians 5:21), and we desperately need to know it as an aid in our journey to truly and miraculously be with and reign with God, not to stand as an end in and of itself.

I used to believe and even argue that things like healing, speaking in tongues and words of prophecy were all a farce, and I tried to prove it from the scriptures. But the further that I dug, the more I found myself having to perform detailed mental gymnastics, piecing together obscure Bible passages and entirely ignoring or explaining away others. Finally, I realized something: if you send any person who wants to know God into a room to read the Bible from cover to cover with no other outside influences, they could only reach the conclusion that what God did then, he still wants to do today. Jesus healed people everywhere — through the 12 disciples and then through 72 unnamed others. He healed through two deacons, Philip and Stephen. He healed the Apostle Paul's eyes through a relatively unknown but obedient disciple named Ananias. He healed through Paul and through Paul's friend, Barnabas. Letters were written to the church about gifts of healing. James instructed all believers to "confess your sins and pray for one another *so that you may be healed*" (James 5:16 - emphasis added) — the same passage where he called elders of churches to pray for the physical healing of those ailing in the church, **expecting** them to be healed, and told believers that our words were no different than Elijah's, the great miracle-working prophet of the Old Testament. If that isn't evidence enough, Jesus himself said that anyone who followed him would do the very things that he had been doing:

"Very truly I tell you, *whoever* believes in me will do the works I have been doing, and they will do even greater things than these, because I am going to the Father" John 14:12 – Emphasis added.

If we have the examples of this great cloud of witnesses, why do some people still teach that ordinary believers today shouldn't expect their lives to look like they did? I believe a big part of the reason is because they deeply love God and his glory. They hold him in high esteem, and they have seen far too many "miraculous revivals" sweep into town, which were full of hype and sensationalism instead of focused on truly knowing God, which then hurt people. I believe it is because they want to see people **love** God and not treat him like an oversized vending machine to dispense some miraculous "fix-all" for their broken lives so that they can continue living for themselves without him. They've seen the scandals, the flesh and the aura of pride of those who say things like, "unless you operate in this gift or that one, you don't really love God." For many of them, they've put themselves out there for God to show up like he did in the Bible, but it didn't pan out like they thought it would, which broke their hearts. All of these reasons kept my focus on plans and steps that I could follow so that I didn't have to step out onto the unknown waters of the miraculous. But in all of our discussions and debates of what happened and what should still happen, we missed the crucial understanding of **why** it happened. Why did Jesus show up everywhere preaching the Kingdom, healing the sick and setting the captives free? Why those three particular things?

**Preach. Heal. Set the Captives Free.**

Why those three? I mean, preaching makes sense. The souls of man are clearly separated from their Father. You'd have a hard time finding any born-again church that didn't preach that Jesus came so that we could enter a relationship with him. That makes sense. But healing and coming against the demonic? I mean, whether you call it spiritual warfare or deliverance doesn't matter much, it's just uncomfortable. Weird, even. Why were those things at the center of Jesus' new order? The answer is simple, contained in the pages of scripture.

"The reason the Son of God appeared was to destroy the devil's work" 1 John 3:8.

This passage reveals the crux of the *reason* that Jesus came, and we must understand what it says. In Greek, the word translated "destroy" means to "loose, dissolve, do away with, or annul."[5] That's significant. "Work" means "the enterprise that someone leads *and any product that has been accomplished by it*" (Emphasis added).[6] So, here it is: Jesus came not to simply take us to heaven but to entirely demolish the enterprise our enemy set up *and* all of the products that were accomplished through it. Look at the garden before he showed up and then look at our eternal home in heaven after he is annihilated. In both places, you see people walk in intimacy with God with no pain, tears, sickness or depression. In both places, people know their identity and walk in their purpose. In both places, they experience joy so profound that words can't fully express it. Sickness, disease, addictions, compulsions, depression, conflict, pain, despair, loneliness — all of these are the products of the enterprise that Lucifer and his underlings brought to the earth. The reason Jesus appeared was to destroy that enterprise and everything that it manufactured. He didn't just come to stop him from causing further damage but came to completely uproot him and everything associated with his kingdom. He didn't send up a flare in the sky to wow the people that would just fizzle out but invited his kids from this point forward to discover their reason for living. The Savior extended his hand to any who would dare to come be with him and reign with him.

God is still speaking miraculously in dreams and visions. He is still healing personally with great delight through his children. We aren't in some kind of circus to show people how holy we are but are just formerly shattered people who have been transformed by the One who makes all things new. Now, we get to run to other precious and broken people to tell them that they have a Daddy who came to do the same for them. That's what it means to be a disciple who makes disciples: our whole existence is simply to be with him and, from the Overflow of that place, to reign with him by doing the very acts of love and power that Jesus did.

We could spend our days becoming expert marksmen who can flawlessly hit hollow targets that will never satisfy us, or we can realize that the journey of life was designed to be overwhelmingly simple — being with God, knowing him as our Daddy and reigning with him. We can join him in setting people free from every place that the enemy of our souls has left his grubby fingerprints, trying to steal, kill and destroy. The journey of "Life in the Overflow" is not for the super-elite but simply discipleship through intimacy. All are invited, and if you are a follower of Christ, it is supposed to be normal Christianity. It isn't complex, but you need to be prepared to tear up your blueprints of your plan for your life because the life of the Overflow isn't something that you have the capacity to hold. It is so much greater, deeper and more gloriously alive than anything that you could experience by your effort. But it will cost you. It will mean trading in everything in your hands and all of your plans for everything that he is offering. It will mean waving goodbye to your right to dictate your life or determine your steps. It will also mean bidding farewell to mediocrity, insecurity and former songs of slavery. Your heart has been crying out for it. Becoming an overflowing disciple is the great goal of your life. Be alert with your eyes wide open. It's time to hit your target.

## QUESTIONS:

1. Have you ever felt that you weren't "cut out" for being a disciple-maker or that you didn't have a clue what you were doing? How did this chapter help you?

2. What "targets" or goals have you believed that you had to hit to be a good Christian? To be enough? To have a successful life? How does it help to hear that God **makes** you enough and that your only target is discipleship through intimacy: to **be** with God and from there, to learn to **reign** with him?

3. What are your thoughts about the idea that Jesus is calling you to do the same things the disciples did: preach the Kingdom, heal the sick and set the captives free? Be honest about your concerns or fears.

4. Ask the Holy Spirit what he wants to say to you about this chapter and be silent for a few minutes. What did he say? What do you feel that he's calling you to believe, receive or do as a result of this chapter?

5. Pray for one another.

## CHAPTER 4

# INTIMACY IS EVERYTHING

Buried in the gospel of Luke, we find the story of Jesus' encounter with two sisters, Mary and Martha. I think part of the reason that I love this story is because I grew up as the only boy with three older sisters, so perhaps a story about sisters where one is so ticked that she's ready to throw down an MMA brawl with the other just feels like home. In addition, I can totally relate to Martha's raw emotion and frustration, and I am enraptured by the picture of hope that Jesus extends to people who really want to please him but are exhausted from tirelessly trying to **do** enough so that they can **be** enough. The story goes like this:

"As Jesus and his disciples were on their way, he came to a village where a woman named Martha opened her home to him. She had a sister called Mary, who sat at the Lord's feet listening to what he said. But Martha was distracted by all the preparations that had to be made. She came to him and asked, "Lord, don't you care that my sister has left me to do the work by myself? Tell her to help me!" "Martha, Martha," the Lord answered, "you are worried and upset about many things, but few things are needed - or indeed *only one*. Mary has chosen what is better, and it will not be taken away from her" Luke 10:38-42 – Emphasis added.

Now, Martha gets a pretty bad rap. You'll hear messages telling you to "Be a Mary," and I even saw a ladies' necklace for sale that read, "I'm _not_ a Martha!" While I understand the sentiment that people are trying to convey, we need to realize that Martha really **loved** Jesus. After all, she was the one who took the initiative to invite Jesus to her house. By this time, he was very well known and would have been highly sought after as a guest. Everyone in the temple recognized an authority in Jesus' preaching that they'd never heard before, and everywhere he went, crowds of people were healed. Jesus was so popular that they had to push him off the shore in a boat just so he could address everyone at once. So many desired his company that the gospels say on more than one occasion that he had to intentionally seek quiet places and times to draw away with his Father. And yet, Jesus chose to dine at Martha's house. This should tell you something of the headstrong and driven heart that beat in her chest.

We also know that Martha loved Jesus because she worked herself to the point of exhaustion to please him. I don't know how it is in your home, but when we are having company, my calm and gracious bride, Jill, transforms into a different person. At the mention of a dinner party, my beautiful princess suddenly becomes a four-star general ready to lead our small army into a detailed and well-organized battle against the infantry of dirt, grime and clutter. She becomes William Wallace, giving the speech on the front lines before the crucial battle in "Braveheart," urging us to keep our eyes focused on the defeating the enemy before us. While she doesn't have it in her to be bossy or rude, she becomes highly motivated. Everyone receives a list of jobs, depending on how special the occasion is. And so it was with the ever-intentional Martha as she prepared for Jesus' visit. She shared the home with her sister, Mary, and brother, Lazarus — yes, that Lazarus. In the hours counting down to Jesus' arrival, I can almost hear Martha feverishly barking out orders: "Mary, you've got to step it up. I can't stay on you the whole time! Lazarus, get your feet off my end table. If I see it again, I will send you to an early grave, and then who's gonna help you?" Martha had prepared her favorite dish and undoubtedly worked up a sweat as she dashed from room to room to cross off each item on her extensive list. She was doing her very best because she wanted to make her home somehow presentable for the King of Glory to enter in. But despite her best efforts, when the knock came on the door, she still didn't feel close to "ready." I imagine that Martha did what many of us do when guests arrive before we're ready: she put on the "hostess face" — that bright-eyed, glossed-over look that we paint over our frustrated face as we do our very best to fake it in the most chipper voice possible.

She showed Jesus in, undoubtedly smiling on the surface as she asked him to make himself comfortable in the living room. Like an iceberg, the bulk of her feelings remained unseen. After a moment or two, she might have excused herself to "check on dinner." In the other room, she warped into light speed, looking for anything still out of place: shoving mail into the junk drawer, pulling the rug over a spot on the floor she missed when she mopped. And then, of course, she probably used the ol' "close the door" trick when the room looks like the cows flew through the air in the movie, "Twister." Just as she made a little headway, she painted her "hostess face" back on to return to Jesus when she saw it.

There, sitting in the middle of the floor — completely oblivious with a goofy grin plastered across her face — was Mary. Her lack of awareness for all that "needed" to be done to clean house enraged Martha. If you are the parent of a child who has ever misbehaved in an important setting, you probably understand how Martha felt. She might have tried to subtly clear her throat or motioned to get Mary's attention, to no avail. She might have positioned herself just behind Jesus so that he couldn't see her giving Mary "the look" — that glare of disapproval that shoots from the eyes so sternly that you think it will knock you across the room. But it didn't work. Martha might have even looked for something inconspicuous to throw at Mary without getting caught. All to no avail. No matter how hard Martha tried, Mary was enraptured by every word that Jesus spoke. And just then, Martha snapped. Do you ever only realize how mad you are about something when you open your mouth and intense emotion starts falling out and then it's too late to take it back? Martha let them have it, first by accusing Jesus of lacking compassion and playing favorites. Then, she commanded him to do what she said — not a good idea. Finally, she called her sister out on the carpet, demanding justice. Court was in session, and Judge Martha wasn't pulling any punches.

I can see her pointing and snapping her finger with her head swaying, as if to say, "Oh, heck no. Not on my special day, you don't. I do not think so!" Here's what she said to Jesus: "Lord, **don't you care** that my sister **left** me to do all this by myself? **Tell her** to **help** me!" Martha had just become a martyr as she attempted to show Jesus that she was the one working hard to please him. Meanwhile Mary, who seemed to get all the attention, just sat on her butt doing nothing. Martha questioned her motives. It isn't just that Mary didn't help. It's that she left Martha all alone. In Greek, the word for "left" means to "abandon or forsake."[7] In other words, Martha was saying, "I'm working harder for your love, and she abandoned me, but she's getting the reward!" She even judged Jesus' love for her. Look at her question: *'Don't you care?'* It's as if at Martha's breaking point, she confessed what she'd been wrestling with this whole time — she was doing everything in her power so that Jesus would care, yet Mary was rewarded for doing nothing. Martha called "foul" and demanded that Jesus make Mary help. The Greek word for "help" means to "co-strive" with.[8] Martha couldn't appreciate Mary's delight because she believed that the only path to be enough with Jesus was through duty. And so, she sternly demanded that Mary be placed alongside her in the yoke of "to-do's" and join her in misery.

Jesus' response isn't a rebuke nearly as much as it is an invitation. In essence, he admonished, "Martha, of course I care. I love you. But just breathe and take a look at yourself for a minute. You're a hot mess — *so* worried and *so* upset because you are *so* distracted about *so* many things. However, you only need to be doing one thing right now — sitting with your sister at my feet." The word "distracted" used here to describe Martha means to "over-occupy the mind" with too many things, leaving her anxious, exhausted and disturbed.[9] How often do we "over-occupy," not only our minds, but our schedules, our energy, our souls — all under the harsh and demanding load of everything that others and ourselves have convinced us that we "need" in order to be enough? Martha's knees were buckling under the pressure, and Jesus refused to grant her request to yoke Mary into that. Martha would soon learn that Jesus didn't come to throw more yokes on anyone but to destroy them. He wants to trade our yoke of burdens for his yoke of grace. The cool thing about that picture is that, like oxen, being yoked together with Jesus means that we are intensely close to him and that he is bearing the workload — it's his yoke! We don't need to work for his favor. He already did all of the work and just wants us at his feet.

Martha loved Jesus, but somewhere, she shifted from the simple relationship of a messy, wide-eyed kid with her Daddy to a heavy, detailed, exhausting list of demands, and when others didn't line up with her requirements, she judged them. When rigid religious rules come face to face with a relationship of rejoicing, judgment and the attempt to "silence the party" results. If we haven't been there, we have likely seen it — our relationship with Jesus is less like a dance and more like getting a root canal. You know that you're approaching a mindset of duty when, like Martha, you shift to judgment of others, anxiety, emotional exhaustion and heaviness. Religious duty pressures you to "clean your house" so that Jesus wants to stay there, and you cannot grasp the concept of grace. How often do we act like we are **saved** only by grace but **loved** by God based only on our performance? Because of that, we boil discipleship down to a detailed checklist of church attendance, spiritual disciplines, how much time we spend in prayer a day or the last time we shared our faith. When these things spring up from the Overflow of grateful hearts, they are awesome but ugly when we make them tools to earn favor.

Another symptom of a duty mindset is an obsession with rules. Now, I am a rule follower. I have a detail-oriented personality, and I find some sense of security in knowing rules and expectations. And certainly, God has revealed his heart and his order, and we find life when we trust what he has said. But my concern is that we become so preoccupied with the rules

— what movies you can and can't watch, what words you can and can't say, what places you can and can't go— that we miss the heart of what really matters. We might even fool ourselves and look down on other believers who don't "follow the rules" as well as we do. See, that's the thing: duty always judges the motives of other people's hearts by how well they follow your rules! We judge other people's devotion to Jesus through lenses and construct boxes of behavior to confine them.

When I was in Bible college, guest speakers came to our chapel services. As a young Bible student, I drank up what these men and women of God shared because they had been at this for some time. I learned a lot of awesome things in chapel, but I also heard a few things that really messed with my head because I believed them. Well-meaning leaders and pastors shared what helped them grow close to God but imposed their standards, such as, "You *need* to do this if you really love Jesus." I took some of their points as the eleventh commandment. One speaker told us that the Bible says "early in the morning, I seek You," so therefore, if you were really holy, you would meet with God in early morning hours. Striving, I tried to set my clock earlier, but it was like trudging through mud, and no matter when I went to bed, I couldn't stay awake. I might have been on my knees, but the only thing I had in common with other people who rose early for prayer is that my eyes were closed! As a result, I showed up morning after morning to my first class, exhausted and frustrated at my failure to do the duty that I "needed" for Jesus to be pleased in my house.

Another chapel speaker told us to journal. That just gave me writer's cramp. I heard detailed prayer plans and other disciplines that I needed for a faithful walk with God. These speakers really meant well, and what they shared worked for them. But here's the problem: there's never been another **you** on the planet. No one can give you a "one-size-fits-all" plan on how to be close to God because the world has never seen one of you before! Additionally, any advice on drawing close to Jesus that starts with rigid demands and requirements completely misses what Jesus did on the cross. He paid it all and offers life — life in all of its fullness. All bought by him. Because he adores you.

Whenever we find ourselves comparing our walk with Jesus with someone else's, duty-filled religion isn't far away. A true dance with our Daddy is like Mary's, who had no time to judge anyone else because she was completely consumed with Jesus! Duty will always leave us worried, tired and upset. No matter what you do, it will never be enough. When you mess up, you can't to lay it down or move on until you "do enough good" to really convince yourself and God that you've changed. Your soul can never rest because duty is like the sandcastle that you're always working on and tweaking and guarding to keep from crashing down around you. You can never stop because if you do, your structure won't last the night. It is exhausting. I know. I have lived there.

Perhaps the heart of the story of Mary and Martha is that duty stays very busy but misses the delight of being with Jesus! Martha loved Jesus, and she tried **so** hard. But in all of her activity, she nearly missed the fact that the King of all creation was right there in her home. She was so focused on managing her mess that she couldn't see him. If we are not careful, we can go to church, read the Bible, spend time in a lot of Christian activity and still miss Jesus! You want delight with Jesus, not a focus on duty. No one wants duty. I mean, just listen to the word: duty. Doodie. It sounds like something that my homeowner's association said that people need to pick up after their dogs. Duty stinks. It really does.

Jesus offered Martha — and us — a beautiful invitation: Stop cleaning. Stop obsessing. Stop trying to earn enough to contribute to what has already been fully paid. Just come and sit at his feet and let him wash over you. Jesus knew that Martha's home was a mess. He knew that stuff was hidden away in the cupboards and that dirt was on the floors. He didn't care. He just wanted Martha's heart because he knew that the clearer Martha saw him, the more she'd know who she really was, and when she saw that, her feet would follow her heart. Jesus sees the messes in your cupboards and dirt on your floors, too, and he yearns to just have you sit so that he can tell you over and over who you really are! We are not accepted by God because we've done enough. We're accepted because of the finished work of Jesus on the cross! And because of that, Jesus isn't nearly as concerned today with what you will do **for** him as he is with what he wants to do **in** and **with** you! We have to stop scurrying to manage messes and putting on "hostess face" to impress people and God, and we must learn how to sit in the presence of the One who loves us perfectly and longs to speak over us! Even deeper, we have to learn to live there!

Mary shows up just three times in the Bible: in this story, when her brother Lazarus dies, and the last time when she anoints his feet with a perfume that cost a year's wages just one week before Jesus went to the cross. Each time that we see Mary, she is in the **same** place — at his feet! Whether she was learning from him, dealing with debilitating grief after her brother's death or worshiping, she lived a life full of the delight of intimacy with Jesus at his feet!

I cannot tell you what that looks like for you. I that know for me, I find that place — his presence in my life — when I have a cup of coffee, my comfy chair, my Bible and pen and highlighter, some Pandora worship music, and time and space. I can also tell you, though, that living at Jesus' feet is **so** much more than a formula of "quiet time." In our culture, we definitely need time to spend in stillness with our Father — copious amounts of time. We need to embrace the simplicity of the already finished gospel. We need to learn to bring all of our heart to our King. Jesus told Martha that only one thing was needed — and that wasn't what Mary was doing with her time, feet or hands. The "one thing" was what Mary was doing with her heart: intimacy. It's **always** been about intimacy. Any spiritual treasure that you seek that doesn't flow from intimacy with your Father isn't Christianity. It's just a religious ladder that you're trying to climb that will never lead anywhere that you want to go. You don't need lots of steps and lists and plans. Discipleship is found when you learn to make him your "one thing" and just keep sitting there.

## BROKEN EQUATIONS

We make following Jesus so complicated. The Pharisees had 613 laws they had to follow to the letter to be "acceptable" before God and their peers. You needed to diligently obey 248 commands, but the lion's share of the list were negative — 365 commands that you should not do! How would you like to keep track of **that** "daily" list? No wonder they were always in a bad mood. They woke up every morning, exhausted from the previous day's performance." Even the Sabbath, their supposed day of rest, was loaded with rules. Like a kid who sleeps with one eye open because of the imaginary monster in their closet, the Pharisees must have walked around in a state of perpetual anxiety, fearfully looking over their shoulder that they'd do something stupid to reap God's wrath. And even beyond their own pursuit of rigid rules, they spent every waking moment going around "tying heavy burdens" on other people's backs. These were the spiritual leaders of Mary and Martha's day — the "rule police." You can see how Martha might have had the idea that she had to work for Jesus' favor, but just because a lot of people try to make a trend — secular or spiritual — popular, doesn't make it right.

If discipleship could've been written as a mathematical equation in Martha's day, it would have looked something like this: "hard work + sacrifice + getting it right = Holiness." It sounds eerily familiar, doesn't it? Here's the problem with that equation: Jesus already did the hard work that we were powerless to do by trying to follow the law (see Romans 8:1-4). If you're dead set on a formula, follow this instead: "Jesus + Jesus + Jesus = Holiness" or said another way, "Jesus + Nothing = Holiness." Jesus already was the atoning sacrifice, which was sufficient (see Hebrews 9:24-28).

Additionally, we're just kids. If you haven't noticed yet, we don't "get it right." I mess up all over the place, don't you? I say dumb things. When circumstances don't go according to plan, I can lose sight of the One who is holding my life and get overwhelmed by stuff that won't even matter a week from now. I sometimes find myself clinging to trinkets like they are some grand treasure. Now I am not saying that we, as redeemed Christians, have to go around sinning. I echo the words of the Apostle Paul, "absolutely not!" In a later chapter on identity, I will share how you really **are** a new creation, and the better your mind comes to understand the change that has already taken place in your spirit, the more sin loses its grip on you.

What I am saying about not "getting it right" is that we are kids growing up with our Daddy, and as we learn who he is and who we are, we are going to miss it sometimes. Most of my not "getting it right" is just because I am in the process of learning, and learning is messy. Most of my falls are unintentional in the same way a kid learning to ride a bike sometimes falls and skins his knees. He doesn't mean to or want to. But even more than he doesn't want to fall, he doesn't want to sit on his porch, watching everyone else enjoy the exhilaration of the ride. His bike invites him on wild and unbounded adventure. He sees many who have gone before him and have conquered bike riding, and he believes that, no matter how long it takes, he can learn to ride. He isn't terrified that he won't get it right because his eyes aren't focused on falling, but he is looking forward to the moment that he feels the breeze rush through his hair as he glides down the street, experiencing the jubilation that he knows is available. Even when he falls, he isn't failing. He's just learning how to do something that he doesn't know how to do yet, and the process is beautiful. Whether you are 8 or 88, your Daddy in heaven sees you as a kid learning how to walk with him in the same way a kid learns how to ride a bike. You weren't called to "get it right." Jesus got it right for you and extends the invitation to fully receive and release his Kingdom, but you have to get on the bike called "Grace."

## EMBRACING GRACE

The Bible adamantly expects us to grasp this concept of grace, mentioning it more than 130 times in the New Testament alone. Paul starts every one of his letters, declaring "grace and peace" over God's beloved. You've likely heard that grace is "unmerited favor" — a gift from God that you cannot earn, similar to being pulled over for going 30 mph over the speed limit and not getting a ticket. That's good news, but the biblical concept of "grace" actually goes much deeper than that: it means "merciful kindness that fills us with great joy and delight." If a cop pulled you over and let you go with a warning, you might be grateful but not "filled with delight." You'd just be really aware of how badly you broke the rules. You might be thankful to the cop, but you would probably feel like you are a bad driver who just escaped a close call. I think that's how a lot of Christians feel with God: like they're still a "bad driver" who should be penalized, but that God patiently overlooks our rule-breaking. While I understand that, what if he really *did* pay the price for our sin and take it away? What if we really *are* a new creation, and what if we really *did* receive a new heart that now beats to love and serve him? What if we really *aren't* "bad drivers" anymore, but people who were born to be behind the wheel and feel the wind rush through our hair as we learn how to walk more fully every day in who we are even though we sometimes misstep? That's what grace for the believer is about: not God overlooking the disobedience of dirty sinners, but him taking great joy in extending kindness to his kids who've been given all they need to serve him and are learning to walk out their identity!

## TEARING UP OUR "TO-DO" LISTS

All of Christianity is just about "one thing." Since my time in Naples, I have had the opportunity to share how to experience life in the Overflow with a lot of people in a lot of different contexts. While it's been beautiful in many conversations, I have seen eyes start to gloss over or even begin feeling heavy when I share the all-encompassing simplicity of just giving Jesus all of you. I think we find some sense of security in a list that we can check off, but I also think that it goes deeper than that. I think that we've been told for too long that our lives are all about us: our happiness, our goals, our own little world. Since we think that our lives are ours, we want to give Jesus the minimum that he requires so that he will bless our pursuit of our goals in our life. We want a list so that we can garner his blessing to acquire the treasure that we really want, whether its acceptance, status, importance, possessions or falling in love. We chase a million other treasures, and all too often, we kick against the idea of not having a list because we want to accomplish enough to earn the right to lead our own lives — similar to the teenage daughter of a millionaire wanting both her independence so that she can make her own decisions and her daddy's debit card.

We seek independence and blessing because we fail to realize that ruling our own lives will only produce fleeting shadows masquerading as blessings. We all too easily treat Jesus like an à la carte menu where we get to pick what blessings we want from him by how much we think they will cost. When I was in middle school, my mom sent me to school with lunch money every day. Students could go through the regular line and eat a balanced lunch or through the à la carte line, which had a bunch of junk food that you bought individually. I never told her, but my lunch every day was a bag of chips, a giant chocolate chip cookie and a Hawaiian Punch. À la carte Christianity gives people the false idea that their life is theirs and that they don't need to "cash in" for anything more than the level of blessing that they think they want. In the meantime, just like my middle school lunch, we fill ourselves with junk that will never satisfy the real hunger of our souls. While that might seem harsh, I think we don't really understand how amazing the cross is and what he is really offering us. Like Martha, I think we are willing to check off the items on our lists because we cannot imagine what it would actually be like to be sons and daughters, adored by our Father.

But please, hear my heart: you don't actually want a list. It makes you worried, tired and exhausted doing what you think is required of you. And Jesus nailed that list to the cross when he demolished the enemy that kept shoving requirements and shame down your throat:

"When you were dead in your sins and in the uncircumcision of your flesh, God made you alive with Christ. He forgave us all our sins, having canceled the charge of our legal indebtedness, which stood against us and condemned us; he has taken it away, *nailing it to the cross*. And having disarmed the powers and authorities, he made a public spectacle of them, triumphing over them by the cross. Therefore do not let anyone judge you by what you eat or drink, or with regard to a religious festival, a New Moon celebration or a Sabbath day. These are a shadow of the things that were to come; the reality, however, is found in Christ" Colossians 2:13-17 – Emphasis added.

This passage is so packed full of ridiculously good truth that you might just want to read it again. You were dead, and God made you fully alive. He forgave all of your sin. He canceled your full debt and took everything that condemned you and everything that said you were not yet enough, and he nailed it to the cross. He took your enemy and completely vanquished him so that you don't need to be governed by a list of rules anymore. Your list was a shadow, a temporary guardian for the uncircumcision of your flesh. But here's the deal: if you are a follower of Christ, that dead flesh was cut off you and removed. You don't want or need a list. What you want is to know your Daddy. What you need is to practically understand how you can! That only happens when you tear up your to-do list and understand that Jesus simply desires to become your "one thing!"

The gospel is fully potent all by itself to cure all of man's ills and restore all of our glory. The gospel is not Jesus and… but Jesus period. He paid it all. We cannot add to it or alter it. Our messiness doesn't invalidate it. Our fear that we're not ready doesn't hinder it. We merely need to receive it. Right now.

Like Martha, you love Jesus. You do. Stop rushing around in a million different directions trying to please him and convince him to stay in your house. He's pleased because you are his, and he's ached to be reunited in your house for longer than you've known. Stop cleaning or trying to put on your "hostess face" to mask what's broken in your world. He sees it and desires to heal all of it, but you have to let him in. Bring all of your worry, all of your tiredness, all of your burdens. Bring them to his feet and stay there. In the next chapter, we will talk about how to keep Jesus as your "one thing" in a world that pulls for your attention in a million different directions. But please, don't rush to turn the page. Right now, in this moment, take your burdens to his feet. Where are you tired? Frustrated? What are you anxious or worried about? Where is life just really tough right now? Jesus is in your house, and he doesn't want you to do anything except sit before him. He wants to meet you there and wants intimacy with you... an intimacy that is completely all that you need.

## QUESTIONS:

1. How can you relate with Martha? Where are you worried, anxious and/or distracted?

2. Do you spend more of your life with God in "duty" or "delight?" Practically speaking, what do you feel you need to "do" in order for Jesus to be pleased in your house? Where is the Holy Spirit challenging you to exchange duty for delight?

3. What would it look like for you to develop a lifestyle of sitting at Jesus' feet like Mary?

# CHAPTER 5

# MAKING JESUS YOUR "ONE THING"

Jesus had his share of run-ins with the Pharisees and the other religious ruling party of his day, the Sadducees. They saw Jesus and his revolutionary teachings as a dangerous threat to their way of life. Not that things are much different today — Jesus does have a way of messing up our little empires with the real thing, doesn't he? They were convinced that he was a lawbreaker and intended to prove it. They continually tried to trap him and demonstrate that Jesus didn't uphold the law. Instead, every time he showed them through his words and actions that he was not only a keeper of the true law of his Father, he was the fulfiller of it. The problem is, when you go toe-to-toe against the author of something by telling him what the words of his own story really mean, you won't win that argument.

One such leader tried to corner Jesus with what he was certain was an unanswerable question. An "expert" in their law tried to hedge Jesus in by asking him which of their many laws was the most important. They hoped that Jesus would trip himself up. They reasoned that if he answered, "Honor your father and mother," they could smugly reply, "So, that's more important than not murdering someone?"

Then, the great "Rabbi" would be discredited as a man who either didn't really know the law or didn't uphold it. Their plan seemed foolproof. While I might have responded to the question by giving the "expert" a wedgie, Jesus didn't do that. Though the man meant it as a trap, Jesus used it as an opportunity to tell anyone who really cared to know what the whole law was about and how to truly fulfill it.

"Hearing that Jesus had silenced the Sadducees, the Pharisees got together. One of them, an expert in the law, tested him with this question: "Teacher, which is the greatest commandment in the Law?" Jesus replied: "'Love the Lord your God with *all* your heart and with *all* your soul and with *all* your mind.' This is the first and greatest commandment. And the second is like it: 'Love your neighbor as yourself.' *All* the Law and the Prophets hang on these two commandments" Matthew 22:34-40 – Emphasis added.

"The law and the prophets" was one of at least two ways of referring to all of the scriptures that had been written to that point, the other being the law, the writings and the prophets. So when he responded, "All the law and the prophets hang on these two commandments," he was saying, "If you fulfill these commandments, you've fulfilled the entire Bible." You don't need 613 laws. You only need to understand and do one thing: "Love God and seek Him with all of you."

Maybe you are wondering if Jesus addressed two distinct commandments. We will get to that in a minute, but suffice it to say, one thing becomes a few things that become everything. All you need flows from one thing: "Love God with all of you." This would have stunned and silenced the people in Jesus' presence, but it was far from a new idea. God has been saying it all along, but we failed to see it. Consider just a small sampling of what the Bible has to say about loving and seeking God with all we are:

"*One thing* I ask from the Lord, this *only* do I seek: that I may dwell in the house of the Lord all the days of my life, to gaze on the beauty of the Lord and to seek him in his temple" Psalm 27:4 – Emphasis added.

"Whom have I in heaven but you? And earth has *nothing* I desire *besides you*. My flesh and my heart may fail, but God is the strength of my heart and my portion forever" Psalm 73:25-26 – Emphasis added.

"How lovely is your dwelling place, Lord Almighty! My soul *yearns*, even *faints*, for the courts of the Lord; my heart and my flesh *cry out* for the living God" Psalm 84:1-2 – Emphasis added.

"You will seek me and find me when you *seek me with all your heart*. I will be found by you," declares the Lord" Jeremiah 29:13-14 – Emphasis added.

"But *seek first* his kingdom and his righteousness, and all these things will be given to you as well" Matthew 6:33 – Emphasis added.

"I am *jealous* for you with a godly jealousy. I promised you to *one* husband, to Christ, so that I might present you as a *pure virgin* to him. But I am afraid that just as Eve was deceived by the serpent's cunning, your minds may somehow be led astray from your *sincere and pure devotion* to Christ" 2 Corinthians 11:2-3 – Emphasis added.

The Love Story of the Bible screams in page after page: "Love God with all you are and come fully alive!" Did you know that Jesus' desire for your walk with him is actually for you to experience "ever-increasing glory," according to 2 Corinthians 3:18? That means that we should be getting more excited each day about who God is and what he has done in our lives than we were the day before. Someone who has known Jesus for 10 years should be noticeably more excited than they were at their fifth spiritual birthday. A Christian of 20 or 30 years should be uncontainable! Regardless of our circumstances, we should be so jubilant and overflowing with hope that we look **nuts** to the world around us because they've never seen such excitement. Not at the Super Bowl. Not at the Oscars. Not at night clubs. Not anywhere. Our joy and our hope should be impossible to ignore. That is natural Christianity.

If you aren't experiencing joy unspeakable, you can only reach one conclusion. The fault isn't on God's side. He is the waterfall that is pouring out every moment. If we aren't overflowing, we aren't living under the waterfall. I hope that stirs something in you because it's not an attack but a soothing balm to your spirit. Realize this: whatever you've experienced with Jesus — your best moment — he offers more than that to you. Remember that time when you understood his grace more deeply than you've ever known? He offers more to you in this moment. Think of that time when you were most lost in the wonder of worship — the teary-eyed gratitude that left you speechless at seeing a glimpse of how he really paid it all or the fiery conquering of "I really **can** do anything through Christ" victory chant when you caught a glimpse of his overwhelming majesty. Right now, he offers more. We will never reach the end of this uninterrupted deluge — a flood of peace, grace, love and life. While it's available deeper than you've ever experienced right now, we have to learn to make our whole life — all of it — about the pursuit of the King.

## OASIS VS. RESIDENCE

I have seen people get really, really excited about Jesus in these three environments: summer camps, mission trips and prison. I have led teenagers at summer camps for a number of years where they experience profound and breathtaking spiritual breakthroughs. Others become completely broken on a mission trip after being suddenly confronted with the depth of need in the world around them. Some pretty shy people erupt out of their shells to become world changers. People behind bars see the light of hope when they encounter Jesus and spend hours a day reading the Bible. A beautiful clarity and peace transforms their countenance. Though their body is chained, their spirit is free. These three places share one very important quality that leads to the break out of revival: people are separated from the normal comforts and distractions of life. They are in a place of surrender where they can listen so that when God speaks, it electrifies them.

These days, I struggle with leading summer camps. Yes, they provide an amazing environment of inspiration that helps people see the life that Jesus has made available to them. But I laid on my face in agony at the last summer camp that I led, weeping just moments before our final session. Miraculously, students were healed left and right at the hands of other students. Ordinary people were receiving powerful visions and insight from God for one another for the first time. Several girls who didn't even know what the gift of tongues was received it in a worship service when it wasn't even mentioned. People were set free from strongholds. Tremendous forgiveness and emotional healing was taking place between people who had carried sharp resentment and judgment. Jesus was flowing through normal people everywhere, doing far more than we dreamed possible. So why the heck was I on the floor, bawling like a baby? I realized in that moment that we'd helped them see how to run to the oasis of the Overflow, but they didn't know how to "live" there. My heart broke with concern that many might return home and within a few weeks, needlessly get on a hamster wheel of performance, when something even better than this moment was daily available for them. I wasn't upset at them but really longed to show these precious people a better way. Only I didn't have a clue how.

I had to be honest. I had been in church for nearly 20 years, leading numerous trainings and spearheading all kinds of spiritual growth campaigns. The thesis of my senior project in seminary had been designing a discipleship plan for the local church. I had preached tons of "how to" messages, but when it came to simplicity, I didn't know where to start. I didn't have a clue how to point them to the simplicity of just abiding with Jesus and "staying" there. I wept because what they needed in that moment was not another sermon, even though as a teaching pastor, I am a huge fan of sermons. The problem when it comes to living at Jesus' feet isn't a lack of information — we have more access to sermons, books, Bible studies and blogs than ever before. I think our problem is that we've been inundated with far too much information and known far too little abiding.

People come alive at summer camp because they encounter the real presence of their Father. It doesn't last because they haven't learned to make it their place of daily reality. Too many discover God as their Daddy in camp just to leave that place and think that he's only supposed to have weekend visitation rights and a few weeks of extended stay each summer. Too many are adopted as children only to continue to live like they're orphans. Jesus doesn't just want to be an oasis in the desert during a crisis. He longs to be more than just a weekly "fill up." While he will faithfully meet you there, a mailbox with your name on it sits right under the waterfall of his presence. You weren't created to visit his presence, but he came so that you could live there.

## THE "ONE THING" REQUIRES LETTING GO OF EVERY OTHER THING

To practically walk this out — where the rubber meets the road — you can't read this section through a filter of "works." If our life is truly about "one thing," our hands cannot afford to cling to other things. Our life cannot bear up under the load of multiple masters — we only have room for one King. Remember the rich young ruler who came to Jesus. This controversial scene even shook the disciples because someone came to Jesus, claiming that he was ready to follow him, but he left sad and empty.

"As Jesus started on his way, a man ran up to him and fell on his knees before him. "Good teacher," he asked, "what must I do to inherit eternal life?" "Why do you call me good?" Jesus answered. "No one is good—except God alone. You know the commandments: 'You shall not murder, you shall not commit adultery, you shall not steal, you shall not give false testimony, you shall not defraud, honor your father and mother.'" "Teacher," he declared, "all these I have kept since I was a boy." Jesus looked at him and *loved* him. "One thing you lack," he said. "Go, sell everything you have and give to the poor, and you will have treasure in heaven. Then come, follow me." At this the man's face fell. He went away sad, because he had great wealth. Jesus looked around and said to his disciples, "How hard it is for the rich to enter the kingdom of God!" Mark 10:17-23 – Emphasis added.

Unless this man was lying, he was a pretty upstanding dude who had closely followed the moral code of the Ten Commandments since his childhood. He seemed adamant about following Jesus as evidenced by his desperation in running up to Jesus and falling before him. The Bible tells us that Jesus looked at him and loved him. This appeared to be a "home run." Why in the world, then, did this same man willfully leave in discouragement just moments later? He walked away when Jesus ultimately invited him to follow him because he was unwilling to surrender his dearest treasure. A casual reader might miss what Jesus was doing, but every good Jewish student caught it. Jesus listed the commandments, starting with the sixth, "You shall not murder." Then he listed the seventh, eighth and ninth commandments before ending with the fifth. Did you catch it? Jesus intentionally skipped the tenth commandment: "You shall not covet anything that belongs to your neighbor" — the one about materialism.

He left because he wanted the spoils of the treasure Jesus offered without laying down the real treasure of his heart, his possessions. Jesus observed that it was really tough for the "rich" to follow him because they think they have something of value that they don't want to give up. Maybe you think about the guy living in the $12 million mansion as you read that, but if you have a roof over your head, functioning electricity and food in your fridge, you are richer than 99 percent of the world's population. Don't miss it: you and I are the rich that have a hard time following Jesus because of the delusion of our treasures. Perplexed, the disciples wondered how this could happen. They might have thought that Jesus should just water down the gospel a little until perhaps the man sees what he's missing. He could always "upgrade" his walk with Jesus from a "by the skin-of-his-teeth Christian" to more of a "disciple" later, right?

Without opening Pandora's Box, Jesus seemed pretty clear that he never intended for believers to be divided into multiple classes. If all of life and complete freedom from slavery to our enemy is available through him, he wouldn't ever want people to just take a little portion for now and then trudge through the mud for the rest of their life. Without speculating on who will or won't make it to heaven, the mere fact that we as believers have to address how much we "have" to give up to follow him means that we don't yet trust his heart or understand that he **is** the treasure. When we come to Jesus, he doesn't ask us to sacrifice great and profound valuables that bring us real joy so that we just settle for him. No. "Every good and perfect gift" comes from him (James 1:17). He asks for empty hands, but he wants us to lay down our striving, emptiness, fear, need for control and our obsession with being wanted that is driven by nagging insecurity. Everything that exudes real life flows from him. He asks us to surrender the imposters that we've used to numb our pain so that he can finally and fully heal us, show us our new identity and fill us with the ecstasy of knowing and walking with him. Look at what the Apostle Paul says about all of his former "treasures" in comparison to what he found in a bright light on that road to Damascus:

"But whatever were gains to me I now consider loss for the sake of Christ. What is more, I consider everything a loss because of the *surpassing worth of knowing Christ Jesus my Lord, for whose sake I have lost all things.* I consider them garbage, *that I may gain Christ* and be found in him, not having a righteousness of my own that comes from the law, but that which is through faith in Christ—the righteousness that comes from God on the basis of faith. *I want to know Christ*—yes, to know the power of his resurrection and participation in his sufferings, becoming like him in his death, and so, somehow, attaining to the resurrection from the dead. Not that I have already obtained all this, or have already arrived at my goal, but I press on to take hold of that for which Christ Jesus took hold of me. Brothers and sisters, I do not consider myself yet to have taken hold of it. But *one thing* I do: Forgetting what is behind and straining toward what is ahead, I press on toward the goal to win the prize for which God has called me heavenward in Christ Jesus" Philippians 3:7-14 – Emphasis added.

Before Paul met Jesus, his contemporaries would've all agreed that he was on the fast track to success. Diligent in his studies, he excelled at his profession. The "Who's Who" of mentors had trained him so that he quickly escalated through the ranks to a place of prominence. He had the privilege and authority to arrest people who preached this new message of a so-called resurrected Savior, Jesus. Christians feared Paul. Admirers adored him, and friends surrounded him. He was on his way to making something of himself. Then, **Jesus** happened and Paul came face to face with the impossible: a Man who was raised from the dead and who had conquered death itself. A man who breathed the miraculous — powerful enough to speak from heaven through a radiant light that showed Paul just how much he couldn't see and powerful enough to completely heal his sight through a stranger. A man who knew everything about him and asked him to know him with everything. Without realizing it, Paul followed in the steps of the 12 disciples: "He left everything at once and followed him." He surrendered it **all**. His position. His reputation. His safety. Every "so-called" friend. He was now seen as a threat and enemy to the very people who once applauded him. He plummeted from "Employee of the Month" to "Traitor of the Year."

You'd think that Paul would be sad. Maybe he'd lament, remembering the "glory days" before Jesus ruined everything. Or maybe he'd go to his room and cry as he thumbed through old photographs and listened to sappy, sentimental songs. That's not what happened, though. Instead, Paul wrote to the church of Philippi that he used to have things that he really treasured, things that he considered "gain." But once he found Jesus, his former treasures — the best that he had — became nothing but a detriment, a loss, to him. Actually, the meaning was even worse. When he lined up his old treasure next to what Jesus offered, the former was "garbage," to sanitize it a bit. In Greek, the word literally means "dung" — animal poop.[10] To put it in today's English, a Christian who has been given the fullness of heaven yet who desperately tries to hold on to what this world offers is no different than a guy clinging to *poop*. How's that for a visual image? He went on to tell the Philippians that he let it all go because he found a surpassing treasure: knowing Jesus and being known by him. Not knowing stuff about him but actually knowing the God of the universe and experiencing the fullness of his presence and power.

Paul said that to get that treasure, he focused on "one thing:" letting go of everything else and reaching forward to cling to Christ. The picture in the Greek provides an image of gladiator games. In order for someone to be victorious on a chariot, they could not remove either hand from the straps or shift their weight to look behind them because they'd lose their balance, causing a deadly fall. They couldn't hold on to anything else, either, because the intensity of the ride required that the solider fully grasp the straps with both hands, leaning all of their weight into the chariot. Paul uses this strong imagery: he held on to other things in the past, but now, he has let go of everything, including his regrets, to put all of his focus onto "one thing:" **knowing** Jesus as his treasure.

See, God is actually "knowable." We aren't supposed to come to him from afar through a priest or mediator like they did in the Old Testament. No. God wants you to lean all of your weight into him because he wants to reveal himself to you. That's what Paul learned, and that's what he prayed for us:

"I keep asking that the God of our Lord Jesus Christ, the glorious Father, may give you the Spirit of wisdom and revelation, *so that you may know him better.* I pray that the eyes of your heart may be enlightened in order that you may *know* the hope to which he has called you, the riches of his glorious inheritance in his holy people, and his incomparably great power for us who believe" Ephesians 1:17-19 – Emphasis added.

Jesus isn't trying to take something great from you. Instead, he's longing to make something great of you! He's inviting you to know him better. He wants to enlighten your heart to know hope. Real hope. He wants to show you your calling. He wants to reveal that all of the riches of heaven are at your disposal because you are now a child of royalty. And he wants you to realize that the same power that raised Jesus from the dead is now alive **in** you and longing to burst **out** of you to shower hope everywhere. All of that and more is available to you today, but he needs to occupy all of your heart. Jesus talked a lot about the Kingdom of God, and in one of my favorite parables, he compared life with him to a field that might not look that impressive on the surface but which contains a treasure of more incredible worth than we could ever fathom:

"The kingdom of heaven is like treasure hidden in a field. When a man found it, he hid it again, and then in his joy went and *sold all he had* and bought that field" Matthew 13:44 – Emphasis added.

Notice three very important details in this parable.

1. The Kingdom is described as something that costs you everything. This man threw his whole lot into just one thing: owning this field.
2. He isn't burdened about bidding farewell to all that he has, making a martyr's march to the real estate office. Instead, he is giddy, even beside himself, filled with delight.

3. He defined what awaited him in the field as treasure beyond his wildest imagination, overwhelmingly greater than what he gave up in exchange. He knows he should never be able to obtain such a treasure and cannot believe that some crazy realtor is putting it within his grasp. That's why he's so giddy and running with joy to capture the opportunity of a lifetime. He wants to seal the deal before they change their minds. Like the NFL team that wins a controversial call and hurries to run the next play before it's challenged, this guy gladly casts aside everything to run and buy this field.

Life in the Overflow demands that you lay down everything, but it isn't a sacrifice. Following Jesus isn't a sacrifice. We give him our broken past and our junk, and he fills us with his peace, unlocking the secrets of our hearts to make us every bit of what we were intended to be. We have to stop clinging to the poop of this world as if it were some grand treasure. Think about the things that keep most people from leaving everything to follow Jesus: cars: poop. Money and possessions: poop and poop. Status and reputation, comfort and entertainment. However you dress it up, it's all poop. Instead, we are offered real treasure. And by "real treasure," I don't mean what Jesus can give us. Just like all good daddies who want to bless their kids, God is a good Father who wants to prosper us beyond our wildest imagination. Even so, some parts of the "prosperity gospel" teach that people give up their stuff to follow Jesus so that he will give them more stuff. That makes me queasy. More money and more stuff isn't the treasure. While this planet provides some pretty cool creature comforts, the truth is that you could "take 'em or leave 'em" if you found the "real" treasure. The real treasure isn't stuff but Jesus himself.

Some might ask, "Doesn't the Bible say, 'Delight yourself in the Lord, and he will give you the desires of your heart?' " Absolutely. But when you find your fullest delight in Jesus, you find that he **is** your treasure. When he gives you the desire of your heart, he is giving you himself. Yes, he gives a million other blessings, but the reason that Paul could be "content with little" or "content with much" is because he found his treasure in Jesus, not in externals. Jesus says that, right now, we live in a kingdom where everything that can be shaken will be shaken. Can I hear an "amen?" Cars break down, and stuff gets old. One month, you have money in the bank, and the next you are wondering how you will pay your bills. People love you one day but not the next. Everything in this kingdom **will** be shaken because nothing here is your treasure. He has given you a Kingdom that cannot be shaken, though, a treasure that will never rust, corrupt or fade. That treasure is himself. We stress out about so many petty things, but if you have Jesus, you have the pearl of great price. You have the treasure. If you have Jesus and you never are applauded by man again, you still have Jesus. If you have Jesus and you live in a home that requires constant repairs, don't fret: you have Jesus. If your time here on earth never holds another external blessing but you have Jesus, for goodness sake, you have Jesus. He **is** your treasure. Forever. As if that weren't enough, he wants to bless your socks off, too. He really does. The God who wants your life to be a dance of love with others really isn't out to embarrass you. He's out to liberate you and make you an ambassador of hope. He longs to give you so much blessing that you cannot contain it, but like Paul, you have to stop clinging to stuff. Enjoy it when it comes, but you don't have to despair when things here don't go your way. You already have the treasure. You have Jesus.

## CLEARING A CLUTTERED HOUSE

You can live every day from glory to glory. But make no mistake, you will need to empty your hands and clear your cluttered house. We cannot be filled to overflowing with the Holy Spirit if we're already filled with a thousand other treasures and demands on our life. We must lay it all down. When you choose to lay down everything, many troubling scriptures will finally make sense. I used to scratch my head at tons of things that Jesus said, stressing over them. I didn't know it, but his words threatened my "poop treasure" that I'd shined and placed on my mantle. I didn't want to let go of it, so like the rich young ruler, I couldn't fully receive what he was saying. Consider some of the crazy sayings of Jesus: "Whoever is not with me is against me" (Matthew 12:30). "Unless you eat the flesh of the Son of Man and drink his blood, you have no life in you" (John 6:53). "You cannot serve God and mammon" (Matthew 6:24 – NKJV). We translated that money, but the Greek actually means "another treasure."[11] He says that you cannot serve God and another treasure because it's a conflict of interest — you will love one and hate the other. It's not just money but any other treasure. You don't have sufficient room in your heart for two masters. They will pull you in opposite directions as they cry out for your unwavering loyalty, and if you have more than one treasure seated on the throne of your heart, you will be in grave internal conflict. You will only ultimately follow one of them while you forsake the other.

Consider this precious gem in the gospel of Luke:

"Large crowds were traveling with Jesus, and turning to them he said: "If anyone comes to me and does not hate father and mother, wife and children, brothers and sisters—yes, even their own life—such a person *cannot* be my disciple. And whoever does not carry their cross and follow me *cannot* be my disciple" Luke 14:25-27 – Emphasis added.

Ummm....What?!? Maybe Jesus was just having a really bad day when he said that. It's confusing to think that God, who is the definition of love itself and the one who told us to love even our enemies, is now asking us to hate mom and dad, spouses and kids, even ourselves. This doesn't jive with, "Love me with all your heart and love your neighbor as yourself" (Matthew 22:37, 39). You might wonder why he is saying that if we fail to do this and "take up our cross," then we're out of the "disciple" club.

However, when you understand that there is only room in your heart for one thing — one treasure — it becomes abundantly clear. The people Jesus listed are those closest to you — the ones who have your loyalty.

When push comes to shove, they are the ones you will listen to and protect. Humanly speaking, they influence you the most. Obviously, he isn't calling us to literally "hate" them. Don't go toilet paper your parent's house or kick your spouse to the curb. He is saying that to follow him, you have to be willing to fully follow. You cannot put what Jesus asks you to do up for a popular vote and judge how it fits with what your "other" counselors say.

Notice that what he asks you to do in those relationships is ultimately what he asks you to do with your own life: to lay it down. To die. He is calling us to come and unapologetically and unswervingly follow him, no matter what. He is calling us to echo the words of the old chorus, "I Have Decided to Follow Jesus," which says, "Though none go with me, still I will follow."[12] Jesus isn't being judgmental or harsh when he says that we "cannot" be his disciple if we don't surrender everything. That phrase isn't a statement of superiority but of reality, and it means that unless you surrender your need for the approval of man, you will not make it. It's as if someone tells you, "If you never train or sign up for an Ironman Triathlon, you won't make it!" "If you sign up to fight on the front lines in a war without going through basic training or firing a weapon, you won't make it!" "If you jump out of a plane and don't have a parachute…." Get the picture?

At some point, Jesus will call you to go somewhere, and others or even you might be inclined to hesitate or object. At some point, voices of logic will try to "protect" you from going out in the deep with your Creator, and if you've "got" to make them happy, you won't make it. I love my parents, my kids and my spouse. They are such an overwhelmingly beautiful group of people. They make me smile and laugh. I would do anything to protect them. But I can't make them my god. Sometimes, they are going to miss it and in those moments, I cannot bow my life to their desires or demands. No. Truly **loving** them requires doing what Jesus calls "hating" them. While it seems like a paradox, my heart only has room for one master. My life is no longer my own, and I will go where he leads.

The real issue here is trust. Do we trust Jesus' heart? Some say that they will follow Jesus fully when they trust him more, but real trust is only built in the place of sustained intimacy. You don't learn to trust someone by guarding your every treasure, keeping them on the outside. Trust is only built as you hand people things that matter to you, and they show you that they are faithful. I tried for years to "wade" deeper with God one teeny, slow, controllable step at a time, but it didn't get me anywhere. I had to drop my guard and be real with him. I had to admit that there were places that I didn't trust him, things I had prayed for and didn't receive the answer that I expected. As Proverbs 13:12 says, "Hope deferred makes the heart sick." I was scared. I had been harboring other treasures in my heart that were keeping my hands too full to really run after him. You can only construct real trust with God when you communicate with real vulnerability.

In the next chapter, we'll talk about coming to a supernatural place where you "Overflow" with his presence every day, but this is by far your most crucial place of decision. If you don't take this key step, nothing else happens. It is time to rewrite the mission statement of your life. Up until now, perhaps you've felt you need to do, be or accomplish many things in order to be fulfilled, but your life is just about one thing: **You really have to know your Daddy!** He is the fount of all life. If you don't do anything else during your day, you have to learn to hear his voice and enter into the wild dance of romance with him. He is so much more ridiculously good than we've realized, and he is for you, but you have to lay down whatever is in your hands to take up the treasure that he offers.

Right now, just slow your heart. Breathe. Be willing to let go of stuff that's keeping you from your Daddy. Begin to open up and learn to trust him. Be willing to put the book down and to talk with him for as long as it takes. Don't wait until you fully understand everything to start opening up because real trust is only built in a place of real vulnerability. Pour out your heart. You really can know him. It's not about a long list of things to do. It's just one thing: give him all of you — all your faults, frailties, hopes, dreams — everything. Lay down your poop. Drop your guard. Let him *be* your Daddy. Learn to make him your "one thing."

## QUESTIONS:

Take some time to quiet yourself before the Lord and be vulnerable.

1. Where is it that you don't trust God? Are there things that you've "swept under the rug?" Examples might include: places you've asked him to come through and didn't see him, traumatic experiences when he seemed absent or prayers for someone sick who wasn't healed. Ask God to remind you of your own situations.

2. What treasures do you need to lay down? You can easily spot them by asking yourself: What do you feel that you have to have in order to be happy? What do you freak out about if you don't have? What do you worry about or stress over? What do you turn to for comfort when life gets tough? Ask the Holy Spirit to expose the other treasures in your heart. Spend some time in prayer. You might need to seek further counsel from a mature brother or sister. Don't be embarrassed to ask for help.

# CHAPTER 6

# BROKEN STAIRWAYS:

*Stop "Climbing" and Use the Elevator Already!*

I have a confession to make. I love running although I didn't used to. For many years, I told people that if they saw me running, they'd better run, too, because it meant that someone was chasing me with a weapon! The very thought of running used to give me side cramps, and I dreaded the day each year in school when we had to complete the one-mile run. But then something strange happened: somewhere along the road, pun intended, I fell in love with it. I find peace as I put on my headphones and listen to worship music or a sermon and breathe in nature. During the last few years, I've run several 5ks, a 10k, and most recently, a half-marathon in quite a few cities across my home state of Florida. I have run on dirt roads deep in the country in South Carolina and down the shoreline of several beaches, waves crashing beneath my feet. I even ran up the same steps that Rocky did in front of the Philadelphia Museum of Art. The only place that I don't enjoy running is on the treadmill. With sincere apologies to treadmill lovers, I just can't get excited about that contraption of insanity! While I certainly didn't mind the air conditioning, I could never move past the fact that no matter how much effort I exerted, I was still standing in the same place. No matter how hard I ran, I never went anywhere. I felt the same frustration with growing in my faith for a long time, too. I just kept jumping on different "spiritual growth" treadmills that exhausted me but always left me feeling as if I was standing in the same place where I started.

Since early in my walk with Jesus, discipleship has been one of my greatest passions. When I read that Jesus' disciples "left everything" to follow him, I desired that as well. Once I entered Bible college, I began devouring books on how to be a disciple, amassing quite an extensive library. With my highlighter and pen as my tools, I endeavored to excavate the depths of some great books about spiritual disciplines and holiness. I sank my teeth into other amazing books about theology and spiritual warfare. I thank God for them and still use and reference them. But each one offered a different "secret" to becoming a disciple. I tried really hard, but I never felt like I was getting anywhere.

I had another problem, too. The more that I read, the more that I came to understand that I wasn't just supposed to *be* a disciple — I was supposed to help *make* disciples who make even *more* disciples. This was overwhelming — I wasn't even sure I knew how to *be* a disciple, let alone *make* them. I started reading books on church spiritual growth strategies to see what they could share to help me "make" disciples. I tried to help lead a "Purpose-Driven" congregation while remaining a "Simple" Church. I tried to balance the "Marks of a Healthy Church" with the "Irrefutable Laws of Leadership." I consumed a mountain of books on small groups and read others about keeping big vision. I went to conference after conference that shared how to make disciples by being missional yet remaining "relevant." While the authors of nearly every resource urged me that it wasn't a "one-size-fits-all" solution and to only apply what worked in my context, I had a hard time listening. They seemed successful to me, and I joined crowds of other pastors and spiritual leaders who tried to follow each plan to the letter, only to ultimately meet with frustration.

Before I go any further, let me first urge you to do something. If you belong to a local church, thank God right now for your pastors. You might want to call or text them or even send a "thank you" card. Take them out for coffee. I have had the joy of being around a lot of pastors for years, and they are some of the most selfless and beautiful people I have ever known. They face so much more than you probably ever realize and have endured so much more than they will probably ever tell you. They pray and work and counsel tirelessly for one reason, and I promise you, it isn't the money or fame! Like me, they really want to make disciples who make disciples! Encourage your pastors and jump in with them because making disciples isn't a "pastor" thing but an every believer thing! In all of the spiritual growth plans, I observed that too much pressure was placed on pastors and too little credit, invitation and involvement was given to the rest of the Body of Christ.

Indeed, we live in a culture where many believe that they should go to church so that they can "be a better person" without understanding that they have been called and empowered to be disciple-makers themselves. I didn't hear a lot about expecting the Body of Christ to rise up and be the Body of Christ. At the same time, I was one of many pastors who felt a deep burden and even a sense of guilt at failing to see church members walk as disciples, a burden many attempt to alleviate by trying harder and working more hours. Yet, the Bible tells us that pastors are just one of five office gifts along with apostles, prophets, evangelists and teachers, whose collective purpose is to "equip the saints" to know God so that together, we can reach fullness and do Christ's work (see Ephesians 4:11-13). Jesus said the harvest of people needing hope is plentiful, and he ripped the veil in the temple because you no longer live in an age where professionals do the reaping. Sons and daughters do.

## CONSUMERS AND SPECTATORS

According to Google definitions, a consumer properly defined is "a person who acquires goods for their personal use and enjoyment."[13] We live in a consumer society. Entertainment and commerce sends the constant message that you are the center of your own world and that you find supreme happiness as you earn, acquire and enjoy the things that you want. It's the reason that advertisers spend so much money so that they can get yours. At every corner, they tell you that you deserve what you want and that you should have an ample menu of selections so that you can get the most for your money. Consumerism drives stiff competition between phone manufacturers, car companies, clothing retailers, even food distributors. Everyone wants your business. Somewhere along the way, that same mindset crept into the church. Too many churches started focusing on keeping people "happy," and too many church attenders started voting with their feet and their dollars when something else vied for their attention. Too many church leaders started viewing other churches as competition while too many families started changing churches more quickly than they drop mobile carriers because they didn't feel that they were being "fed," and another congregation grabbed their attention. Our obsession switched from fully equipping people to embody the gospel to fully impressing people to want to show up for our really excellent services. Because of this, we've rolled out a full menu of classes, "catchy" and entertaining message series and a continual restless tweaking to do whatever it takes to "keep people engaged."

The problem isn't that we desire creativity. The closer that we get to Jesus, the more that we are set free to run and dance in our myriad of expressions. Creative ideas, drama skits and videos, well-crafted worship anthems or anything that flows from the confines of creativity should be birthed in our intimacy with our Father. Christians need to unashamedly let creativity ring through our lungs. My concern isn't necessarily about programming — it is about the heart that drives it all. When we start making decisions based on what people will like instead of based on asking what our Daddy wants to release, we are in trouble.

I hope you don't hear judgment and that you will hear what I am saying. We may live in a consumer-driven culture, but we are not called to be a consumer-driven church. Too many people are leaving churches because they view it like a product where they are supposed to be the satisfied customer, but Jesus didn't birth his church as a competitive consumer organization. He birthed it to be a united family, an equipped army, a compassionate hospital of healing and an environment where regular people become disciples who make disciples who turn the world upside down. But we can never become that if we run from church to church like a revolving door when we don't feel as if it meets our needs. People leave the church for so many reasons:

- They don't like the message series.
- It's too big.
- It's too small.
- They don't offer enough programs.
- Someone failed to greet them.
- A leader said something they didn't agree with and
- Too many other reasons to name.

More than 50 percent of Christians don't belong to any local body.[14] While there are a lot of reasons for people joining the so-called "dones," a big one is consumerism. A popular move has been spreading where people just occasionally watch YouTube videos or catch sermons on TV instead of attending a local church. If that's you, I don't mean to offend. But I also don't want to see Christ's Body segmented and separated anymore. Christ built his church for so much more than just a place where you can view messages, even really good ones. He calls you a member of his Body, and he says that his Body cannot be complete without you! Consumerism is seeping into every area of our lives. Please don't let it happen with you and the church. Maybe a church really hurt you. If they did, as a pastor, I am so very sorry. It breaks my heart, but your church experience isn't all that's out there. Christ built his church, and he wants you in it. This isn't about you checking off something from some list to make God happy. It's about the Body becoming all that it can be, and you becoming all that you can be. Jesus designed the church as an environment where you can grow. If you've stalled in your church search, I encourage you to restart. Some awesome churches out there really are working to make disciples — I serve in one of them — but no church gets it all right. It is made up of messy sons and daughters learning who they are. Don't run if you see something broken in your church. See how you can be part of the solution. You weren't created to consume a sermon Sunday after Sunday. He wants to release springs of living water out of you in your church and everywhere.

Pastors and church leaders, just as I've seen too many church attenders think like consumers, I've seen too many pastors try to do everything. They do all of the preaching, counseling, answer all of the questions and so much more. That leaves the church members to be nothing more than spectators. I know from experience that most of this stems from a servant's heart, but all too often, people who have been in the church for years don't ever feel ready to embody the gospel. Whenever most of the people in the church are sitting and observing the gifts of a few select others, making disciples will take a back seat to molding "evaluators." People will go to church, listen to a worship team, listen to a sermon, listen to some prayers and then go home. If they are really involved, they might go to a small group where they answer a few questions, but they mostly listen to what the leader has to share. For many people, they become spectators who evaluate how the service made them feel: whether they liked the message and the topic or not or whether they liked the sound or not, but there's so much more. Jesus didn't say, "Follow me, and I will make you really good evaluators of fishermen." He said, "Follow me, and I will make you fishers of men" (Matthew 4:19 – ESV).

Pastors, I bless and encourage you to shake off the spectator mentality that is so prevalent in our culture and provide opportunities everywhere for people to hear God and respond. And, yes, it will be messy as it always is when kids learn how to walk. But we have to be less concerned with excellence and more concerned with creating safe environments where sons and daughters actually learn to take their first steps without fear of falling. We have to raise the bar of what Jesus has made fully available and attainable for ordinary believers and give them tons of opportunities in every ministry to practice it. We have to remove any mystical rock-star lens that wants people to be impressed with us or our church by our glossy presentation because all that does is intimidate people, hindering them from seeing their own distinct beauty. We have to stop being ok with allowing a few people to carry the load. Like Moses' father-in-law told him when he was leading the Israelites, it will wear you out. It will also leave out a whole lot of unique gifts that make your church great. Please, make your church a safe place for hungry sons and daughters of God to participate in the work of the gospel. And when they do, please don't pick apart their offering through the "excellence" filter. Instead, become a place that applauds every time you see someone step out for their King and partners with them for continued equipping. The gospel is simple, not complicated. Let's remove the intimidation and release the infantry.

## BROKEN STAIRWAYS

All of the discipleship plans that I drew up for our church focused on steps. Step one: Salvation. Step two: Baptism. Step three: Spiritual Disciplines. Step Four: Freedom. But all of the outward or "miraculous" stuff — preaching, healing and setting the captives free — fell to the bottom of the list, always just out of reach because we don't yet feel "ready." As a result, people can be in the faith for 20 years and still not feel prepared to share the gospel.

All of the stairway models that we've set up, much like our school system, carried the idea that you had to graduate each "step" before being ready to move on to the next one. This created a real problem. For example, some people grew up not knowing about healing and convinced themselves that they didn't need to address it while others who grew up understanding healing and speaking in tongues thought that they had completed the necessary steps, reasoning that they'd graduated from matters of "spiritual disciplines" and "character" long ago. Others carried an aura that looked down their nose at anyone who didn't practice their miraculous lifestyle as if everything they were doing was merely "baby stuff." While I am making broad generalizations, the struggle was real. One part of the Body needed confidence that they really could manifest the Kingdom but felt ill-equipped to do so, sensing that they were being judged and belittled for it. Others really needed to see that the gifts were supposed to flow from intimacy and not stand as ends in and of themselves to showcase their spiritual worth, but they couldn't see this perspective.

For all of them, the stairway model made it really difficult to mess up. After all, if you had already *graduated* from the step of knowing your identity and were now ready to share your faith, but you suddenly awoke one morning and couldn't see your worth clearly, it felt like you had been held back a grade and needed remedial classes. So many Christians operate under that "I should know better by now" mentality. In addition, my "stairways" required lots of details and effort, and everyone's journey was made to look identical — cookie-cutter versions of each other. I kept trying to tweak it or fix the same stairway another way. Then, one day, God gave me a clear vision. He told me they were all broken stairways. I kept putting more doors into stairways on the ground floor of a building called discipleship. Each stairway made it up a few flights — some further than others — but they all abruptly ended, and none of them came anywhere close to the top. My own pursuit of discipleship felt the same way — as if I were running hard but ultimately hit a dead end no matter what route I took. Just then, I heard God say, "Stop climbing stairs and take the elevator already."

"What?!?" I responded. I was floored — yes, pun intended! I wanted to know what he meant.

He continued, "I already paid it all. All the stairways that you are constructing are because you think that you are the power behind discipleship, but I am the power. I am the motor. Just get in the elevator, hit the button, and I will take you where you need to go!" Holy cow! That is such good news and a great picture of exactly what he did.

"His divine power has *given* us everything we need for a godly life through our knowledge of him who called us by his own glory and goodness" 2 Peter 1:3 - Emphasis added.

Just as Jesus paid for everything necessary to save us, he paid for everything to mature us, too. He already gave you all that you need to live a godly life and to fully know him. It's true. You don't need to work hard to climb your way up the stairs. He's the motor. Beyond that, while all our manmade plans might progressively "unlock" new levels with God as we graduate past the lower levels, he doesn't operate that way. All of the riches of heaven are yours right now. Healing and making disciples aren't down the road at the Ph.D. end of the spectrum. You are his, and as you live under his waterfall, it is all available now!

## ONE THING BECOMES A FEW THINGS THAT BECOME EVERYTHING

If you remember, Jesus told the experts of the law that the entire Bible would be fulfilled if we'd love Jesus with all of our hearts and love our neighbors as ourselves. Those two commands are not separate from each other. Jesus told us to love him with all of our hearts, all of us. "All" is not the same thing as "the best portion" or "the majority." It is not just 95 percent, but "all" equals 100 percent of us. If we give Jesus all of our heart, we have nothing left to give to anything or anyone else.

When we love Jesus with "all" of our heart, he pours all of himself into us, resulting in the Overflow. God says that his desire is for us to "be filled with all the fullness of God" (Ephesians 3:19), and he calls us to "be continually filled with the Holy Spirit" (Ephesians 5:18). The word "fill" means for something to be occupied to its maximum capacity.[15] When we give all of us to him, he "fills" us. It gets even better. Jesus promised that he would send us the Holy Spirit, and he said that when the Spirit came, "rivers of living water would flow from within them" (John 7:38). The Apostle Paul said that when we come to the place where we trust in God, we begin to "Overflow" with hope (Romans 15:13). So as we do one thing — love God with 100 percent of us — he fills us with his love for us.

We are called to "love our neighbor as ourselves," which requires us to know how to love ourselves. Some people question this because they feel that it sounds selfish or narcissistic, making more of themselves than anyone else, but this misses the point. Loving ourselves is not about being "self-centered" or "self-serving." In fact, the only people who obsess to make everything about themselves are people who haven't yet learned to truly love themselves. When we love God with all of us, he shows us how he sees us and enables us to love ourselves the way that he loves us. And as we love God with all of our heart and are able to lift our head and properly see our worth, loving others becomes easy because they are no longer our competition. One thing becomes a few things.

Jesus and the disciples traveled around preaching, healing and setting the captives free, not putting on some kind of circus but manifesting love to the people. Preaching demonstrates love and brings our spirit back to our Father. Healing demonstrates love that sets people free from sin's effects on our bodies and unites them with the kindness of God. Setting captives free demonstrates love to bound souls so that they can come out from under the bondage of slavery and find the joyous freedom of being his child. Jesus tells us to preach, heal and set the captives free because these are manifestations of love. But all of it — **all** of it — flows from just one thing. One thing that becomes a few things that changes everything.

## MORE THAN YOUR VESSEL CAN HOLD

I will deal with more practical steps for healing and setting the captive free in the chapter on authority, but to close this chapter, discipleship never means that you climb a stairway of steps of your effort. What Jesus is asking you to do as a carrier of the gospel is impossible. You cannot train yourself for his miraculous power to manifest through you. You can only position yourself under the waterfall where he Overflows. When you live every moment, learning to stay in the place where you love Jesus with all of you, you are under his waterfall. In that moment, he is pouring out of you. Jesus said that the Father came to give you the Spirit "without limit" (John 3:34) or without restriction. This is similar to those massive buckets that fill with water above kids' heads at water parks. They fill up a little bit at a time until the bucket starts swaying back and forth and then all of a sudden, **boom**...it erupts everywhere with a barrage of water. Once, my young son stood under one such bucket, completely unaware of what was coming. As the bucket started to sway, I hurried to him and whisked him out of the way in the nick of time. He would've been knocked over, completely drenched by that much water. It would've been too much for his little body to contain. That's how your Daddy pours out his love into you when you love him with all of your heart. You cannot contain it. It has to come out.

You don't need a complex stairway. Instead, you need to stay where his love pours over you. While you might tire of me saying this, I am going to repeat myself because it is everything. I do not have another message. His Kingdom will flow out of you as you stay in a focused place where you love him with all of your heart. You do not need more "steps" to Overflow. He already paid it all. You do not need more "study" to Overflow. The streams that he wants to pour out of you are more profound than what you can comprehend. Remember, he changed history with "ordinary, unschooled men," according to Acts 4:13. You do not need to wait before you Overflow. It isn't the gospel of tomorrow but the gospel of right now. You do not need more "breakthrough" before you Overflow. Two thousand years ago, Jesus broke through and gave you everything you need.

Stop climbing. Take the elevator. Get ready for a wild ride!

## QUESTIONS:

1. Can you relate to being a consumer or a spectator in God's Kingdom? How is the Holy Spirit challenging you to change that mindset?

2. Do you feel that God is pleased with you now? What "stairways" do you find yourself building in order to make yourself pleasing to him? These might include spiritual disciplines, activities, etc.

3. Read 2 Peter 1:3 again. What do you feel you "need" to be successful in life? What do you feel you lack to consider yourself "godly?" Jesus already gave us all we need, and we come to understand it "through our knowledge of Him." Take the places you feel inadequate and unqualified to his throne — talk to him honestly and ask him to wash over you with his truth. Don't rush — let him transform you there.

# CHAPTER 7

# INTIMACY WITH GOD:

*Slow Down and Embrace the Process*

I love my lead pastor, Len Harper, who is actually so much more than a lead pastor. He's a spiritual father, a mentor and a friend. I have served under his leadership for nearly 15 years. He has blessed Jill and I by investing in our marriage since before day one, leading our pre-marital counseling and serving as the officiant at our wedding. He has been with us when it mattered most, including celebrating at the hospital when all five of our kids were born. When I became aware that I needed to be set free from rejection, Len prayed me through it. When I needed direction on whether or not to continue in seminary while working full-time, Len was there. And seven years later, when I needed a mentor to oversee my senior thesis, Len spent a plethora of hours wading through it all with me. As I've needed advice about life, family, ministry…time and time again, Len has been there. I sometimes hear horror stories of pastors who serve on staff under their lead pastors. It breaks my heart, but thankfully, I have not experienced this personally. At every turn, Len has honored, protected, served and elevated us. He has been the exact same person in his office and in his home as he is standing before our congregation. I am a far better man of God, husband, father and pastor because of Len Harper.

I have come to know Len quite well over the years and recognize certain quirks of his. I know, for instance, that when we go to a restaurant that he will probably order salads for both of his sides and ask for two different dressings for each of them, on the side, of course. If he orders pasta, he will ask for "extra, extra cheese" and "extra, extra, extra sauce." I know that if he goes to someone's home for the first time, he will likely go into every single room even if he is not invited. Just ask my wife how we know that one! I know that if you are telling him a story and he doesn't understand something, he will keep asking questions until it makes sense to him. Whether it is numbers or a company's policies or how something works, Len really wants to understand the details and becomes very uncomfortable when they aren't clear. At a meeting, if anyone suggests a potential direction for our church, Len will ask one question, which just might be his favorite. "What does that look like?" If all of life is really about intimacy with our Father, and if all of the fruit that we'd ever want to bear overflows out of us when we stay in the place of intimacy, we'd be wise to ask that same question: "What does that look like?" What does it "look like" for you to walk in intimacy with God? The answer will probably surprise you. Drum roll, please.

I cannot tell you.

I am not you. You have been uniquely made, so it might look quite different for you than it looks for me. Len, for example, feels particularly close to God when he sits in his hot tub or goes for a quiet run. He stays up late hours praying and reading magazine articles. His spirit is lifted as he reads through his Bible plan, which he has followed for nearly 20 years. This is his "happy place." That looks really different than the way it looks for me. I feel close to God when I dig deeply into passages of the Bible. Reading plans don't work for me. Some days, I camp in a few verses. Other days, I'm all over the scriptures. I also love sitting down at a piano and singing my heart out to my King. I "think out loud" a lot and process verbally with people, often realizing something new that I never before expressed even while I'm talking. I also love walking — especially out in open spaces —

when I pray. Len's times of intimacy with God look similar from day to day while mine are all over the board. You don't have to find a "right" way to connect with God. If intimacy is your goal, then you have to discover how you connect with him. At least two important qualities need to be present in all of our lives to truly have intimacy with God since it's about a communing from heart to heart. We must communicate with God, and we must allow him to communicate with us!

## SLOW DOWN: LEARNING TO LISTEN

God has always been the God who speaks. When he created Adam and Eve, he walked with them in the garden, and he talked with them, telling them his heart and their purpose. He talked with Adam's son, Cain. God spoke to Noah, directing him what he needed to do to save the world from the flood. He spoke to the patriarchs, Abraham, Isaac and Jacob. He spoke to women — Sarah about her coming son and also to the dejected Hagar, comforting her and promising her an inheritance. He spoke to Moses, who eventually delivered the children of Israel from the Egyptians, through a burning bush. He spoke to judges, starting with Gideon and to prophets, starting with Samuel. God spoke to King David and many of the kings that followed him. God spoke to Job when life didn't make any sense and to Job's "friend," Eliphaz. He even spoke to the fish that swallowed Jonah to tell it where to spit him back up on land! In story after story, all through the Old Testament, God shows himself as a God who speaks to his children.

When you turn the page to the New Testament, God shows us that he has never changed, speaking to his kids in visions, dreams, words of knowledge and prophecy, bright lights and simple, straightforward promptings. If anything, his voice only intensified when he sent the Holy Spirit. Make no mistake about it: God is a relational God, and he desires to connect and personally speak to us. In an incredible passage in John 10, Jesus compared his relationship with us to a shepherd leading his sheep to the place of pasture. I encourage you to read this chapter, but for the sake of our discussion, I'll give you just the highlights:

"The one who enters by the gate is the shepherd of the sheep. The gatekeeper opens the gate for him, and the sheep *listen* to his voice. He *calls* his own sheep *by name* and *leads* them out. When he has brought out all his own, he goes on ahead of them, and his sheep *follow* him because *they know his voice*. But they will never follow a stranger; in fact, they will run away from him because they *do not recognize a stranger's voice*...I am the gate; whoever enters through me will be saved. They will come in and go out, and *find pasture*. The thief comes only to steal and kill and destroy; I have come that they may have life, and have it to the full...I am the good shepherd; I know my sheep and *my sheep know me—just as the Father knows me and I know the Father*—and I lay down my life for the sheep. I have other sheep that are not of this sheep pen. I must bring them also. They too will *listen* to my voice, and there shall be one flock and one shepherd...My sheep *listen* to my voice; I know them, and they *follow* me. I give them eternal life, and they shall never perish; no one will snatch them out of my hand" John 10:2-5, 9-10, 15-16, 27-28 – Emphasis added.

Did you get all of that? God speaks to us *individually*: He calls us each by name. He speaks to us *directionally*, charting a specific course to lead us where we need to go. God speaks to us *clearly*, distinguishing his voice from that of a stranger. He speaks *revealingly*, fully disclosing who he is to us and unveiling who we are to him.

But it gets even better. God doesn't just want to speak externally *to* us. Jesus said that he would send the Holy Spirit to speak *within* us.

"All this I have spoken while still with you. But the Advocate, the Holy Spirit, whom the Father will send in my name, will *teach* you *all* things and will *remind* you of *everything* I have said to you. Peace

I leave with you; my peace I give you. I do not give to you as the world gives. Do not let your hearts be troubled and do not be afraid" John 14:25-27 – Emphasis added.

Jesus told you and me that he would send the Holy Spirit to "come alongside" us to help us run the race that God marked out for us. That's what "advocate" means: "one called alongside you to help you."[16] But did you catch what he said the Holy Spirit would "come alongside" us to do? He said that the reason the Holy Spirit came was to **teach** us and to **remind** us. Even more, the Holy Spirit would teach you **all** things: about God, about you, about life. How long do you think that it would take for you to learn all things about God? We could start talking now and expend multiple lifetimes without once taking a break to breathe, and we wouldn't be able to do more than scratch the surface of all things of his majesty. He has so much to say that it will take all of eternity to hear it. That's exactly the point. If the Holy Spirit is to teach you all things about God, you and life, then he has a lot that he wants to say to you, starting now.

1 John 2:27 says that the Holy Spirit is the "anointing who teaches you about all things." That word "anointing" means to "smear or coat something in a messy manner."[17] Some brides and grooms do this when they serve each other their wedding cake. My wife and I played it nice, but some of these couples smash cake in each other's faces with such intensity that you don't know whether to laugh or call an ambulance. They have cake everywhere, in every single crevice — in their eyebrows, hair, up their nostrils and in their ears. They look like performers for the Blue Man Group. That's what it means to be "anointed" with something. The Holy Spirit's desire is to come so completely and so powerfully upon you that he fills every crevice.

In addition to teaching us, the Holy Spirit will remind us of everything that Jesus said. That brings me such great comfort because I used to see some things a lot more clearly than I see them at this moment. Have you ever had a day where you just had a hard time grasping the fact that God really loves you? If you grew up anywhere around a church or a Vacation Bible

School, you learned the song, "Jesus loves me, this I know, for the Bible tells me so," as a very young child.[18] You don't need to be taught it, but you need to be reminded of what you already know, because the circumstances of life have attempted to knock that truth from its rightful place. As you love God with all of your heart, the Holy Spirit will continually remind you of what you might have forgotten. He will breathe over you and help your mind reacquaint itself with who your spirit already is. Most beautifully of all, he will do it without any condemnation! That's why Jesus speaks peace over you and tells you to not be troubled or afraid. The Holy Spirit is always speaking truth over you. He has come to teach you all things and to remind you of everything that you forgot. The question is not whether or not God is speaking to you but whether you've learned to discern his voice from the voices of strangers.

When I share about God eagerly desiring to speak supernaturally and individually to us about specific situations in our lives, some people get nervous. People comment, "God spoke to us fully in the written Word, and the canon is closed." Some even take verses in the book of Revelation out of context, arguing that if you believe that God gave you specific counsel, then you are adding to scripture. Someone quoted Hebrews 1:1, 2 which says, "*In the past* God spoke to our ancestors through the prophets at many times and in various ways, but in these last days he has spoken to us by his Son…*" (emphasis theirs). They insisted that we are in the "last days" when God doesn't speak through prophets anymore because Jesus ended that. However, the book of Acts uses the exact same phrase with a very different conclusion:

"'In the *last days*, God says, I will pour out my Spirit on *all* people. Your sons and daughters will *prophesy*, your young men will see *visions*, your old men will dream *dreams*. Even on my *servants*, both men and women, I will *pour out my Spirit* in those days, and they will *prophesy*" Acts 2:17-18 – Emphasis added.

Indeed, the words of Paul and all of the events of Revelation show that in the "last days," God is speaking through prophets and releasing signs and wonders all over the place. Beyond that, the passage my friend quoted in Hebrews seems to say that however far or near we are from the end of all things, we are currently in what God considers "the last days." The author of Hebrews wasn't making a statement about whether or not "prophets" still spoke at all, but was instead proclaiming that the One that all of the prophets spoke about is now here. The context of Hebrews 2 and 3 is that One greater than the prophets is here, and we need to hear him. In fact, the Apostle Paul assumed the ongoing necessity for prophets, talking about their role within the church and strongly charging us to not "treat prophecies with contempt" (See 1 Thessalonians 5:20).

Even so, some individuals still get upset when people start saying that "God" spoke to them. Sometimes, some of us who say that we hear from God act pretty strange. For example, John the Baptist lived alone in the desert, wore a "hair robe" and ate bugs. If you're a little eccentric, I'm not attacking you. Be exactly who God made you to be, but remember that sometimes prophetic people alienate others by acting weird and making something natural a little too mystical.

People also become concerned about hearing God because they've seen some people attribute some pretty funky things as "God's told me" to them that actually contradicted the Word that he already gave us. People say that God told them to leave their spouse, quit their job or leave the church. Some say that God "told" them that something he clearly called a sin in the Bible was "ok" for them, like having sex outside of marriage or involvement in an affair because this person makes them "really happy." We live in an age that is growing increasingly biblically illiterate. What I mean by that is that some are quick to speak for God based on their feelings without knowing what he's already said. He gave us his Word as our definitive plumb line for living. If what you believe about God doesn't line up with his Word, what you believe needs to change!

"And we have the prophetic word *more fully confirmed*, to which you will do well to pay attention as to a lamp shining in a dark place, until the day dawns and the morning star rises in your hearts, knowing this first of all, that no prophecy of *Scripture* comes from someone's own interpretation. For no prophecy was ever produced by the will of man, but men spoke from God as they were carried along by the Holy Spirit" 2 Peter 1:19-21 (English Standard Version) – Emphasis added.

Peter calls the Bible "the prophetic word more fully confirmed." I like that. The word means "the more stable" word from God, which is why it's so important to know our Bible.[19] In it, our Daddy has spoken to us. Everything that you know about God, about yourself and about life that you hold to be certain — absolutely everything — is from the Bible. You might not know it. You might think that you heard it from your parents growing up or read it in a book somewhere, but the Bible is the more sure word of prophecy that we need to test every other word of prophecy against. Otherwise, we won't be "carried along" by the Holy Spirit but by our "feelings" and by the wave of popular opinion. You can exponentially increase learning to hear God's voice practically in your life by digging into and falling in love with his Word. Before we look into that topic further and learn how to really come alive and become confident in God speaking to you in your everyday life, I need to give one word of caution.

## NO ROOM FOR IMPOSTERS

Leaders and lay people alike struggle when someone says "God told me." Once someone is convinced they've heard from God, you might find it nearly impossible to prove otherwise. When they **have** truly heard from God, they are fueled by his personal revelation to them, which gives them a strong resolve to cling to what he said — what a thing of beauty! But when what they've "heard" goes against something that God has clearly said in his Word, too many respond, "well, I see it says that, but I know what I heard."

Exodus 20:7 says to "not take the name of the Lord your God in vain," which means to attribute something "false" to God and "empty" his name of its worth. It means to say that "God said" something that God did not say. It's the fourth commandment of God's "Big Ten" — a big deal! We take God's name in vain when we misattribute what we hear or feel to suit our own agenda. Comments beginning with "God told me" often raise red flags for many believers, including me. We have to learn to recognize the voice of our Father and discern what he is and isn't saying. We have to weigh what we're hearing against what the Bible says. We have to be connected with men and women of God we trust who also walk with God and can help us confirm that what we're hearing is accurate.

But it is a very different thing to say "be careful what you attribute to God" or "guard against imposters" than it is to say that "God doesn't want to speak personally to you today." God *is* speaking, and you **must** learn to recognize his voice! I'm not really a fan of lists because they seem so canned — like a television infomercial. "Do these three simple steps and get these amazing results." But even so, I have three steps to share with you to help you daily hear the voice of God. We live in a culture where most people don't experience everything that God says is available. For that reason, we need to learn how to live so that hearing God is our normal experience. The three things are:

1. *Learn* to love his Word,
2. *Learn* the priority of stillness and
3. *Learn* to lay down our own agenda.

If we will do those three things, we will live in the place where we hear him.

## LEARN TO LOVE HIS WORD

I used to really hate reading the Bible. I viewed God as harsh and thought that he would "get me" if I didn't act right or prove my devotion. And so, I isolated myself in my room and forced myself to read three chapters of the Bible every day. I'm not exaggerating. I *literally* locked the door — probably to keep myself from escaping. I was going to read the Bible if it killed me. I must have read the first half of Genesis — and even a little further — a hundred times. But I could never survive all the laws of Leviticus. By the time I started reading what the people needed to do if their skin spots had a hair in them, I quit. I tried to pretend that I enjoyed the Bible. I even tried to convince God that I enjoyed it, but like a 10-year-old kid who opens a box full of new underwear for Christmas when he wanted an Xbox, I couldn't mask my disappointment with the story.

The Bible is the #1 bestseller of all time. Nearly 9 out of 10 Americans own a Bible, and the average household has over four Bibles.[20] Yet, over half of Americans who own a Bible say that they don't read it regularly. Why? The enemy of our souls accuses us of not loving God enough, but I think the real reason is much simpler than that.

My favorite movie series of all time is the "Lord of the Rings" trilogy. When I was ordained, I received a replica of Aragorn's sword to hang in my office along with the charge to "leave behind the calling of Ranger, and take up your place of royalty." I just initiated my two oldest boys into the ingenious parable of J.R.R. Tolkien through the nearly 12-hour-cinema story in small segments, and they loved it. However, the first time that I saw the "The Fellowship of the Ring," I hated it. Maybe I grew up under a rock, but I had never heard of Tolkien and knew nothing about the story. All I saw were short people with hairy feet who talked funny and had a strange fascination with jewelry. They talked with such urgency as the musical score intensified, building to something important, but for the life of me, I couldn't understand what the big deal was. I fell asleep less than an hour in and woke up during the last scene as one hairy, short guy pulled another one into the boat because he apparently couldn't swim. I turned it off, muttering something to my wife like, "That'll never sell."

A few years later, our church was hosting a "men's movie night" at someone's home that included friends and plenty of chicken wings. I needed no further motivation to attend. When I arrived, my friend, Russ, excitedly told me that we'd be watching "The Fellowship of the Ring." I didn't know that Russ was one of the world's biggest "Lord of the Rings fans," so I began to complain about the movie. Big mistake. Since I had only watched a third of it, I had no clue what I was talking about. Without judgment, Russ asked me if I wanted to know what the story was about. For the next 10 minutes, his eyes lit up as he told me about hope lost, a powerful enemy and the most unlikely band of heroes who had been counted out by most but who had a destiny far greater than they knew. He told me what to watch for. When he was done, I knew that I had either really missed it the first time or that Russ needed to get his head checked out. What he described sounded awesome, but I didn't remember any of it. I decided to give it a second look and glued myself to the screen for the next 3 1/2 hours, overcome with wide-eyed wonder. When it was over, I sat on the edge of my seat. I *had* to know what happened next! I only hated the "Lord of the Rings" because I didn't understand the story.

Author John Eldredge succinctly summed up our problem with understanding the Bible and how it fits with our lives:

> "For most of us, life feels like a movie we've arrived to forty minutes late. Sure, good things happen, sometimes beautiful things. But tragic things happen too. What does it mean? We find ourselves in the middle of a story that is sometimes wonderful, sometimes awful, usually a confusing mixture of both, and we haven't a clue how to make sense of it all. No wonder we keep losing heart. We need to know the rest of the story."[21]

For many of us, the Bible is like an epic movie with lots of random scenes. But we have no idea how they fit together or why they matter. We know about Noah and the ark, Moses and the Red Sea, Jonah and a fish, Jesus and a cross, but what do they have to do with each other? And what do they have to do with me?

I hated the Bible before I understood the story. Now, I cannot get enough of it. Maybe the Bible is overwhelming to you or you grew up feeling like only "theologians" were supposed to understand it, spin it, make it interesting and spoon feed it to us with some practical application for today. But the Bible wasn't written for theologians. It was written for you. Even if you don't understand it now, you can understand it in the future. It wasn't written over your head and is completely accessible for adults and even kids. But it is a treasure, which will require some digging. The history and culture behind it differ greatly from your own, but it isn't just 66 separate treatises, haphazardly glued together. No. It is one story about you recovering "one thing." It is God's story. It is your story, too. Even if you don't understand it today, you can understand more today than you did yesterday and more tomorrow than you do today. We become great in small steps, a little at a time.

Dig deeply into his Word. Buy a study Bible — they have great notes that help explain word meanings, culture contexts, historical perspectives and more. My favorite is the "Life Application Study Bible," available in several versions. Ask lots of questions. I encourage students at church not to run away from challenging passages of scripture that don't make sense but to wrestle through them. Ask. Ask. Ask. The truth is always your friend, and you learn by asking. Surround yourself with people who understand the Bible better than you do. They guide you like Russ did for me with "Lord of the Rings," and they will help you understand the Word in depth.

If you're a reader, two resources have helped me more than any others when it comes to understanding an overview of the Bible. I referenced the first a few pages ago: "Epic" by John Eldredge. Despite the short length, he did a better job than anyone of helping me understand that the Bible is really just one basic story. For people who want to dig a little deeper, I strongly recommend "The Drama of Scripture" by Craig G. Bartholomew and Michael W. Goheen. Much like Eldredge, the authors help you understand the big picture of the Bible, but then they analyze each section to help you understand what is going on in that portion of scripture. A lot of people have various ideas for what you "need" to be a faithful Bible student. Plans are really helpful, but you can easily become bogged down by them. Ask the Holy Spirit about going somewhere in the Bible that really seems to set your soul on fire. Whenever I am really excited about what I am reading, I am following his direction because he's the One that put the excitement there. Lastly, do not allow the enemy to intimidate or bully you with guilt about your level of understanding of the Bible. He uses this tactic because he is terrified that you will discover who you really are. Don't be deterred. Don't worry about how much you are reading, either. Wherever you are today, your goal is intimacy with your Daddy: knowing him. Focus on that above all else.

## LEARN THE PRIORITY OF STILLNESS

As people of the 21st century, we sure send out mixed messages. We say that we're too busy, yet we keep committing to more activities. We say that life is too noisy, yet we're the ones holding the devices that create all of the noise. We say that we need more rest, yet we stay up too late. We are always running. Mark Schultz penned these words to one of my favorite songs:

> I am driving
> I am late for work
> Spilling coffee down my whitest shirt
> While I'm flossing and I'm changing lanes
> Oh Yeah
>
> Now I'm driving
> Through the parking lot
> Doing eighty, hey what the heck, why not?
> Watch it lady, Cuz you're in my spot
> Once again, It's early to work
> And here's a surprise, I got a
> McMuffin for just 99 cents today
> I think they ran a special
>
> I can't stand still
> Can I get a witness?

Can you hear me?
Anybody, Anybody?
I think I am running just to catch myself
Mark Schultz, "Running Just to Catch Myself"[22]

We are very optimistic about how much we can accomplish with our time. Our culture does not value, much less cultivate, stillness. Instead, we spend all of our time trying to create shortcuts and to manage the overabundance of lesser things that are toppling off our plates. You can live in a place where you hear God, but you need to learn to prioritize stillness. He often speaks in a gentle whisper. The number one concern that I hear from people is that they don't feel like they hear God speak to them the way the Bible says is possible. The question that I often ask is, "Are you ordering your life with the kind of stillness that creates space for you to just be quiet and listen?" It's tough to hear God on crucial life issues if we're always mentally or digitally plugged in somewhere else. Stillness is a real issue for us.

My good friend, Richard Mull, has mentored me in Kingdom principles. He authored "The Jesus Training Manual," which I highly recommend. Richard has helped me learn how to hear the voice of God more than anyone else. Years ago, he came to our youth summer camp. He first laid a foundation in the Bible that God wanted to speak to each one of us. He showed us how God speaks in dreams, visions, words, promptings and pictures. He helped everyone move past the fear of "missing it." We needed to learn the difference between confidently attributing something to God that he didn't say and learning how to hear his voice. One misses it and refuses to listen, change or alter their direction. That's prideful and foolish. The other might miss it, even by a lot, yet God is giddy about it. Why? Because of the posture of their heart. I only want to warn you that if you aren't going to walk in humility, you will hurt people in the process when you make a mistake. Most people fall on the other end of the spectrum, though, and are petrified that they will assign something to

God that he didn't say and ruin everything. They walk in humility, but they also walk in fear, and they don't want to miss God, so they're hesitant to step out and try. If that's you, stop fearing. God is pleased with you. "God opposes the proud, but gives *grace* to the humble" (James 4:6 – ESV – Emphasis added).

Richard then encouraged us to close our eyes but not to "try" super hard to clear our mind, taking our time and asking God to speak to us. All around the room, some 30 students and leaders followed directions, waiting quietly for about three minutes. Then, he asked us to open our eyes and share what we heard, sensed or saw. Nearly everyone saw a picture or heard a phrase. For some, the picture looked like a movie playing inside their eyelids while others received more of an impression. Some heard an inner voice. Others saw words written out in their mind. There isn't just one "right" way to hear God any more than there is one "right" way to show someone that you love them. Our God, who is vast and creative, delights in using the full arsenal of his creativity. As teenagers and adults shared, some immediately knew what God was telling them. They had been asking him for wisdom about a particular decision and now heard a clear answer. Others were a little more perplexed and almost hesitant to share because what they saw didn't make sense. I related to the dilemma.

One of the first times that I did this activity, I saw a guy riding on a unicycle while my eyes were closed! When it was time to share, the leaders asked anyone who saw anything, regardless of how bizarre, to share what they saw. All of these leaders, who I greatly respected, shared these profound words. As I listened to each one, I clammed up a little more on the outside as an argument raged on the inside. Like the angel and devil on each shoulder, a back-and-forth tennis match ensued. The conversation went like this:

Angel: "They *did* ask everyone to share. Maybe what you saw is significant."

Devil: "Are you insane? I am not sharing mine. I'm listening to all these beautiful, cascading images of glory being shared effortlessly with Bible verses to back up the stories. I am **not** sharing that I saw a guy on a unicycle.

Back and forth the argument went until someone finally asked, "Anyone else?"

I tried to keep my mouth shut, but just then, I blurted out, "I saw a guy on a unicycle!" Sheesh. I thought that was the end of my church career. But moments later, someone shared something profound — that silly unicycle pinpointed a place for deep healing from a wound long ago — the exact answer they needed.

As I looked at these nervous teens here, I reflected on what had happened to me. I was thrilled when they started blurting out what they saw without regard for how "foolish" they might seem. They were taking their first steps toward a lifestyle of hearing from God. In John 5:19, Jesus said that he could do "nothing" except what he saw the Father do and say. This echoes what he told us in John 15: "apart from me, you can do nothing." Imagine what could happen if we really started believing that we could hear our Father and began following through by saying or doing whatever he tells us.

We live in a super-fast-paced, multi-tasking society. We obsess about progress and struggle with sitting still. We have our phones next to us while we use our tablets while we watch TV while we try to carry on a conversation. In the middle of this chaos, God wants to speak to you. A lot. Every day. But you have to slow down and recover the lost art of stillness. You have to learn to stop "doing." God gave us a Sabbath because we require rest: physically, emotionally and spiritually. You cannot always be going, accomplishing and running. If you do, you are a branch attempting to be a vine. You are trying to grow fruit by your own efforts, and you aren't really stopping to let him pour over you. If we could understand this one thing as Christians, I'm convinced that we'd see revival. We read books filled with steps because we want shortcuts to let us hear God, bear fruit and make a difference without having to change the pace of our lives. You need to meet God in the quiet. Though he was the perfect Son of God, Jesus regularly drew away from all of the demands and expectations of people and the busyness of life just to be with his Father:

"Very early in the morning, while it was still dark, Jesus got up, left the house and went off to a solitary place, where he prayed" Mark 1:35.

"Immediately Jesus made his disciples get into the boat and go on ahead of him to Bethsaida, while he dismissed the crowd. After leaving them, he went up on a mountainside to pray" Mark 6:45-46.

"At daybreak, Jesus went out to a solitary place. The people were looking for him and when they came to where he was, they tried to keep him from leaving them" Luke 4:42.

"The news about him (Jesus) spread all the more, so that crowds of people came to hear him and to be healed of their sicknesses. But Jesus often withdrew to lonely places and prayed" Luke 5:15, 16.

We need to learn to be still but not to try to somehow appease God or make him happy. We need stillness because we were made to be with him. When I go on trips away from my wife and kids, it is actually painful for me. I remember again just how much they mean to me, and I count the hours until I can go home and be with them again. At this exact moment, I am away on a writing retreat, and how I miss them! In addition, I normally only interact with others for one brief moment each day. Today, I saw a group of 80-year-old ladies in the lunchroom. That was a real treat!

My wife came to visit me at this beautiful and isolated retreat location. I loved our time together here. Less than 10 minutes after she left, I texted her this:

*"Dang. This place is so less beautiful without you in it. Excited to write, though. Gonna press on and see where it goes. I love you. Be safe and let me know when you get there. I'll be eating dinner with some 80-year-old ladies!"*

Why did I text my wife, so overcome with emotion just 10 minutes after she left? Because I was made to be with her. To me, the world really is less beautiful when I'm not with her. Still majestic, sure, but when Jill is around, its beauty is uncontainable. I feel the same way about my incredible kids. I was made to be with them. The day I arrive home from this retreat, I plan to declare an "Ammons' family holiday" so that we can sit in our PJs and just enjoy being together. I plan and protect family time, not because they'd be mad at me if I didn't. I do it because I belong with and yearn for them. You need to develop stillness with your Daddy for the same reason. David stated it this way:

*"You, God, are my God, earnestly I seek you; I thirst for you, my whole being longs for you, in a dry and parched land where there is no water. I have seen you in the sanctuary and beheld your power and your glory. Because your love is better than life, my lips will glorify you"* Psalm 63:1-3 – Emphasis added.

Do whatever it takes. Lay down less important stuff that's tying up your time, simplify your schedule or stop binge watching Netflix. While entertainment is a beautiful gift, it can't substitute for a King. Your busy activities for yourself or your family or your community are wonderful. Hobbies provide enjoyment and relaxation. But we have to stop letting good things keep us from the "one thing." If your life is really "too busy," let go of whatever it takes to find stillness with him. You were made to be intimate with God.

## LEARN TO LAY DOWN YOUR AGENDA

I started this chapter by telling you about my favorite question from my mentor, Len. I will end it sharing one of his favorite quotes. "God's will can never be clear if you've already got one of your own." If we're honest, we often ask God for things that we already have worked out in our minds. If we aren't careful, we can allow our will to overshadow his. But he really is who he says that he is. He really is your creator who knows you better than you know yourself. He really is Lord of all, holding all of creation in his hand with all of the resources of heaven at his disposal. Nothing is too difficult for him, and he can accomplish whatever he wants whenever he wants. He moves the hearts of kings and princes. He promises that he hears you and answers when you call to him with a sincere heart. What you really want is not your will but his will. If you can remember that, hearing him will become so much simpler. Now, when I pray, I tell God that I am ready to hold on to or let go of whatever he says. I just want to go with him where he wants me to go. This attitude has saved me from some really dumb decisions.

## MESSY VULNERABILITY: EMBRACE THE PROCESS

I also want to encourage you to embrace the process of becoming completely vulnerable with God. They call it spiritual "growth" because, although we've been given everything we need, growing up is a process. It is messy. We aren't supposed to be fully formed and, believe it or not, God wants to hear you be honest about what is really going on in your heart. Don't sanitize or censor it to sound like what you think a "good" Christian should say. God isn't offended by your shortsightedness, and he isn't intimidated by your doubts. You can be "you" with him. Everything you believe, feel and do are simply the manifestations of what is really going on in your heart, so the quicker you can be honest about it, the sooner and fuller you will find the hope — and the God — you're longing for. You were made to know God as your Daddy and your closest friend, and you can. But it requires slowing down from our fast-paced lives to cultivate real stillness to listen to him and messy vulnerability to establish trust in him. You will know what he means by ever-increasing glory when you embrace the process of being a son or daughter. What are you waiting for? You've got a Daddy who has a lot he wants to share with you!

Let me make one final point about intimacy with God. Most of this chapter has been about learning how to listen to him because he really has a lot more to say than we think that he does. Even so, communication is a two-way street, and God also wants you to bring your heart, all of it, to him. Don't "church it up" or try to make this look super spiritual. Read through the Psalms. David is incredibly honest with God about the full range of human emotion. He seems to accuse God and then praises him, sometimes even in the same sentence. He pours out his heart in gut-level vulnerability about how people have wronged him and the injustice of it only to soar into some of the most profound declarations of trust in his God just a moment later. He laughs. He cries. He screams in despair, and he shouts in delight. The reason his prayers were recorded in scripture and even sung out by thousands as their spiritual anthems is to give us an example of how God wants us to come to him. Real. Gritty. Unpretentious. If you are mad at God, don't stuff your feelings. Run to him instead. Tell him everything. If you are scared, be honest. Don't try to sound holy by using spiritual words. He knows you better than you know you. Drop your guard and open up.

## QUESTIONS:

1.  Do you struggle to hear from God? If so, I encourage you to do the same exercise that Richard led us through at camp. Close your eyes and ask the Lord what he wants to say to you. Don't try to figure it out. Just listen and don't hurry. After you spend some time in quiet solitude, write down what you see or hear. If you didn't see or hear anything, don't worry. Share what you sensed with a trusted friend or leader — someone who walks with God like you do. Ask them for their input. This little exercise can help you "prime the pump" so that you can start hearing God speak to you.

2.  Do you need to reevaluate your schedule to make room for the process of developing intimacy with God?

3.  Do you know how to be vulnerable with God, sharing everything that's in your heart, even the messy stuff? Take a few minutes to be honest with God about where you struggle to trust him and where life is overwhelming right now.

# CHAPTER 8

# UNEARTHING OUR IDENTITY:

*Learning to See Yourself as God Sees You!*

---

Long ago, great glory arose from the dirt. God took something common, pulled it into his embrace, shaped it with his own hands and then he breathed into it. As a result, we became living beings, uniquely made in his image, the object of his great love. This is the story of the origin of mankind — our roots. We were a miracle, magnificent and complete. We have to remember that, because we have an enemy who would like nothing more than to erase our story from our minds and completely rewrite it, stripped of its purpose, compassion and beauty. He'd love for you to think that your existence is nothing more than the result of a long series of random genetic mutations or mistakes. What better lie could he perpetuate than erasing God and telling you that you have no purpose? Only one: vilifying God and paralyzing you with fear that you will never achieve your purpose. That just might keep you up at night.

What better revenge could he exact against God and us than to convince people who really want to please God that they will *fail* to measure up to impossible standards: to make God seem like an unreasonable taskmaster and man an endless disappointment, and thus run the names of both of them through the mud? Your enemy has always wanted to push you back into the dirt to before that act of majestic and glorious love. He has tirelessly spray painted his vile and corrupt messages across our minds like graffiti in an attempt to deface God and the masterpieces of his creation. We have to go back to the beginning, back to what happened in the dirt to excavate the truth because we aren't some random accident. We are a decision of intentional love. We weren't "commissioned" by a taskmaster but chosen by a Father. And we were not created to toil and fail but born to reign and rule. As John Eldredge says, "we've heard quite a bit about original sin, but not nearly enough about original glory, which comes before sin and is deeper to our nature."[23]

We need to know the dignity that we were made in because Jesus restored us to it. The first Adam lost the garden. Christ, the second Adam, ushered us back into all of its benefits. Everything you believe to be true about yourself will drive you, your dreams, your feelings of worth and ultimately, how you spend your days. It is all about identity. You have to see what God sees when he looks at you because that's who you were created to be. If you are born again, he has again pulled you into his embrace as his hands have lifted you up from the miry clay to breathe his Holy Spirit upon you. While the first Adam was made in the image of God, the second Adam came to completely conform you to the image of God. You have to see what he sees when he looks at you because that is who you really are. You have to see how he sees you, because when you do, you will love yourself like he loves you. And when that happens, you won't be able to keep from loving others and seeing them the way that God sees them, too!

## HE SEES YOU AS PLANNED AND WANTED

I **love** my kids. Being a daddy is one of the greatest joys of my life. I can remember the restless excitement as I awaited the birth of each of my children. I am a pacer. When I am excited or nervous, or even just deep in thought, I pace. When I talk on the phone, I walk a "race track" into the floor of our home over and over again, which cracks up my wife because now all my kids do it, too. I'm sure I wore down some floors, pacing the halls of the hospital where my five kids were born. I anticipated their arrivals and could not sit still. I couldn't wait for the indescribable feeling of looking upon my precious babies for the first time and holding each one of them in my arms. I wanted to be a daddy, and I delight in my kids.

But perhaps you didn't experience this growing up. Maybe you didn't know one or both of your parents. Maybe you were told that you were unplanned. Maybe your relationship with your parents is strained, or maybe, for whatever reason, you are presently going through life feeling unwanted. Alone. Invisible, even. You might be surrounded by people every day at your work, at church or in your hobbies. You might project a confident image and warm smile as you talk and joke about world events. You might amass tons of friends on social media and be constantly surrounded by people yet feel completely alone. When Adam stood without human companionship, God proclaimed that it was "not good" (Genesis 2:18). Part of his announcement was about the beauty of marriage, but part of it was that it's unnatural and contrary to our design to be isolated. It is "not good" because you were not made to be alone.

God always wanted to be a Daddy, too. He planned the day of your birth, pacing the hospital floors in anticipation. Your parents might not have planned you, but the God of the universe certainly planned you. Some days, you might not feel wanted here, but you have been more profoundly wanted than you have ever realized.

In Jeremiah 1:5, God says, "Before I formed you in the womb, I knew you, before you were born I set you apart." That word "knew" is "yada" in Hebrew, which means to "know at the deepest level by experience."[24] One of the enemy's greatest schemes is to tell us that if people truly knew who we were in the core of our being, they would reject us. The God who formed you knows you. He knows when you sit and when you rise. Before even a word is on your tongue, he knows exactly what you are going to say. One of the signs of any great friendship or love is being able to finish each other's sentences. He knows you even better than you know you because he hand knit you, and he takes great delight in you. Psalm 139, one of my favorite passages in the Bible, shows us so powerfully how God sees us. Read it through slowly, really thinking about what God is saying, and then, read it again!

"You have *searched* me, Lord, and you *know* me.
You *know* when I sit and when I rise;
you *perceive* my thoughts from afar.
You *discern* my going out and my lying down;
you are *familiar* with all my ways.

Before a word is on my tongue you, Lord, *know it completely*.
You *hem me in* behind and before, and you *lay your hand upon me*.
Such knowledge is *too wonderful* for me, *too lofty* for me to attain.

Where can I go from your Spirit?
Where can I flee from your presence?
If I go up to the heavens, you are there;
if I make my bed in the depths, you are there.
If I rise on the wings of the dawn,
if I settle on the far side of the sea,
even there your hand will *guide* me,
*your right hand will hold me fast.*

If I say, "Surely the darkness will hide me
and the light become night around me,"
even the darkness will not be dark to you;
the night will shine like the day,
for darkness is as light to you.

For you *created* my inmost being;
you *knit* me together in my mother's womb.
I *praise* you because I am fearfully and wonderfully made;
your works are *wonderful*, I know that full well.

My frame was not hidden from you when I was made in the secret
place, when I was *woven together* in the depths of the earth.

Your eyes saw my unformed body;
all the days ordained for me were written in your book
before one of them came to be.

How *precious* to me are your thoughts about me, O God!
How *vast* is the sum of them!
Were I to count them,
*they would outnumber the grains of sand—*
when I awake, I am still with you"
Psalm 139:1-18 – Emphasis added.

David says that God really knows us, and if we understood how well he
knew us, our brains would be overwhelmed with the knowledge of his love.
That sounds like an Overflow of love showered upon us. Why? Because he
knows us intimately, flaws and all, and yet, he wants us. Every day, before
you can even open your eyes, God has already thought more thoughts
about you than the number of individual grains of sand that fill every
beach that has ever existed! All of those thoughts about you are precious:
something that God "deeply esteems because he holds them with such
great value." And that's before your feet even touch the floor!

If you could see what God sees when he looks at you, you would Overflow
with love because he overflows in love for you! Just the thought alone is
mind boggling — more precious thoughts than the sand on the seashore.
If God had a computer, your hard drive would be overloaded, unable to
receive any more messages, because it would it be filled to capacity with
love letters from him to you. The Gmail servers couldn't contain the sheer
volume of messages that he sent, detailing how great he thinks you are.
The "like" button — no, the "love" button — on your Facebook page
would explode from overuse. All of the data on every webpage across
the internet could not even begin to express the precious things that God

**119**

thought about you before you even rose from bed just this morning! He knows you, and he desires so deeply for you to know that you are wanted.

## HE SEES YOU AS HIS POEM

Psalm 139 also tell us that God individually and lovingly hand-crafted every intricate detail of our body, soul and spirit for the exact purpose that he had in mind. He knit you together stitch by stitch in your mother's womb. He made your frame just the way he wanted. He had a grand plan for the beautifully unique life that you would live, and he ordered your days, bestowing gifts upon you and breathing a one-of-a-kind personality into your soul — your way of seeing and interacting with the world around you. Psalm 139 says that God didn't approach your creation like the cookie-cutter options of most housing subdivisions with just four different models. Instead, he created the exact shade of your skin, hair and eyes and made each one of us spectacularly diverse. God could have made you any way that he wanted, but you need to know with every breath that you breathe today that you aren't just wanted. You are purposefully and deliberately crafted in every detail as the masterpiece that he chose to create.

Heaven has no shortage of resources. You'd think that we believe it does when we look in the mirror since we often wish that we could change our height, hair, eyes, smile or our figure to look like a certain friend or celebrity. We wish that we had a personality like so and so or the sense of humor like that one comedian that everyone wants to be around or the creativity or giftedness of our favorite star. You'd think that we actually believed that God ran out of supplies and only used the really great options on someone else. But that's not what he says:

"For we are God's *handiwork*, created in Christ Jesus to do good works, which God prepared in advance for us to do" Ephesians 2:10 – Emphasis added.

The word translated "handiwork" is "poiema." Our word, "poem," which means "masterpiece," stems from this Greek word.[25] Let that sink in for just a minute: you are God's *masterpiece*. Just as a sculptor works painstakingly to chisel away everything that does not hold the full glory of his final product, God chiseled you. Just as a master artist draws their eye near their work to place every single stroke and every color in its place, so God painted you. As a master craftsman cuts, constructs, sands and finishes a one-of-a-kind custom cabinet, so God crafted you. And as a songwriter patiently and intentionally guides every single melody line and perfectly places each syllable, so God wrote you. You are God's song. You are his canvas. You are his poem. You are his masterpiece. And God is a writer, a sculptor, a painter and a builder who simply cannot make junk.

"You are *precious* and *honored* in my sight" Isaiah 43:4 – Emphasis added.

We cannot afford to ever look in the mirror and judge what looks back at us as second-rate or unworthy. We cannot afford to spend our days harboring the covetous desire to have what everyone else has that we have deemed worthy. We cannot afford to obsess over beauty contests and strongman competitions. We cannot afford to want to be everyone else except who we were created to be because envy is stealing our joy and robbing us of the opportunity to fully be who God made only us to be. No one in the history of mankind possesses your exact DNA or owns your fingerprints. They say that "everyone has a twin" and while others might resemble you, even twins are distinct people. There has never been another you. Don't spend so much time obsessing about trying to be someone else that you miss being you!

The Israelites got in trouble because they didn't walk in their identity. God called them to be distinct. Different. The one light in the whole world that could display the hope of God to the rest of mankind. Instead, they continually wanted to be like the other nations. God was their king, but instead, they asked for a human king. God made you to be distinct, and your enemy hates your uniqueness, so he tries to bury it by getting you to want to be like everyone else. But when God says that in his sight you are precious and honored, he gives a picture of an explorer unearthing a rare treasure. The world is digging to find a treasure they've never seen before: you. And only you can answer that call.

When you were growing up, maybe you were teased because of your looks or because others thought your particular passions were weird or nerdy. Maybe you've hidden the distinctness of who you really are, shoving it way back in a dresser drawer because you tried expressing it years ago and were bullied. Bullies only bully because they are incredibly insecure, and they think that they can only attain worth by attacking other people physically, emotionally or verbally. After working with teenagers for years, I have learned that the "popular" and loud kids with an entourage that follows them everywhere — the ones with perfect style who exude such confidence, the ones who everyone wants to be — are often the most insecure of all. When you know who you really are, you have no need to belittle others. In fact, the people who are the most confident in their own true worth will encourage you the most to find your worth because they know what worth looks like, and they can see it in you.

Don't listen to popularity polls. Don't listen to bullies - pray for them and love them, but don't cave to them. Don't let people box you into a predetermined stereotype. You can love hunting and poetry. You can be a princess and a warrior. Or, as "High School Musical" tells us, you can be a jock and bake a mean crème brûlée! Don't be ashamed of your passions. If you have a unique sense of style, run with it. Every great fashion trend and technology breakthrough started with a super creative person who was unafraid to look at things differently than everyone else. Whatever the case, God planted a uniqueness within you for the awesome work that he has for you. Embrace it.

## FULLY YOU, FULLY IN LOVE WITH JESUS

I talk with many high school and college students who want to find the love of their life and live happily ever after. They are so driven by style, fashion and popularity that they stress about projecting an image of what they think is required to be desired. This can lead to a lot of foolish decisions and eventual heartbreak. You will never be more attractive to the one person who you will spend the rest of your life with than when you are fully you, fully in love with Jesus. If God "ordered all your days," then he has been intentional about the one person who he has for you to marry. If you are called to be married, he created someone for you and had the two of you specifically in mind for each other. Like puzzle pieces, you are meant to fit perfectly together.

As a teenager, I bought that lie that I needed "an image," which put me in relationships where a lot of people were hurt. I sacrificed my purity and personality to fit whatever made me "wanted." When I met Jill, I noticed something so different about her. I don't know if it was love at first sight, but a whole host of my friends from high school could tell that I put her in a category that no other girl has ever occupied in my heart. We dated *four* separate times in high school and early into college. Each time was short-lived. I was working so hard to fit an image that I was actually hiding me.

I tried to be dignified. Serious. Suave. But that wasn't who I really was. Finally, in a weak moment, I showed Jill a video tape of funny skits that I made with my young cousin. The central skit was about a superhero named "Ballerina Boy," and my female cousin owned a tutu. You can figure out the rest! Jill watched, laughing, with tears in her eyes. She later told me that was the first moment she started falling in love with me, which makes sense because I was finally being me for the first time.

Just be you. Don't sell out. Don't compromise. Being fully you, fully in love with Jesus is the greatest magnet for the love of your life. This applies to your future career path and other major life decisions, too.

People sometimes ask what to do if they feel physically unhealthy, out of shape and overweight. Or they wonder about issues in their soul, such as insecurity, anger or lust. We will deal with this in our chapter on surrender, but for now, we need to distinguish between your worth, which never changes, and your work, which is how you properly take care of your body, soul and spirit. The God of the universe has knit worth into every fiber of your being. You will never have to work to achieve worth or strive to maintain it. God built you as his temple of great worth. Your work is to steward your temple so that it reflects all of the health and worth that God designed for it. Don't view this sense of work through a lens of legalism but rather in the same way that Adam "worked" in the garden to properly maintain and rule over what God made. Our rule with the Holy Spirit needs to start with our own temple because it possesses great worth!

Consider the following analogy. If you sign the papers to buy a beautiful eight-bedroom, 3 1/2 bathroom mansion on 3 acres of land with a media room, state-of-the-art kitchen and a bowling alley, you own it. No matter what kind of day or week you have, you will still own the same eight-bedroom, 3 1/2 bathroom mansion on 3 acres of land with a media room, state-of-the-art kitchen and a bowling alley. You own the title. Your performance doesn't change the blueprints, the height of the ceilings, or the legal status of the property as a residential mansion on 3 acres of land with the state. It **is** a mansion. Your worth is similar. You live in this beautiful mansion called "you." You could live in a beautiful eight-bedroom, 3 1/2 bathroom mansion on 3 acres of land with a media room, state-of-the-art kitchen and a bowling alley and refuse to mow the lawn outside. You could choose to continually ignore basic maintenance until the home springs a water leak. The mansion will be the same, but now you will reside in a dwelling that looks like a jungle outside and smells like a swamp inside! That isn't about worth but about maintenance.

You are God's temple, glorious, and nothing will change that, but don't allow the temple to fall into disrepair. This is not about guilt or shame. If you need to start taking better care of your body, ask for the Holy Spirit's anointing and obey as he leads you. If you see somewhere that you need to guard or repair your soul, pay attention to it as you quiet yourself in stillness and ask your Daddy to reveal what he wants to do. We should not ignore the health of this beautiful life that God has given us. I'm just asking us not to confuse our body's maintenance with its magnificence or our soul's servicing with its significance!

## YOU ARE NOT A SINNER SAVED BY GRACE

If you are a follower of Christ, please do me a favor. **Please** stop saying that you're "just a sinner saved by grace." While that's a popular sentiment, it is a complete lie. The truth is that you *were* a sinner, and then you were saved by grace and now, God doesn't consider you a sinner anymore. In the New Testament, God doesn't once refer to a Christian as a sinner, yet 66 times in the Greek, he calls us saints or "holy ones, pure and blameless," people who have been set apart for a great purpose.[26] If you see yourself as a sinner, you will live like one and strive to manage your sin. If you realize that you are no longer a sinner, but a saint, you will rise up and act like it. Even if you sin, you don't ever have to sin because it isn't your true nature anymore.

The Spirit of God wants to totally fill you all the time, which is attainable now. Wherever you are filled with his Spirit, you "*cannot* gratify the desires of the flesh" (See Galatians 5:16 – emphasis added). In Greek, "cannot" is the double-negative "ou me," which translated means, "it is absolutely impossible" to fulfill the desire of your flesh where God's Spirit is filling you.[27] I am not preaching sinless perfection or some kind of self-sufficiency or pressure to never mess up. You're a kid who will make mistakes. But theology that treats the "sin nature" as if it is a natural part of you will always trip you up. I have heard and learned so much about these two warring natures in us as if every day is supposed to be the battle between your shoulder angel and your shoulder devil. If we believe that, we will excuse a lot of wrong behaviors in our life as "just being human." We will also settle for so much less than what Jesus bought. When you look at what the Bible has to say about "sin nature," you can only draw one conclusion:

you shouldn't hold on to it any more than a butterfly holds on to its dead cocoon.

I used to think that the New Testament was flooded with places talking about "my sin nature" because I studied a Bible that mistranslated it as "flesh." "Flesh" has two different meanings. The vast majority of the instances in the New Testament that refer to "flesh" are actually talking about being a human being: "flesh and bone." For instance, John 1 says that "the Word became flesh," which obviously doesn't mean that "Jesus became sin nature" but that he took on humanity. The Bible does not say that we are "sinners saved by grace" with a supersized, scary sin nature. Only five passages in the entire New Testament, all written by the Apostle Paul, refer to a sin nature: Romans 7:1-8:17, Romans 13:12-14, Galatians 5:13-25, Ephesians 2:1-7 and Colossians 2:9-15. You can study each of these incredible passages in their full context, but for the time being, read the highlights of Paul's conclusions and the italicized key words in these verses about the sin nature to see what he is saying:

"What the *law was powerless to do* because it was *weakened by the flesh*, God *did* by sending his own Son in the likeness of sinful flesh to be a sin offering. And so he *condemned sin in the flesh*, in order that the *righteous requirement of the law might be fully met in us*, who *do not live according to the flesh* but *according to the Spirit*…Those who are in the realm of the flesh cannot please God. *You, however, are not in the realm of the flesh* but are in the realm of the Spirit, *if indeed the Spirit of God lives in you*" Romans 8:3-4, 8-9 – Emphasis added.

"The night is nearly over; the day is almost here. So let us *put aside* the deeds of darkness and put on the armor of light. Let us behave decently, as in the daytime, not in carousing and drunkenness, not in sexual immorality and debauchery, not in dissension and jealousy. Rather, *clothe yourselves with the Lord Jesus Christ*, and do not think about how to gratify the desires of the flesh" Romans

13:12-14 – Emphasis added. "Those who belong to Christ Jesus have *crucified the flesh* with its passions and desires" Galatians 5:24 – Emphasis added.

"As for you, you *were dead* in your transgressions and sins, in which you *used to live* when you *followed* the ways of this world and of the ruler of the kingdom of the air, the spirit who is now at work in those who are disobedient. All of us also *lived among them at one time*, gratifying the cravings of our flesh and following its desires and thoughts. Like the rest, we *were* by nature deserving of wrath. *But* because of his great love for us, *God*, who is rich in mercy, *made us alive* with Christ even when we were dead in transgressions—it is by grace you have been saved" Ephesians 2:1-5 – Emphasis added.

"In Christ you have been brought to *fullness*. He is the head over every power and authority. In him you *were also circumcised* with a circumcision not performed by human hands. *Your whole self ruled by the flesh was put off* when you were circumcised by Christ, *having been buried* with him in baptism, in which *you were also raised* with him through your faith in the working of God, who raised him from the dead. When you *were dead* in your sins and in the *uncircumcision* of your flesh, *God made you alive* with Christ. He *forgave* us *all* of *our sins*, having *canceled* the charge of our legal indebtedness, which stood against us and condemned us; he has *taken it away*, nailing it to the cross. And having *disarmed* the powers and authorities, he made a *public spectacle* of them, triumphing over them by the cross" Colossians 2:10-15 – Emphasis added.

Pay attention to the word pictures. Look at the verb tenses and what Paul says happened in the past that is not part of our present: We *were* dead in sin. We *used to* follow the ruler of the air. We *used to* gratify the sin nature and obey its thoughts. We *used to* have a nature deserving of wrath. We *used to* be ruled by the uncircumcision of our flesh. But God condemned its power in our lives so that righteousness could be fully met in us. "Fully" means all of one thing and none of the other. Paul says that when we came to Christ, we crucified the sin nature and all of its passions and desires. God took that old part of us and cut it off entirely, nailed it to the cross, made a spectacle of it and buried it. He threw it aside as useless, just as a butterfly tosses aside its dead cocoon, leaving it free to soar into its true destiny.

Other Bible passages confirm this, telling us to count ourselves entirely "dead to sin" and to not let it reign because we've been brought from death to life (Romans 6:11-13). Colossians 3:9 says that we already "put off our old selves." The Bible does not present the sin nature as a living counterpart intended to war successfully with the new you. Jesus condemned it and cut it off you. He invited you to nail it to the cross with him in great triumph. Paul tells us that a Christian no longer wrestles with their sin nature, which would be like digging up the old, dead corpse that used to enslave you and wearing it around like a coat, which is why sin feels so unnatural if you are a believer. Sin is no longer your identity.

However, we do still sin even when we don't want or intend to. It should grieve us, and we should run straight to the throne of grace for help in our time of need with no condemnation because though we're an entirely new creation, we live in a fallen world where the enemy of our soul continually blasts us with his lies. The system of this world has believed him. We still fall because we're still kids here.

I used to needlessly fall a lot more, which wreaked great havoc in my life because I didn't understand that Jesus died for much more than to ensure that I would go to heaven. I thought that I was just a sinner saved by grace, and since sinners sin, they eventually come up with exhausting plans to keep it under control. But he no longer sees you as a sinner but a saint and a glory bearer!

## HE SEES YOU AS A GLORY BEARER

Pottery was a big deal in Paul's day. Cups, bowls, pots, dishes and more were all made from clay. The containers were beautiful but frail. If you dropped one, it cracked. Paul made an interesting observation: you and I are like clay treasure boxes. On the outside, we are frail and weak, including flaws such as love handles, wrinkles and more. Before you feel insulted that Paul called you clay, remember that God himself said that he molded you like clay as the work of his hand, his poem! Second, Paul said that the important part was not the clay but the treasure contained within. Far from being a "sinner saved by grace," you are a "glory bearer!" You literally carry a treasure every place that your foot treads. You carry a light within you, the "all-surpassing power" of Almighty God, flowing through an ordinary vessel in a way that shows the whole world that it is "from God and not from us" (2 Corinthians 4:7). That's what Jesus meant when he said, "You are the light of the world." He didn't say that you could be the light in the far off future. He said that you are the light now. Whether or not you know it, you carry treasure and bear glory. He says that "Christ in you *is* the hope of glory" (Colossians 1:27), that you "shine like a star in the universe as you hold out the word of life" (Philippians 2:15), and that you bear a glory even Moses couldn't contain:

"Now the Lord is the Spirit, and where the Spirit of the Lord is, there is freedom. And we all, who with *unveiled faces contemplate the Lord's glory*, are being *transformed into his image with ever-increasing glory*, which comes from the Lord, who is the Spirit" 2 Corinthians 3:17-18 – Emphasis added.

When Moses encountered God on Mt. Sinai, he heard God give him the law for his people, but Moses wanted more. "Show me your glory!" Moses asked God (Exodus 33:18), and God did just that! God passed by in front of him, but Moses was only permitted to see the back side of God. Still, the experience was so overwhelming that when Moses came off the mountain, he radiated brightly. He was a human Lite Brite! As you can probably imagine, the people were petrified and asked him to put a veil over his face. But as Paul said in the above passage, we've been invited to sit in the place where we see God's glory without any veil to hide it! As we sit before the Lord, we are being transformed into ever-increasing glory. The word "metamorphosis" comes from the word "transformed:" we bear glory now, but as we come to him in the stillness, he continually encourages us to stretch our wings and soar as butterflies. We have to stop acting like caterpillars who cannot fly or "sinners saved by grace" and start flying like butterflies, "saints full of the hope and glory of God."

## YOU ARE HIS BELOVED (OR "NOBODY PUTS BABY IN THE CORNER")

Understanding your identity is so crucial to living "Life in the Overflow," and some of the lies we've believed have been deeply ingrained in our minds from so many different directions. The most significant way that God might see you is as his *beloved!* Right after Jesus was baptized, God spoke from heaven about his heart for his Son. "This is my *beloved* Son. In Him, I am well pleased" (Matthew 3:17). "Beloved" means "dear, respected, worthy and *favorite.*"[28] Yes, God spoke from heaven to Jesus saying, "You're my favorite!" Now, as any good parent knows, you should never favor one child above the others. In my home, we talk a lot about making no one the favorite, but what if we're thinking about it wrong? What if instead of playing no favorites, a parent played **only** favorites? What if each kid actually *was* their parent's favorite because each kid was receiving the maximum amount of favor that their parent could possibly bestow upon them, according to their unique needs? God treats us like this: He says that Jesus is his favorite, and you are his favorite and his beloved, too.

"Therefore be imitators of God, *as beloved children*" Ephesians 5:1 (ESV) – Emphasis added.

"But we ought always to give thanks to God for you, brothers *beloved by the Lord*, because God chose you as the first fruits to be saved, through sanctification by the Spirit and belief in the truth. To this he called you through our gospel, *so that you may obtain the glory of our Lord Jesus Christ*" 2 Thessalonians 2:13-14 (ESV) – Emphasis added.

You are called to look like your Daddy because you are his highly favored, dearly loved kid, and you are to live a life of extreme gratitude because God chose you to receive the **same glory** that Jesus has! You could never be just another face in the crowd to him. On all of the planet, no one turns his heart quite the way that **you** do. I understand a little of this because as a daddy of five incredibly unique kids, they are all my favorite. God sees us the same way. When we fail to understand his perspective, we allow the enemy, others and even ourselves to push us back in the corner, settling for mediocre dreams because we don't see anything special about us.

Growing up, my sister and I spent every summer in South Carolina, half of the time with my dad's mom, who we called "Mema." She has since gone home to be with Jesus but stands as a "hero of faith," a woman who embodied the love and power of God at the same time. I can still remember her singing "I'll Fly Away" in church with tears streaming down her face. While some others might have been thinking about "flying away" to the lunch buffet after church, my Mema was lost in the wonders of her future home with her present King. She lived in intimacy with God. How I miss her, but she is dancing on golden streets, every moment breathing in the wonders of the place she sang about so joyously.

We spent the other half of the summer with my mom's parents, who we call "Nana and Papa." I soaked up such a rich heritage of faith during those summers. My Papa showed me what "love in action" looked like, a hard worker who spent himself to radically bless and serve those who crossed his path. He was the first one to recognize the call of God on my life and told me as a young boy that I was destined to be a preacher. I so hoped that he was wrong! Church bored me, and we sang stale songs that made my throat hurt with words that I needed a lexicon to define. No one looked happy to be there. I thought, "Please tell my Papa that he was wrong and that I'm supposed to be a movie star or football player. Please, please, not a pastor." I'm so glad he was right and spoke into me.

My sweet Nana is one of the most pure-hearted, unassuming, radiantly beautiful of all of God's creations. She has been a rock of encouragement, a listening ear and hands that just finished making the most delicious pound cake. I sat with Nana in the middle of the day, watching soap operas or her favorite movie, "Dirty Dancing." The movie follows a young, innocent girl named Frances, but her very strict father still calls her "Baby." She's learned good morals but has been placed into a "box" of everyone else's "safe" expectations for her and has never dared to dream her own dreams. Enter Patrick Swayze who plays Johnny, the ritzy country club's dance instructor. Johnny colors outside the lines and has made some pretty questionable life decisions, but he can see *greatness* in Baby. Something unique, inspiring, beautiful. Her feet have never dared to dance, but he sees a song buried deep in her heart that is screaming to get out that's about more than just the music. He sees something in *her*. As he teaches her to dance, he falls in love with her in the way of typical 80s movies: during a three-minute music montage. Johnny doesn't do everything right, but he cherishes Baby and under the eye of his love, she begins to come alive and believe in herself in a way that she never did before. But *spoiler alert*: Johnny loses his job just before the big end-of-summer dance and right at the end of the movie, she sits in the very back corner of the room, feeling ordinary, unexceptional, invisible and foolish for having dared to dream that a caterpillar like her could ever become a gorgeous butterfly.

Just then, when all hope is lost, Johnny bursts through the door, struts straight to the back of the room and boldly declares one of the most iconic lines in recent film history: "Nobody puts Baby in the corner." You might think that you are ordinary, unexceptional or even invisible, but you're not. You might feel foolish for daring to dream that your life could really matter, but you're not that, either. You're *beloved* and right now, your King has set his eye on you and is standing at your table, telling any who would seek to put you in a box that nobody puts you in the corner anymore. The dance is in you. Your feet might not have dared to dream yet, but it is knit in your heart, and you are being invited onto the dance floor to take the leap into his arms. He has plans that you cannot even begin to imagine: his very best plans because that's what you do for a *beloved*. Stop sitting in the shadows and go to him. It's going to be "The Time of Your Life."

## LEARNING AND REMEMBERING YOUR IDENTITY THROUGH INTIMACY

Jesus said that the reason the Holy Spirit came was to *teach* us all things about God, ourselves and life and to *remind* us of all things. A big part of teaching and reminding about "all things" includes our identity. We talked about who God says we are now. We apply that in our lives and put it into motion in the place of intimacy. Everything that God wants to accomplish in our lives is only found in the place of intimacy. Instead of giving you detailed steps and campaigns to help convince you of your true identity, I will just leave you with this simple picture.

Imagine your life as a blank canvas. Every day, the Holy Spirit wants to paint things on your canvas: things that he wants to *teach* you and things that he wants to *remind* you. Maybe right now, he wants to really teach you that you are a saint and not a sinner. Let that be the canvas for your place of stillness before him today. Do not have any other agenda but just listen to him to speak to you about that. Dig into his Word, pour out your heart and go where he leads you. Don't be in a hurry to solve it or to move on to the next thing. Just dance in intimacy for as long as he wants to paint on the canvas. If you spend the next two months breathing in that beautiful part of your identity, take the necessary time. You are dancing with him, which he loves. The process will become so much more natural when we make true intimacy our only goal. Then, he can show us what hinders us or where he wants to grow us.

This short story portrays what it means to remember our identity. Even when you forget who you are, he hasn't! Commit to stay in his presence.

Prioritize stillness. You'll learn who you are in ways that you've never known before and remember things long forgotten. You'll be able to breathe again.

## BREATHE AGAIN

They met when they were just teenagers, but it wasn't exactly love at first sight, at least not for her. He was smitten, but she barely noticed him. Quiet and awkward around strangers, he didn't exactly encourage the "vibe" of a lifetime love. Their friendship moved slowly and deliberately as she began to trust his character and started to open up to him as a friend. He found 100 new reasons to fall in love with her each day, and 101 reasons to keep quiet about it.

Slowly, without even realizing it, he forgot to be awkward around her. His personality and humor began to shine through. She saw his confidence grow, which made her take note, since she had known him for years. She felt safe and comfortable in his presence. They spent hours on the phone and nearly every day off work together. They'd been to the movies, the mall, the beach, even ice skating. She thought they were just really good friends, But suddenly, she felt something very different that almost scared her. This mattered. **He** mattered. She didn't want to admit it, but for the first time, she was actually falling in love — not the infatuation that calls itself "love" but is really just a fickle imposter. No, this was actual "love." Substantial and true.

Four years seemed to pass by like the blink of an eye. This once awkward boy was now a man, and she couldn't imagine her life without him. They found something real, and she never intended to let go. In the sight of God and their closest friends and family, they made the promise to love each other as long as there was breath in their lungs. And with "I do" and a kiss, they started a journey that legends are made of.

They moved to a tiny, one-bedroom apartment while they both worked full time to put him through school. The quaint apartment wasn't the ideal place to raise a family, but baby #1 didn't seem to care much about her parents' timeline. Just like that, they became a family of three, their hearts stolen by this little princess who could do nothing except be adorable. Eighteen months later, they moved into their first house, just in time to welcome a little boy into their lives. Three years later, their third, a girl, arrived. rounding out their family.

The years followed in a beautiful mosaic: colorful, messy and worth more than ordinary people should be able to afford. Between homework and dance recitals, living-room dodgeball games and bedtime stories, they lived an adventure and loved every minute. Wise with their money, they helped all three of their kids find their way to their future. Then, they paid off the house, inspired to do something crazy — sell it to travel the world together. Through 12 amazing years and four breath-taking continents, they crafted more memories than most have in a lifetime.

But her failing health and strange forgetfulness oddly led them back to where they'd started: a tiny one-bedroom that was nice...and quaint. A full staff cooked their meals, and social gatherings, like Bingo Night, kept them busy. They didn't even really miss their independence but simply enjoyed being together.

Soon, a routine doctor's visit led to further tests that concluded what they both feared: Alzheimer's. The last few months were excruciating yet beautiful. As the oldest daughter, I will never forget that last Tuesday before Jesus took her home. Those events spoke to their character and to what I want mine to be.

My dad was helping my mom put on her shoes to go down for lunch when she looked at him in confusion. "I'm so sorry," Mom stated. "I know you're important, but everything in my head is so foggy. I'm afraid you'll have to tell me who you are." She dropped her gaze from Dad's because though she couldn't say why, it broke her heart to be so confused.

Without hesitation, he tenderly placed his hand on her cheek and lifted her head. As she looked at him, his eyes gazed straight into hers with the same intensity they held decades ago on their wedding day. "Don't worry. I know who *you are...even when you can't remember.* On the days you can't look into my eyes because you've forgotten who I am, *I will always love you. And I will always know exactly who you are.* Good days and bad, *you're always my girl.*

He must've reminded her a hundred times in those last months, every time with as much passion and conviction as the first. She held on to him and wiped a tear away from her eyes. She didn't need all of the answers — she could rest simply because she knew that she was safe in the arms of a love that would never forget or forsake her. Her confidence came solely from the joy and love that she saw in his eyes. She could *breathe again* because though it didn't make any logical sense, when she looked at him, she somehow remembered who she was mirrored in the reflection of his eyes.

Your Daddy knows who you are even when you don't. You can breathe again and see it when you gaze into his eyes.

## QUESTIONS:

1. Meditate upon the scriptures in this chapter in your time of stillness with your Daddy. Let him breathe over you with them. Which one speaks the most to you?

2. Learn to see what he sees when he looks at you. Where does your perspective need to change? His opinion will change everything!

3. Through past experiences with parents, school, friends, church or romance, nearly everyone struggles with rejection. Is it easy or difficult for you to feel "wanted" by God? Why or why not? Read Psalm 139:1-16 again and ask the Holy Spirit to allow his love to wash over you.

4. Re-read Ephesians 2:10. It is often far easier to recognize value in other people than in ourselves. Nonetheless, we need to embrace who God made us specifically to be with gratitude. You might want to consider traits about yourself that you struggle to embrace. Take these into the place of intimacy with him and ask him for his perspective. Break wrong agreements you've made about yourself. Next, list five traits or strengths and ways God crafted you in your body, soul or spirit. Express your gratefulness to God out loud and thank him for choosing to make you the way he did.

5. Meditate on the scriptures in this chapter in your time of stillness with your Daddy. Let him breathe over you with them. Which one speaks the most to you?

## CHAPTER 9

# THE BEAUTY OF SURRENDER:

*Release What You're Holding to
Receive What He's Offering!*

---

We were born as worshipers. The desire to pursue something greater than ourselves is hard wired into us. Worshipers run after what they worship with abandon, and they sacrifice, going way beyond what most deem as "normal" limits to receive the spoils from their gods. While surrender might not seem to relate to worship, it does. At the core, surrender problems are almost always worship problems.

Jesus said, "Out of the overflow of the heart, the mouth speaks" (Luke 6:45 - Holman Christian Standard) and "Where your treasure is, there your heart will be also" (Matthew 6:21). What we talk about, what we hold on to, actually, all of our actions are the result of what we believe in our heads and what we pursue with our hearts — what we are worshiping. Although this list could include much more, people have historically sought after four key needs:

1. Acceptance/Approval — **to be loved**
2. Worth — **to be enough**
3. Significance — **to be great**
4. Pleasure — **to be satisfied**

Everywhere you look, back through time, people have been running tirelessly and sacrificing enormously to possess those four things. The longing for each one is like a growling deep within our emotional stomachs. Everyone hungers for those things because God placed them in our DNA. However, he wants us to find our fulfillment for each one in **him**. He is love. He is our sufficiency. He gives us significance and greatness. And he wants to deeply satisfy us.

Our problem isn't our hunger for those four things but that we have tried to fulfill them in wrong ways. Our choices have corrupted our hearts and darkened our understanding. The answer to all four of those drives can be found only in our relationship with our Daddy. In him, we have *all* we need, but our enemy wants us to be discontented so that we chase after something more. We got in trouble in the garden because we listened to the enemy's lies:

We weren't truly loved.
We weren't fully enough.
We weren't yet great, and
God was withholding some immense pleasure from us.

Ever since then, we've been looking for satisfaction, trying to fill the hunger of our hearts apart from God.

The trouble is that what the world offers is like a Chinese buffet restaurant. Like a lamb led to slaughter, I used to flock to them with a goofy grin on my face, forgetting what happened every time I ate at one. I loved going to the Chinese buffet because I was getting so much for my money! Something about Chinese food allows us to eat a lot of it. It's salty. It's fried. They have such catchy names for the entrees, and the walls are painted with bright vibrant colors. You load up on plate after plate until you finally leave, nearly rolling out the door like Violet Beauregard from "Willy Wonka and the Chocolate Factory!" But two hours later, it seems like you never ate at all! You are famished. If you're especially "lucky," you'll have one final surprise from your trip to the Chinese restaurant that comes with many opportunities to sit and think about your decision to eat as much as you did.

That's *exactly* what the world's substitutes do: they promise such satisfaction but leave us empty or worse yet, sick. Ask yourself these questions to see if you're filling your soul with a spiritual Chinese buffet:

1. What do I feel I need to <u>become</u> or <u>accomplish</u> in order to feel wanted, recognized or admired?
2. Where am I striving to <u>prove</u> that I am strong, beautiful, talented, funny, popular or respected enough?
3. What do I believe that I need to be, accomplish or acquire in order to be "<u>successful?</u>"
4. What am I <u>trusting</u> to make me happy, numb my pain or make life easier?

You seek the things that you seek and do the things that you do for a reason. The hunger that is driving you is revealing something about unmet needs that you feel in your heart. Honestly ask those questions. We really do find all that we need in him, but when we look to other sources to fill us, we draw from a polluted well. Like Frodo and the Ring, it destroys us, yet we feel strangely attracted to it and begin to defend why we should be able to keep it.

Just think about your life for a minute as you answer this question: Are you living a fully surrendered life, ready to follow Jesus anywhere that he wants you to go and ready to do anything that he asks you to do? If not, what's holding you back? What are you holding on to that you don't want to release?

Personally, I struggled with acceptance and worth, so I knew that one thing that kept me from following Jesus fully was my desire to protect my reputation. I worried what people thought of me. An integral part of this included my struggle with purity. I spent my teenage years until the age of 20 addicted to pornography and chasing relationships that compromised my purity. I didn't believe that I was enough as a person or as a man, so I looked for approval and acceptance from the opposite sex. None of these relationships lasted very long. When the "butterflies" in my stomach, which I confused with love, were gone and when another girl caught my attention, I shallowly ended my current relationship to quickly jump into a new one. Other times, I gave a girl my heart only to have her say, "Thanks, but no thanks." I was obsessed with my "need" to be in a relationship, and I didn't realize that all I was doing was playing with girls' hearts without the necessary maturity to focus on commitment, love or marriage. I convinced myself that this was "love," but all I was really doing was saying, "I'm willing to risk whatever this might cost both of us for how it will make *me* feel better about myself temporarily." That was a far cry from "Love does not seek its own!" As I grew older, relationships became progressively more physical and train wrecked all of the commitments I'd made at "True Love Waits" rallies. I wish I could take back everything that happened. I missed great opportunities to have beautiful friendships with some remarkable young ladies because I wasn't content to develop friendships based on a biblical picture of love. A distorted view of relationships had become my god, which I willingly served to meet those needs.

But this left me feeling empty and dirty, and every step I took into impurity only drove me further away from knowing my true identity. The enemy works through lies and deception, trapping you in sin. Finally, through a lot of patient prayer and help from my best friend, Chris Thomas, who is also my co-pastor, I was able to completely leave an addiction that dominated my life for years and spend the last 18 months before my wedding learning what *real* love looked like.

## DEALING WITH PAST TRAUMA AND LOSS

Half of the issue is what you're holding that you think you want. The other half is about our past, and sometimes our present — what happened to us — broken dreams, heartbreak and trauma. We can hold onto those things, too, in an attempt to defend ourselves from being hurt again. You cope with pain the way that you do for a reason.

Our heartbreak, unfulfilled dreams and our pain can result in the use of different substances to numb ourselves. While rest and hobbies rejuvenate you, unhealthy addictions, such as food, television, social media, shopping, substances, sex, gambling and more, hurt you. Some people involve themselves in everyone else's drama in order to make themselves feel significant. Others attempt to fill the void with busy schedules, excessive activities, vacations or constant noise and activity so that they don't have to stop and face the emptiness that they really feel.

Whatever we turn to for acceptance or success and whatever we use to numb the pain is something we are holding in our hands. The Holy Spirit wants to fill us to overflowing, but he cannot do that if our hands are already filled with counterfeit saviors. We have to release what we're holding to receive what he's offering.

Your core problem isn't the behavior that you are manifesting. The behavior is manifesting because of something going on in your heart. When you address the heart issue, the behavior will take care of itself. For example, if you are wrestling with an addiction to pornography, your core problem isn't pornography but is likely a deep-seated insecurity that you are not really enough. The insecurity, in turn, drives you to compensate for those feelings via porn. If you are wrestling with harsh judgment or anger against someone and you cannot seem to forgive, the core issue isn't that you are just a mean person. Instead, you've likely had some rejection that is making it hard for you to trust God to truly take care of you if you let it go. Of course, the behaviors need to change, but you need to find the core problem because otherwise, you will waste a lot of time putting Band-Aids on symptoms and never find the root of the real issue.

Our enemy tries to bury us in shame by taking our eyes off the real issue and making some nasty accusations. He will tell you that you are dirty, pathetic, evil and selfish. He will tell you that you are the only one who has your struggles and that "if people only knew" the real you, they would be so disappointed. He will try to cripple you with fear, overwhelm you with guilt and blind you to who you are and how your King already disarmed and made a spectacle of him. He doesn't want you to uncover his lies about your emotions and behavior because if you recognize his lies, you can discover Christ's truth that will see you free (John 8:32). And he doesn't want you to know that you've been given the authority to make him flee because when you do, all of his empires will fall.

"For though we live in the world, we do not wage war as the world does. The weapons we fight with are not the weapons of the world. On the contrary, they have divine power to *demolish strongholds*. We demolish arguments and every pretension that sets itself up against the knowledge of God, and we take captive every thought to make it obedient to Christ" 2 Corinthians 10:3-5 – Emphasis added.

Your enemy wants to build castles of beliefs, fears and convictions within your mind that are against the true knowledge of God. He wants to tell you that you are not truly loved; you are not enough; you are failing at what you were designed to be and that you cannot find true, lasting freedom from the things that have held your heart in bondage. He only has power in a believer's life who comes into agreement with his lies. When you do, your false perception becomes your practical reality — you live like it is true, though it is not.

With every lie, he desires to cement another brick in your world so that you struggle to fix or forget about your "problem" through your own effort. Though God loves you perfectly, offers complete healing and gives everything you need for sufficiency, completeness and abundant life, your enemy tirelessly tries to get you to bite into lies intended to enslave you. And though he is defeated, when you agree with your fallen foe, you open the gate to let him set up a vile shop of deception in the corridors of your mind. Some of the lies might have been there so long that you cannot see how absurd they are. You can recognize when you are under the lie of the enemy when you logically know that something is not true, but you cannot stop believing it for the life of you. He has constructed a castle of lies that needs to topple. You can deconstruct it by entering the place of intimate vulnerability with your Daddy, tearing down every lie that has taken root, flipping the enemy's tables and driving him away from your body — your house of prayer.

Appendix 4 provides a guide to questions to ask yourself — and others — in greater surrender. Appendix 5 includes a list of open doors to help you examine your heart and walk in greater personal freedom. I strongly encourage you to bring it to your time of intimacy with God! You cannot wait until you feel like you want to forgive someone before you forgive them. That moment won't ever come, but if you will let God in, he will walk you through it with you. Forgiving those who have wronged you will lift immense burdens off your shoulders and usher you into a place of more beautiful freedom than you can imagine. He has so much that he wants to give you. He is "a father to the fatherless, and a defender of widows" (Psalm 68:5). He has seen every person who has wronged you and promises that you are not a pawn in some cosmic chess game. He is dealing with it and will do so fully and without fail. Further, he calls you to be a victor, not a victim, and stands ready to supply all you need. Someone else's foolish decisions cannot derail the grace, glory and purpose that God wishes to release over you right now. He wants to replace past hurt with present wholeness and crippling fear with conquering faith. He wants to break addictions to substances and give you an addiction to the One *of* Substance. Bring him what is in your hands. Stay at his feet and lay all of your burdens there. I promise; it's worth it!

## QUESTIONS:

Maybe you'll need to be vulnerable about some things that you'd rather keep hidden. The following brutal questions lay us bare before the Lord. But if we trust our Savior, we will know that we are safe enough with him to be honest. He wants to bring healing to your deepest wounds. Be open and ask the Holy Spirit to reveal these answers to your heart.

1. What do I feel I need to become or accomplish in order to feel wanted, recognized or admired?
2. Where am I striving to prove that I am strong, beautiful, talented, funny, popular or respected enough?
3. What have been my greatest heartbreaks or losses?
4. What substances do I turn to when life gets difficult? What do I seek to comfort me when I just want to escape?

# CHAPTER 10

# LEARNING TO LOVE:

*What Happens When You Stop Seeing
People as Competition*

Some years back, all the members of our church went on a 40-day journey to read "The Purpose-Driven Life" together. Our pastor challenged us to find someone to invite to join us who wasn't already a part of our congregation. I thought about several family members or an old friend from high school. But instead, God led me to a man who I will lovingly call "Homeless Steve." My encounters with him profoundly impacted my life, but they didn't start as anything special or super holy. In fact, they began one morning in a Burger King drive-thru because I wanted a Croissan'wich! As I took my grease-saturated paper bag and pulled away from the window, I saw this scruffy, rough-looking, older homeless man with long, unkempt hair and a full beard. His frail frame sat next to an equally scruffy dog that looked like some type of Heinz-57 variety. Just then, the Holy Spirit prompted me to give him my breakfast sandwich, so I obeyed. I rolled down my window and extended the bag, saying "God Bless You." Nothing profound happened. He simply thanked me, and I went about the rest of my day.

But then, in a crazy way, I found myself looking for this man, and sure enough, every day he sat in the same place, so every day I pulled through the drive-thru and bought him and the dog something to eat. He recognized me, and I began parking my car to go and sit for a minute or two. He introduced himself as Steve and explained that his dog was just a "mutt" like him! He smelled like he hadn't showered in months. Nonetheless, I found myself drawn to him, staying a little longer every day. I found myself caring about Homeless Steve, not just as some kind of charity "project," but as a person, even a *friend*.

As we sat and talked, I sometimes watched nice cars pass by with dignified, well-dressed drivers glaring at me in disbelief or even disgust. They seemed to view him as a second-class citizen, deserving of his hardships, and they viewed me as a traitor to have the audacity to identify with him. The contrast between them and Steve was ironic — they looked polished, clean, even regal on the outside, but the reflection of their hearts looked greatly neglected, untended and filthy with judgment. Steve's shell might have looked rough, but I was starting to see a beautiful heart beneath it all. Maybe that's what Jesus meant when he warned us not to be "whitewashed tombs" like the Pharisees — impressive on the outside but filled with dead men's bones within. How quick we are to judge books by their covers. I wish they could have seen Steve through my eyes, heard his story and listened to his heart and emotions and dreams and experiences. Just like me, he was made in the wondrous image of God. Just like them, too!

I brought Steve some clean jeans and shirts from my closet, which he gratefully accepted. He shared about hitchhiking all around the United States. Our conversations turned to God when I told him what I did, and he spoke affectionately when he told me that the "Big Guy" was watching over him, but he didn't know much about a personal relationship with him. Just then, I had the craziest idea — what if I went through my 40-Day "Purpose-Driven Life" readings with Steve? I thought that much of the book wouldn't exactly apply to Steve's situation. I wasn't even sure if Steve could read, but I asked him anyhow. He responded that he would like that, so I gave him his own copy of the book to keep in his backpack. Day after day, I stopped to read to Steve, ending each day's reading by talking with him about it and then praying with him.

One morning I came out to freezing weather, an unusual occurrence for Florida, especially since winter wimps like us natives were not used to it. I wore a favorite sweater, one of the nicest clothing items that I owned. I am not one to focus on clothing, but I loved this sweater. I drove to work, looking *good*, and despite the cold weather, I stopped to read to Steve. I approached him as he huddled over in a futile attempt to keep warm, wearing the same worn flannel shirt and a pair of ripped jeans. I knew before I even asked what the answer would be. Yes, he was cold, and I found myself quickly removing my favorite sweater to put on Steve. I sat shivering and smiling in my white t-shirt as I read to him about God's incredible plans for his life. In that moment, my attachment to the sweater no longer mattered. I'd grown to love "Homeless Steve" more.

Love makes us do crazy things. If you've ever been in love, just think for a minute about some of the outlandish behavior that you've displayed. I once bought a dozen expensive long-stemmed roses, drove 30 minutes across town and petitioned the staff of Busch Gardens to let me in without a ticket to deliver them so that I could publicly declare my love to a girl. It must've worked because she later married me! When the time came to pop the big question, I concocted an elaborate "beach proposal mission" at the very spot where Jill and I shared our first kiss three years earlier. Ever since then, I had been working on a song called "Jillian" that I couldn't bring myself to finish until it was "just right," and unknown to her, both the song and the man who wrote it were now fully ready to present themselves to her in the hopes of a life-long "I do!" The day *had to* be perfect. My meticulous planning of our date included: pottery painting, which she'd always wanted to try; lunch in the historic part of town; and a walk on the beach to exactly *that* spot! I recruited a few friends and worked painstakingly through a detailed chart of the location. Their task was to sneak my keyboard, an amp, a blanket, candles and the works to that remote spot. We researched how to run electricity out there and talked through how to be inconspicuous enough to keep from being arrested for trespassing on private, beachfront property. We had a timeline planned out, a map with a picture diagram specifying the location of each item and a covert communication system through our cell phones so that we could keep in touch throughout the day without getting caught. The exhausting and exhilarating plan emerged as one of the most beautiful moments of our lives! All of the effort, the crazy plan and the desire to go "overboard" beyond the bare minimum was because I *love* that girl, and love makes us do crazy things!

Maybe our problem isn't that we don't know how to love. Maybe we've drawn the line too strictly on *who* to love. Maybe we really do understand more about love than we think we do, but we've just restricted it to a few people when it is supposed to spread like a wildfire, lighting everyone in our path. We sometimes treat love like rationed survival meals, like we only have so much of it to give, so we'd better be really cautious about who we choose to share it with because we don't want to run out. We try to make people prove that they are "worthy" of our love and guard our hearts so that we don't get hurt. But if you have experienced the love of Jesus, you were the "Homeless Steve" in the story — just a rough-looking, haggard, restless wanderer looking for something to get through another day. You didn't just receive the gift of a sweater and some breakfast sandwiches. Your King laid down his own *life* for you while you were broken, giving you a new nature and his whole Kingdom. Love goes out of its way to show crazy kindness that isn't earned or deserved.

As Jesus said, when you love those who love you in return, you aren't doing anything special. It's like paying cash and getting groceries in return — an exchange of goods. As Christians, our love isn't supposed to be like that. Instead, we are raised with Christ and seated in the heavenly realms with him. We are covered, protected, provided for and furnished now and forever with all that we ever need. We can't lose, so we are free to drop our guard and stop rationing love as a logical exchange of goods, and instead, to start radically showing the kindness of God to people. We are so continually and relentlessly overwhelmed by a love from our Daddy, and we can neither deserve nor contain it. It just spills out into a kindness that shows people their forgotten dignity. Look at how God calls us to love:

"A new command I give you: Love one another. As I have loved you, so you must love one another. By this *everyone* will know that you are my disciples, *if you love one another*" John 13:34-35 – Emphasis added.

"Be *devoted* to one another in love. *Honor* one another above yourselves" Romans 12:10 – Emphasis added.

"Let no debt remain outstanding, except the continuing *debt to love* one another, for whoever loves others has *fulfilled the law*. The commandments, "You shall not commit adultery," "You shall not murder," "You shall not steal," "You shall not covet," and whatever other command there may be, are *summed up* in this one command: "Love your neighbor as yourself." Love does no harm to a neighbor. Therefore *love is the fulfillment of the law*" Romans 13:8-10 – Emphasis added.

"Do *everything* in love" 1 Corinthians 16:14 – Emphasis added.

"May the Lord make your love *increase* and *overflow* for each other and for everyone else, just as ours does for you" 1 Thessalonians 3:12 – Emphasis added.

"Above all, *love each other deeply*, because love covers over a multitude of sins" 1 Peter 4:8 – Emphasis added.

And these verses don't begin to scratch the surface on what the Bible says about love.

Jesus said that everyone would recognize that we belong to him, not by our really trendy Christian t-shirts or the fish emblem on the back of our car or by the way we say, "I'm *blessed*" as secret "Christian code" when people ask how we are doing. Instead, he said that people would spot us a mile away if we'd just *love* the way that he does. Love is the only debt that we have that we need to continually pay to everyone we meet. Everything should be done in love as an Overflow out of us to others! When you are at a restaurant talking to a waitress, it is an opportunity to love. When you are in the checkout line at Walmart, it is an opportunity to love. When you are in the waiting room of a doctor's office or in a staff meeting at work or on the phone with someone about a wrong charge on a bill, they aren't inconveniences. They are opportunities to *love*. We need to recognize that every moment that we spend with people is an opportunity to demonstrate the love of our Father. We need to slow down, see them and ask him how he specifically wants to display his love through us to them. All of us need a greater manifestation of our Father's love today — Christian or Muslim, American or foreign, male or female, polite or rude, middle class or little class. If we could remember that, we'd realize that our mission field is where ever a person is because every person is a target for the love of God! We need to understand what love is and isn't because we're surrounded with limitless opportunities, and Jesus said it is the foundation of everything we do!

## LOVE ISN'T RECRUITING SOMEONE TO YOUR PYRAMID SCHEME

For several years, I had the joy of ministering at the YMCA in my community. Honestly, I felt a calling to go there because as a pastor, I spend a lot of time with people inside the four walls of the church, but my schedule had become increasingly segmented from the rest of life. I wanted to make friendships and be a light to my community on a wider scale, and the Y was the perfect place. I started working out there and signed up to volunteer anywhere I could help. First, I scanned membership cards. Then, when they learned that I had some experience with teens, they invited me to take part in their Teen Leaders' Club. I built relationships with these incredible kids and even joined them for an inspiring week up in the Blue Ridge Mountains where they learned how to impact the world around them. Before I knew it, I was serving as a volunteer on the Board of Directors and was eventually honored to serve as the Chairman of the Board. I built so many amazing relationships with a group of diverse people, who I came to really love. We laughed a lot together as we worked in the trenches to strengthen our community. God opened up many opportunities for heartfelt conversations and prayer with people as I counseled them through tough times. He placed me there strategically for that moment, and those precious friends impacted my life much more than they will ever know. When I knew that my time there was ending, it was bittersweet because I really came to *love* them.

One morning, God "set me up." Maybe you've been there, too. I walked into a situation planned by him in detail, but I had no idea what was happening until it was over. By then, I thought, "Ok, I see what you did there." After my shift volunteering, a staff member introduced me to a man who had survived a horrific car accident. He began to share his story with me and how he'd found hope in God in his place of brokenness. I was meeting a new friend and moved so deeply by his story. I was fully "in" that moment with him. All of a sudden, a sweet, 80-year-old lady interrupted our conversation: "A new *friend*," I thought!

She observed, "I see you are both Christians." She then quickly proceeded to invite us to join her business on the ground floor! Whipping out a business card, she shared how this really "fit" with what we were doing as men of God. I really didn't see any connection, but that didn't stop her. With undeterred stamina, she highlighted a few ways that we would greatly benefit from her plans, gave us her contact information and then disappeared just as quickly as she arrived. I couldn't believe it: I'd been had by a sweet, old lady. I thought of the words of Jim Carrey in "Dumb and Dumber:" "And I didn't even *see it coming*!"

I walked to the locker room to try and shake off the strange encounter and ready myself for work. A very outgoing man approached me: "A new *friend,*" I thought. He took great interest in me, asking all kinds of questions. "Wow, what a nice guy," I thought. When he'd gathered enough information, he quickly moved the direction of our conversation into, an "opportunity" to join *his* pyramid scheme. While he was in an entirely different business, he also "happened" to have a business card right at his fingertips. I was enjoying speaking with a potential new friend, but he just wanted a new client.

While he might have meant well, I walked out of the locker room feeling used. As I exited the Y that day, God showed me that he "set me up," saying, "That's *exactly* how most people see Christians." I was stunned but realized that he was absolutely right. All too often, I started a conversation with small talk, asking questions just so that I could shoot them with my Jesus bullet. I hijacked conversations that were going in an entirely different direction so that I could help someone pray a prayer of salvation. Most Christians hesitate to share their faith because they don't want to be seen as MLM recruiters, but many of us believe that God expects exactly that from us.

We are ingrained with the idea that we need to show people hope in Jesus by practically beating them over the head with the gospel and pressuring them to join our club by praying our prayer. We do this with great urgency, compelled by good intentions, but to the rest of the world, we sound like mafia hit men. "Turn to Jesus, or bad things could happen." <Insert strong Italian accent.> If we take our cue from Jesus and not from culture, we will see that he was heavy on compassionate love while uncompromising his stand on the truth. He invited the hungry to find life in him. When we believe that our job to "love" the lost is simply to rush into a gospel presentation, we will fail to listen to them or to truly know them. We might put another notch in our spiritual belt so that we feel really holy, but we will fail to love them.

I believe that Jesus Christ **is** the hope of the entire world. I believe in a real and literal heaven and a real and literal hell. I believe that he alone is "the Way, the Truth and the Life." I also believe that he wants lost people saved and restored much more than I do and that the Father, not my forced presentation, draws hearts for all men to be saved (John 6:44). So, like Paul, I ask my Daddy for "open doors" to the gospel (Colossians 4:3-6) so that I can see where God is leading me and be faithful to recognize and walk through every door that he opens instead of forcibly kicking down doors that he isn't opening. But all too often, we are overbooked and too busy, so we don't have "time" to slow down and stop for the one. But they **are** the mission field — the important thing.

If we really desired for the Holy Spirit to flow through us, and if we really slowed down to see people and get to know them so that we could truly love them, we'd recognize a lot more opportunities to be light. I think we'd see a lot more people come in the Kingdom with a lot more depth to their walk, too, because they would have been walked into the Kingdom a step at a time in love.

I'm certainly not saying that the Holy Spirit won't prompt you to spiritual conversations with strangers you might only meet once. Of course he will! But in those moments, your goal isn't to fire off some memorized sales pitch to "close the deal". It is to really slow down to see them and love them so you can hear what their Father wants to say to them. If you focus on seeing that person as a dearly loved child constructed in God's image, you'd see their unique beauty and stop presenting the gospel on auto pilot. You'd also see their pain and how he is calling you to personally demonstrate the love of their Father to them. I am not saying that you should be sharing the gospel less. Instead, if you let the Holy Spirit drive, you will be talking about the cross, forgiveness, hope and healing naturally because you won't be working so hard to force a conversation somewhere. You will be simply responding to how their Daddy wants to love them in that moment so that you both stand amazed at the relentless pursuit of the Father for our hearts! If we just love, it won't matter how simple or how complex "our part" is in someone else's rescue story with their Daddy. We will just be grateful to dance in their story for however many pages it takes because they found life!

## LOVE ISN'T JUDGING SOMEONE ELSE'S KIDS

Our problem can sometimes run deeper than merely confusing love with the pressure to present the gospel. We sometimes think that we are responsible to tell everyone else how wrong they are. We mean well, but we emphasize what we don't agree with and who we don't stand with. Putting people into boxes of how "acceptable" or "holy" they really are to God and how "safe" they are for us to interact with makes us feel qualified to judge. Accordingly, we adjust how vulnerable we will be with them and how much we will allow them to be a voice in any area of our lives. We've supersized the idea that we should "have nothing to do with fruitless deeds of darkness," (Ephesians 5:11) which is correct, but sometimes our fear of being corrupted has led us to stereotype some really remarkable people who God has called us to serve. If, like Jesus, we could walk unafraid of "sinners" getting us dirty, we could get close enough to break off some of the ridiculous clichés and generic boxes that we've put people in and instead, start to love them.

We could let people see the great hope that we are *for* instead of letting them know everything we are *against*. We could stop judging others by their external behavior, acting as if we were the second Holy Spirit. One Holy Spirit is sufficient, and he called us to draw near to others and *love* them. We cannot ever lift someone up while looking down on them. We judge *most* what we understand *least*. When people wrestle or struggle with something that is different than our struggle or our experience, we all too easily quip, "Well, they just need to stop that."

In my senior year of high school, one of my closest friends came to me on the night of prom in tears, wrecked. He was one of the pillars who had originally brought me to church — an all-star in the youth group, well loved and respected by everyone in our little community. Through his tears, he confided his secret, no longer able to hide it. "I'm gay," he sobbed. The look on his face betrayed his inner struggle. More than struggle, though, I saw fear. The entire church community had embraced and loved him for years. What would they do if they found out about this conflict in his heart? He needed a safe place to share his whole heart without judgment. He needed a place, just like me, to find out what God said about his identity, but he feared that he had crossed a line in the sand that would alienate him from everyone he loved most. Sometimes, the people who most need the direction and compassion of the church in their time of crisis feel too "unacceptable" to even share what's happening in their hearts. My dear friend held this burden for many years and as I consoled him, I quietly wondered who would be there for him now to help him make sense of his feelings and his understanding of God.

I loved my dear friend then and love him still. I just wish I had known how to bring the Body of Christ around him in that moment so that he wouldn't have had to walk that road alone. Needless to say, I have a difficult time when I hear church people say things like, "God made Adam and Eve, not Adam and Steve," or make insulting comments, lumping all homosexuals together in one group instead of viewing them as individuals with their own hopes and dreams. Worse yet, certain segments of the church unfairly assert that they are all on a crusade to destroy traditional values. No wonder so many people use words like "hateful" and "judgmental" to describe us. Most who make insensitive comments about homosexuals aren't hateful people. They are just judging what they don't understand. Since they've never had a same-sex attraction, they glibly say, "Well, they shouldn't feel that way." However, if that same person views them instead through their own lens of temptation or struggle, they become more compassionate and tender and quit making generalizations from a distance because they understand the struggle up close. They don't write off people because they personally know the need for grace and freedom in their own struggle. Real love requires humility.

"Be completely humble and gentle; be patient, bearing with one another in love" Ephesians 4:2.

The power of God is true, and the truth of God is powerful, fully able to heal the sick and set the captives free through us. But if we don't approach others from the overwhelming *love* of God for his kids, our spiritual car is left without an engine and will never arrive at the anticipated destination. Perhaps, all that will be coming out of us are fumes that no one else wants to breathe! We need to stop trying to be everyone's savior and instead slow down to hear their stories, to know them, to love them and to really pray for them to more deeply encounter their Savior. I like how author Bob Goff worded it:

> "I don't think Bible verses were meant to be thrown like grenades at each other. They were meant for us to use to point each other toward love and grace and invite us into something much bigger."[29]

We must have a heart attitude of humility that says, "I don't act like I am better than you because I recognize that I was crafted by the same Artist as you." Humility says, "I don't need to discredit you because you hold a distinct beauty just as I do." Humility includes love without pretending to know all the answers. Humility runs after the One who is **the** answer and invites you to join the pursuit. Humility doesn't judge people's "hidden motives" by their actions. Humility refuses to group people into "stances" and instead prefers to see "faces." But an attitude of humility alone is not enough. Love must not only have the right attitude but the right *content*. If love is a house, humility is atmosphere — the warmth that makes it feel like home. Truth, however, is the floor upon which the home is built — the foundation. Humility must be the attitude of our hearts while the content that comes out of our hearts is truth.

## LOVE IS MORE THAN TOLERANCE

We need a foundation of truth although popular opinion suggests that it is subjective and determined merely by your personal views and situations. Truth is like math. Go anywhere in the world and take a math test. On every continent, "2 + 2 = 4." No matter where you go, "2 +2 ≠ Fred." Everyone agrees that "Fred" is the wrong answer. You cannot say, "Well, 4 is *your* truth, but Fred is *my* truth." Objective truth is not just limited to the world of mathematics. The reason every culture holds to a similar set of values transcends time or personal preference. Globally, people generally view a husband cheating on his wife or a teenager going into a theater with a gun and shooting innocent bystanders as unacceptable behaviors. Why? We have a Creator who wrote the blueprint on how we are supposed to function and act. We embrace the concept of morality because God placed it in our hearts.

Now, of course, you will face a billion unique situations. God might allow behavior for someone else because it doesn't sway their intimacy with their Father in the least while he asks you to stay away from it. The Bible addresses this in 1 Corinthians 8. For example, intense movies, such as "I am Legend," deeply disturb my wife. Meanwhile, I'm chomping on popcorn and giving high fives around the room because they don't bother me in the least. In this case, the Holy Spirit guides our hearts as to what it takes for us to best follow him.

With the tolerance movement, we've begun acting like everything fits into that "I'll do what works for me; you do what works for you" mindset. But we have a higher authority — our Daddy, who has spoken in many concrete ways about truth. Jesus said, "You will know the truth and the truth will set you free" (John 8:32). When we ignore the truth, we walk into lies that bind and hurt us. We have a real enemy and are in a real war, and if we are going to truly love people, we need to stand on a firmer foundation than popular opinion. Look at what Jesus said when he compared our lives to a house:

"Therefore everyone who hears these *words of mine* and *puts them into practice* is like a wise man who built his house on the *rock*. The rain came down, the streams rose, and the winds blew and beat against that house; yet it did not fall, because it had its foundation on the rock. But everyone who hears these words of mine and *does*

*not put them into practice* is like a foolish man who built his house on *sand.* The rain came down, the streams rose, and the winds blew and beat against that house, and *it fell with a great crash"* Matthew 7:24-27 – Emphasis added.

Whoever listens to Jesus builds their lives upon a foundation that is capable of withstanding any storm so that they don't collapse. The tolerance movement has brought global awareness to end bullying and embrace diversity and uniqueness. I applaud this beautiful message.

But to *tolerate* someone is not to truly *love* them. The core value of tolerance is to never disagree with anyone about anything that they want to do. Regardless of your religious convictions, relationships built on love are honest, safely sharing their thoughts and opinions without censoring. Those closest to me open up the most and tell me what they are really thinking. They are the people who I would expect to speak up if they felt that I was about to harm myself. If my daughter were running into the middle of traffic, I would not apathetically sit back and say, "Well, she believes that will make her happy, so who am I to tell her otherwise?" I would instead stop her because that's what love does.

Most of what drives tolerance isn't love but self-preservation driven by insecurity. We want to walk in humility without acting like we know it all, but the key reason that we cannot tell others that we disagree with them is because we want them to like us. We don't want them to think that we are bigots or mean and judgmental people. Admittedly, Christians who spout their opinions when they aren't asked have made matters worse, but as a culture, we've taken political correctness and tolerance way too far. Our culture tries to silence anyone with a different opinion. Because of insecurity, we want to believe that we are right and do not want anyone to tell us otherwise. Like toddlers, we throw sophisticated temper tantrums in the form of lawsuits, petitions and social media rants against anyone who doesn't agree.

Yes, we desperately need humility. But we cannot truly love someone without leading them to life, which only comes through living and speaking truth. The Word tells us to "speak the truth in love" (Ephesians 4:15) and reminds us that Jesus was full of both grace and truth (John 1:17). We are not truthful or gracious when we put a silent "stamp of approval" on what everyone says, especially when their feelings agree with their enemy and not with their Father. We need to take the time to build loving relationships with people. When the Holy Spirit makes us aware of harmful behaviors in the life of loved ones, we can do several things:

1. Ask the Lord to reveal any places where we have aligned our hearts in harmful ways. Jesus said to remove the "plank in our own eye" so that we can see clearly to address the speck in someone else's (Matthew 7:1-5).
2. Pray that the Holy Spirit changes their heart and moves upon them.
3. Ask the Holy Spirit, like Paul did, for an "open door" to share hope with them. People rarely accept counsel unless they ask for it.
4. In some instances, the Lord might tell you to initiate a conversation and address a blind spot in the life of someone you love. When he does, obey and ask him for guidance in your words, keeping a gentle attitude of humility while you share the truth. Remember that those you love are in the hands of your loving Daddy. Don't take responsibility for their response or put that yoke on your shoulders. They are his kids, and he will take care of it. Just love him, slow down to love them and obey whatever he tells you!

## THE POWER OF LOVE

You have no idea of the power of love. For my 80s music fans, it's more than a Huey Lewis song. A few years ago, one of the students in our youth group, Jacob, decided that every person and leader needed to know that they were loved at Christmas time, so he purchased a personally meaningful Christmas present for each one. He asked questions of each person to ensure that he bought each one the perfect gift. He didn't ask his parents for the funds but spent his own hard-earned money. His parents, some of the most generous people I have ever known, instilled love in him. I wish that you could have seen the unbelievable shock and how his gifts impacted our group that Christmas. Some of the youth felt misunderstood and overlooked by the whole world. The expression in their eyes showed that Jacob saw them. He cared. He told everyone that the Holy Spirit prompted his heart to help them see how precious they are. If that isn't preaching the gospel through love, I don't know what is. Their family's culture of generosity changed our church.

Last year, our church threw a community yard sale as a fundraiser to benefit an orphanage that we support in Haiti. Our youth led the way, and people brought various items from their homes: furniture, clothes, books, appliances and more. My wife and I contributed some baby items, including a quality lifetime crib. Made of real wood, the bed could be converted to fit children all the way to college, but we had so many kids that we put them in bunk beds like a military barracks! We could have probably sold it for hundreds of dollars online, but we wanted it to benefit Haiti. Just before we started, our event leader, Billianna (Jacob's mom), felt prompted to tell the rest of us that God wanted us to show love to Haiti but also to our community. She encouraged us to keep our eyes open for anyone who might want to buy something but who could not afford it. She instructed, "Have a heart ready to bless them." I love my church!

Just before we officially called it a day, a mom and her pregnant daughter pulled up on our property. They "happened" to approach me about the crib, wanting to know the price. Immediately, I was overcome with love for them and was reminded, "Be ready to bless someone." I didn't know anything about them, their means or their situation. I didn't need to. I knew what my Daddy said.

"How much is the crib?" the lady, whose name was Judy, asked.

"Take it," I replied. She thought that the crib was sold and started to leave. I realized that I hadn't been clear, so I caught up to her. "No," I insisted, with a wide open smile. "Take it. I want you to have it." She broke down in tears and hugged me as she explained that it was her daughter, Elizabeth's, first baby. They were all so excited but not in any financial position to prepare for this unexpected blessing. Elizabeth's husband was working hard, and Judy and her husband were contributing as well, but they were especially stressed as they prepared for the arrival of this precious little one. Overcome with emotion, I asked them to follow me, and we walked through the yard sale, grabbing every other baby item that we could find. They were blown away. I introduced them to my wife and shared that we probably had a few additional baby items at home. I wrote down her email address. They were ecstatic and hugged me several times. But the story gets better.

My wife and I shared what happened with the college group that we lead, and they wanted to do more. We felt the Holy Spirit calling us to have a "shower for a stranger." In fact, our whole church wanted to throw her a shower and to help meet every need for this precious family. We weren't trying to get them to church or to have a write up in the newspaper. We weren't looking for a "pat on the back." God had opened our hearts to this amazing opportunity, and we felt his love for these beautiful people.

Judy and her family had been giving to the community for years. At the age of 12, her son, Jared, started a food pantry to help combat hunger among the homeless across our county. This was a family of givers, so when I emailed Judy to ask if we could bless Liz and her husband, Jason, and their soon-coming baby, she agreed. I kept in touch with them during Liz's pregnancy. She was having a beautiful princess, Claire.

The week of the shower, our whole church bought everything on the registry and more! We prepared all of the food and decorations and threw one of the nicest baby showers that I have ever seen. One of our members painted a picture for the nursery as she felt the Lord directing her: a purple-

and-green dinosaur with a personal prayer. When the family arrived, they saw the painting amidst the other gifts and gasped in amazement. "How did you know to paint *that*?" Liz asked. She told me that everything — the colors, the painting, the message — were like they'd been perfectly selected for them. We told her what we'd said all along — their Daddy saw them and dearly loved them. We were just sons and daughters willing to do the same!

The harvest is abundant right now. Today, your Daddy wants you to manifest his amazing love and incomparable power to others. We can only give that kind of abundant love to others when it is springing up out of the well of our love relationship with our God. Do you want to love the people who you encounter radically and beautifully? It doesn't come from trying harder. It simply flows from you when you live in the place of focused intimacy with the One who **is** love itself!

## QUESTIONS:

1. When you think about a lifestyle where you regularly tell/show people the hope you've found in Jesus, do you feel overwhelmed? Why? What would change if you saw everything through the lens of just slowing down to love people and only sharing what the Holy Spirit prompts you to — no matter how simple?

2. In this chapter, Chuck wrote, "We judge most what we understand least." Be completely vulnerable and ask the Holy Spirit, "Are there any particular groups of people I find myself judging, disliking or looking down upon for their lifestyle, religion or habits?" How is the Holy Spirit calling you to slow down and love them?

3. In an age when any disagreement with someone's lifestyle decisions is viewed as "intolerant" or even "bigoted," how can we walk as people full of grace and truth? How can we stand upon unwavering convictions and unapologetically point people to the hope found in Jesus with hearts full of compassion and humility?

4. Where is God calling you to slow down and "see faces?" Who is he calling you to more intentionally love?

## CHAPTER 11

# SEIZING AUTHORITY:

*The End of the Age of Intimidation*

Growing up in Florida, we rarely had cold weather. Even when the natives thought that it was really cold, all of the winter snowbirds were wearing shorts, probably laughing at us bundled up in our wool coats. I didn't see snow until I became an adult. The first time that I saw it, I discovered a past time that I would grow to love: skiing. But the start of my journey on the slopes was filled with frustration and fright. At the time, my wife and I were still dating. I went with her and some of her family to Snowshoe Mountain in West Virginia. I was anticipating the adventure until we were almost to the mountains. Jill decided to give me a few warnings to help prepare me for the adventure of skiing:

- "When you get to the top of the ski lift, you have to get off quickly because people are coming right behind you."
- "After you get off the lift, you only have a little area before you go down the mountain."
- "You need to stay on the slope because the sides drop off steeply."
- "The only way to stop is to 'snow plow.'"

If you've ever been skiing, you can attest that everything she told me was accurate, but since I had never seen a ski slope before, I had a very different picture in my mind.

I won't sugar coat it. I quickly moved from calm to completely terrified. Images rushed through my head of a high lift quickly dumping off people, one after another, and then an incredibly steep, long drop that I had to maneuver with two "spears of death" strapped to my feet. If I didn't know how to stop, I might plunge off the side of the mountain forever! I was now very motivated to learn exactly how to "snow plow." You could understand my frustration when my only instructions on how to keep alive were: "Just turn your toes in toward each other." She reassured me that I could practice on a "bunny slope" that wasn't steep at all, and she could show me what to do. That calmed me down until I actually got on the mountain and quickly learned two things. First, the bunny slope was on a different part of the mountain, which meant moving our entire practice to a more advanced slope. Second, despite the instruction I'd been given, I had no idea how to "snow plow!" As I started gaining speed, I tried to turn my toes in as I'd been instructed, but I was traveling far too fast, and my feet weren't cooperating. I flew past Jill and her family like a bullet being shot out of a gun, shouting, "**I. Can't. Stop!**"

Behind me, voices called out, "Fall! Fall! Fall!" Jill told me that falling didn't hurt, but she also said that "snow plowing" was easy! I really didn't want to fall at this high speed, but I was approaching an "edge" of no return, so I dove to the side and rolled through the snow.

I wish I could say that I laughed. I wish I could say that I dusted myself off and quipped, "If at first you don't succeed, try, try again." I wish. Instead, I popped the skis off my feet and angrily stormed back up the mountain to turn them in and call it quits. Fortunately, Jill sent her brother, Josh, to the rescue. Jill gave me the same instructions that she had been told when she learned to ski as a child, but I didn't understand and required more help. Josh, who is not only my brother, but also a tremendous friend, fought the urge to laugh at my self-induced crisis and calmly reassured me that skiing was completely within my grasp. In about 30 seconds, he demonstrated exactly what muscles I needed to move in order to snow plow, and I found that I was able to do it immediately. I then questioned him about what I would find at the top of the mountain, and Josh offered to ride up the ski lift with me the first time. Josh's confidence removed the worry from me because he'd already conquered this mountain. He was the fearless skier who raced down Black Diamond trails. So I trusted the judgment of someone who conquered the mountain when he told me that I could conquer it, too. Within minutes, I was on that mountain having the time of my life. Intimidation was replaced by exhilaration.

You have been called to a journey to ski down a mountain called "Authority." On this mountain you, as just an ordinary child of God, can see people cross from death to life as you preach the Kingdom and watch them trust Christ as their Savior. You can touch sick people and see them healed. You can encounter people bound by lies of the enemy and see them set free. Maybe you cannot picture what that's like, or you've just seen little glimpses, so you are intimidated and just want to turn in your skis and leave the mountain. But take heart: you were made for this, and the One who already conquered the mountain is asking you to take his hand and join him on the lift. You don't have to be afraid. It will be the ride of your life!

## MADE FOR THIS

To understand our authority, let's go back to the beginning of the story. You and I were created with great glory and great purpose: we were made to be with God and to reign with him. He placed Adam and Eve in the garden where they walked with him and responded to his beautiful invitation to rule with him over all the works of his hands. Adam even had some creative input when he named them. And what bizarre names! What on earth was he thinking? Duck-billed platypus? Hippopotamus? Sea cucumber? But the specifics didn't matter since the ultimate Author was delighted as his kids started to write upon the canvas that he had made.

We were his crowning achievement, the exclamation point of creation, the only creatures made in the image of God and the apple of his eye, but a war broke out in heaven, and a very jealous general staged a rebellion. Lucifer, an archangel, arguably the most beautiful angel ever created, betrayed his Creator King and took one-third of an innumerable host of angels with him. They fell to earth with a hatred for God and a revenge plot to obliterate his beloved in the foulest way imaginable: to entice the creation to abandon their Creator. Lucifer took the form of a serpent and lied to mankind about the character and intent of our God, which he continues to this day. He told them that God was not a loving Daddy but rather One who was holding something back from them, a secret knowledge. He told them that the whole reason that God prohibited them from eating one fruit in the garden was because eating it would make them "like God."

I used to wonder about the fall. What was the big deal? Why was God freaking out about fruit? Don't parents tell their kids to eat fruit? Why the separation, disease, death and hell, all because of fruit? But it isn't about the fruit at all. It's about what we thought the fruit would give us. When the enemy "promised" if we ate the fruit that we'd become "like God," he wasn't insinuating that we would be holy, loving or forgiving. After all, he'd just told them that their God was a monster who willingly held back beneficial knowledge to pull the wool over their eyes and keep them under his thumb. This wasn't about character. It was about power. To say that they'd be **like** God meant that they'd have all the knowledge they needed to be in charge so that they wouldn't **need** God anymore. The sin in the garden was that we were created for intimacy but instead chose autonomy, independence from God. We tried to write our own destiny apart from him. We chose separation. We left.

Before the flavor of the fruit had settled on our taste buds, the effect of our choice became evident. The fruit might have looked pleasing to the eyes, but I'm convinced it went down bitter. Lucifer promised "the knowledge of good and evil," but we quickly learned that only one side of that equation was not already in our possession. God had already given us the "good." Now we became all too familiar with "evil." A previously foreign feeling now coursed through our veins: shame, guilt and the desire to hide. God immediately confronted Lucifer, promising one day that he would send "the seed of a woman" to crush the traitor's head at great cost to himself. He promised that he would redeem us, but he also told us that our choice had a cost. Sin had entered the world.

In Greek, one of the definitions for sin is "to miss the mark and therefore to forfeit."[30] We forfeited the right to reign and placed it in the hands of a tyrant king. His rule brought all that comes with sin: sickness, disease, depression, confusion, separation from God, despair, loss and more. We were no longer ruling, but sin was ruling us. While we awaited our Deliverer, God gave us all kinds of laws that reflected his heart, but we couldn't keep them. Laws couldn't save us. Judges couldn't save us. Kings couldn't save us. Prophets couldn't save us. Instead, voice after voice after voice called for us to look ahead, longing for the King who would come and free fallen man from our enemy's oppression. Enter Jesus. Indeed, he came as the King who would die in our place and free us from the penalty of sin. But he came to offer so much more than just a "get-out-of-jail-free" card. He came to restore us back to the fullness of his design for us. As Todd White put it, "Jesus didn't just come to get us into heaven. He came to get heaven into us!"

We have been hard-wired to be with him as sons and daughters and to rule with him as princes and princesses. We have misunderstood his intent and have made Christianity about so much less than what he offers. We have made it about just being recipients of a rescue mission, like flailing, drowning people who should be thankful they made it onto the safety raft. While that's true, the more accurate picture is that we are like Navy Seal divers who have temporarily forgotten how to swim. We're still supposed to rescue the people drowning everywhere around us. Jesus came, not just for eternity, but to restore us to our original glory here and now. We're the restored now called to be restorers. At the beginning of his ministry, he called 12 men from different occupations who would turn the world upside down. They marked the inauguration of a new Kingdom — one that would overthrow the kingdom of our enemy and make a spectacle of him. Jesus could have done it all alone. He could have just placed us on the safety raft. It would have certainly been more efficient. Quicker. Quite a bit neater. But Jesus wasn't just coming for an intervention. He was returning to extend a long-awaited invitation.

Jesus was like a new sheriff who came to a lawless town to restore order and establish a new law. Not long after choosing the 12 disciples, he shared something shocking in the synagogue:

He went to Nazareth, where he had been brought up, and on the Sabbath day he went into the synagogue, as was his custom. He stood up to read, and the scroll of the prophet Isaiah was handed to him. Unrolling it, he found the place where it is written:

"The Spirit of the Lord is on me, because he has anointed me to proclaim good news to the poor. He has sent me to proclaim freedom for the prisoners and recovery of sight for the blind, to set the oppressed free, to proclaim the year of the Lord's favor."

Then he rolled up the scroll, gave it back to the attendant and sat down. The eyes of everyone in the synagogue were fastened on him. He began by saying to them, "Today this scripture is *fulfilled* in your hearing" Luke 4:16-21 – Emphasis added.

The word translated "fulfilled" in Greek is "pleroo," which means "to bring to realization, or to reach its consummation."[31] It is the picture of a cup being filled to its highest point before water spills all over the floor everywhere. As a dad of 4–year-old twins, trust me, I know exactly what this looks like! Quoting Isaiah, Jesus said that his coming fulfilled God's promise of restoration. This wasn't a pipe dream for the future but the cup had reached its tipping point at that very moment. The people could now expect to see it pouring out everywhere.

And pour out it did.

## IN THIS KINGDOM, BUT NO LONGER "OF" IT

We are born in the kingdom of this earth, a fallen world. God created it to be our kingdom, our home, but the entrance of sin darkened it beyond all hope. Yes, we still see glimpses everywhere of the goodness of our Creator. Though his creation left him, he never left us. In every sunset and every flower, we see his beauty. In every bolt of lightning and crashing wave, his power. In every laugh and embrace, his goodness. He is everywhere, and by his grace, he sustains the beauty of creation and sings over this world with joy. This world, though beautiful, isn't home anymore. This world as we know it will end. It has to. Sin was the iceberg that sunk our Titanic, and the ship is going down. It sounds dark, but understanding that fact is at the core of our hope. Since the days of Jesus, he promised that he has been preparing a new heaven and a new earth where he invites his beloved to be with him forever, our true home. And that Kingdom is already very much alive!

Yes, we are born into this kingdom, but when we are born "again," we become citizens of a new Kingdom. Though you probably didn't know it, from the first time that you took a breath after giving Jesus your life, you've belonged to a different Kingdom. Understanding which kingdom we belong to will help us make sense of these chaotic times. When the Bible refers to our relationship to this world, this kingdom, it uses three key words: foreigners, strangers and exiles.

The word "foreigner" means "someone who lodges somewhere temporarily that isn't their home, a guest."[32] If you want a picture of what the Bible considers a "foreigner," imagine checking into a hotel to attend to some business in another city. If your stay is an extended one, you might unpack your suitcase into the dressers in the room, but you would not buy new bedding or rearrange all the furniture. Likewise, you would not invest money or time into painting the walls and changing the drapes to match "your" style. You wouldn't renovate the room to make the floorplan

**171**

suit your needs because you don't actually *live* there. It isn't your home. We usually don't stay in a hotel for the hotel, and we certainly don't get attached to it. The facilities act as a temporary living space that allows us to accomplish a much greater mission. Because of that, you can go to a hotel for a few days and endure tight quarters that are less than ideal because you know that when your business is done, you will return to your home.

This world isn't our home. It's our hotel. It is beautiful, but some things on this side are not as they should be. We have a true home. We only woke up in the hotel of this earth this morning because we have business to attend to before going home. We should be grateful for this world and do our best to take care of it, but we don't need to cling to it as if this is all there is. We are "foreigners" here.

The second word the Bible uses to describe Christians living in the kingdom of this earth is "stranger," which means "someone who travels to a strange land and culture that is not their own."[33] Jesus says that we are not to be friends with the system of this world because "the whole world is under the control of the evil one" (1 John 5:19). You aren't supposed to look like the rest of the world around you. You aren't supposed to put down roots, spending your energy obsessing about being accepted by the standards of this world. It might be popular, but it is unnatural to who you are now. You have traveled to a strange land, and you are quickly passing through it. As you live in the tent of your earthly body and temporarily camp in a place that isn't your final home, you aren't supposed to blend in. You're supposed to stand out, like an LED Maglite. You are a city on a hill, the light of the world. You are a beacon of hope that shines like a solitary star in the middle of a pitch-black sky.

Hebrews 11 lists the greatest heroes of our faith — men and women we are to learn from and emulate. The unifying quality among them was that they lived as "foreigners and strangers" on earth. The Bible says that they spent their days here unafraid to stand out for their King because they eagerly desired a "much better country," their true home. The reason Jesus calls us to stand out in a strange land isn't because he desires to embarrass us but rather to liberate us to know and reflect who we really are. We can embrace being "strangers on earth," not because we are alienating ourselves from or elevating ourselves above other people, but we are urging them to desire a greater country, too. Our whole journey after finding Jesus is to show them that they don't belong here anymore than we do. If we could see that, we would understand that our temporary sojourn here is, in fact, the inaugural days of our eternal reign with him.

The last word the Bible uses to define a Christian's relationship to the kingdom of this world is "exile" or "one who doesn't live by the rights of the land because he isn't accepted as a citizen."[34] When someone is "denied rights" and rejected as a citizen of a much-desired kingdom, they are heartbroken. They are locked out of the country and not privy to their laws or policies. However, the land that denied your citizenship might be an awful kingdom that had once made you a slave. The "denial" of your rights here is because you now belong to an opposite and far more glorious Kingdom.

When we came to Jesus, we received a new nature and completely shifted kingdoms. You are no longer a citizen of this kingdom and do not need to submit to the rules of that snake anymore. Instead, you are a citizen of the Kingdom of heaven, which means that all the rights of that Kingdom are now at your disposal. Discipleship is learning to live more gloriously alive every moment as a full citizen of heaven while you are on mission to set people free from their former kingdom. The Kingdom is already here within you, and while we await its final consummation, we need to see clearly:

"Therefore, with minds that are alert and fully sober, *set your hope on the grace to be brought to you* when Jesus Christ is revealed at his coming. As obedient children, do not conform to the evil desires you had when you lived in ignorance. But just as he who called you is holy, so be holy in all you do; for it is written: "Be holy, because I am holy." Since you call on a Father who judges each person's work impartially, live out your time as *foreigners* here in reverent fear" 1 Peter 1:13-17 – Emphasis added.

Set your hope on what is coming. Set your hope upon who you are now and when the battle will be fully over and when you will be home. Thank God for every breath here, but don't you dare set your hope here. Don't place your expectation in a broken kingdom that you no longer belong to because hope deferred will make your heart sick (Proverbs 13:12). Many live under the burden of stress, anxiety, fear and resentment because things are broken and unresolved in the here and now. They have failed to understand that the "here and now" is only here now! It is quickly fading and "not worth comparing to the glory that will be revealed in us" (Romans 8:18).

I don't want to minimize your heartbreak or the injustice that might be occurring in your life right now. My dad died when I was 6, and it ripped out my heart. I watched one of my closest friends lose an excruciating battle with cancer in his early 20s. I prayed intensely for his full healing, and I really struggled when he passed. I miss him still. My world was rocked by the loss of my sister, my nephew and my uncle. Some people who I have loved have believed lies about me and left my life. My pain might be nothing compared to what you might be going through. But this isn't home or our final "happily ever after." We woke up in enemy territory, a land ruled by one that despises us and will ruthlessly pillage us without hesitation. And yet, he is a defeated foe, and his days are numbered. Our God reigns here and now and will always "work all things together for the good of those who love him." We are not a pawn in a chess game. The enemy does not have the final victory in the life of a believer. Everything will be made right, and we are victors, not victims today. We are not home yet but are foreigners, strangers and exiles, called to manifest the coming Kingdom, which is already alive within us so that dearly beloved sons and daughters can discover what the true King has made available.

## THE UNBELIEVABLE INVITATION OF "TODAY"

A lot of Christians put down their roots here and now because it's comfortable. Media further complicate matters due to how heaven is portrayed in movies, cartoons, art, etc. Heaven is **not** a place where pudgy *Precious Moments* babies play harps as you float on a cloud in a white baptismal robe, drifting aimlessly in a wispy, eternal dreamlike state. That **isn't** heaven. It honestly sounds more like the "other" place! No wonder we don't like thinking about eternity.

Heaven won't be like a dream but will be more real than anything we know. When we leave this earth and open our eyes there, it will seem like we are waking up from a coma. Earth will seem like the dream. We will step into a reality with new colors and dimensions of creation that we cannot even presently put into words. As the book of Hebrews says, this is the shadow. That will be the substance — the reality. Still, when I encourage people not to become overwhelmed by their ever-shifting circumstances and to keep their eyes focused on eternity, I often see their eyes glaze over and hear comments like, "Yeah, but that really doesn't help me today." We wrestle with today because we cannot even begin to picture our eternal tomorrow. We can't scope it out. We don't have all the answers, and as people who all too often like the illusion of having control, we wrestle with concepts that are out of our control.

We love this world and fear leaving it. Just look at how we view death — as unnatural. For the believer, death is the graduation ceremony from your mission field to your true home — a glorious day! God took something that was not part of his original plan and now calls the death of his saints "precious" (Psalm 116:15). Even so, we cling to this world like a child clings to his mom on the first day of kindergarten. We fear the unknown, but the same architect who built **this** world built **that** one, and he promised that heaven is abundantly better than earth. If we truly understood what awaited us, we'd "sell the field" and spend every moment of **this** life reflecting him so that people will want **that**! This world is the preview while heaven is the main attraction. If eternity is a glorious mansion, then this life is only the coat room. Don't fret. You're just passing through. In the place that awaits us, we will have no tears, no pain, no struggle, no enemy, no loss, no goodbyes, no misunderstanding, no sickness, no rejection, no heartbreak — nothing hurtful. In **that** world, you'll never be left out, looked over, undermined or betrayed.

We will worship with perfect abandon in heaven! Here, the Bible says that we see Jesus "dimly, as looking through a mirror" (1 Corinthians 13:12). In the first century, they didn't have mirrors like we do today. The best parallel would be trying to look at your reflection in a pot in your kitchen. You would see colors and some features, but you wouldn't send that picture to the family for Christmas. The real you has so much more definition and beauty than that. It is the same with God. Creation screams of his glory, and we can spend this whole lifetime just scratching the surface of all that he has revealed to us. And yet, all of that is still just a dim reflection. We will see him face to face.

We will walk in perfect unity in heaven. No one will cut you off in traffic because they are updating their Facebook status, and you will never again put your foot in your mouth by speaking without thinking. We will know who we are and whose we are. We will experience perfect joy in heaven. We will even eat better in heaven. We can do **everything** better from heaven! Do you ever wonder why Jesus doesn't just "beam us up" to heaven when we accept him as Savior? Why do we have to stay on this fallen battlefield? Why live here in brokenness when our destiny has already been paid in full? That question came up in the Apostle Peter's day, and he made it clear that we woke up here because we can do everything better from heaven except one thing…we cannot bring people from darkness into light once we're there:

"The Lord is not slow in keeping his promise, as some understand slowness. Instead *he is patient with you, not wanting anyone to perish*, but everyone to come to repentance" 2 Peter 3:9 – Emphasis added.

We are still here because God desperately loves his kids, and he is patiently waiting for people to "turn around" or "change their mind." The journey is about: Being with him. Reigning with him. Sons and daughters. Princes and princesses. It's all been purchased. Man doesn't have to live under a tyrant king anymore, but just like the days in the Garden of Eden, man has a choice. Love must always be a choice. We chose autonomy. Intimacy is available again and, for those of us who have discovered it, we act as ambassadors of hope so that we can come out from under the "enterprise" of the enemy and all he brought. Today is not a day for you to simply suffer and endure as if you were in an ER waiting room. Today is not a day for you to become a recluse who avoids all contact with "sinful" people in fear that they will contaminate you with their "sin germs" or "cooties." Today is not a day for intimidation as if the enemy is winning the war with you as his personal target. No.

Today is an invitation for sons and daughters of God to rise up and know their identity. All of creation has been groaning for you to know what is within you. You are here on mission. You are on offense, not defense. We are not cowering and hiding under a powerful enemy, just hoping to survive the night. Instead, we will overthrow a tyrant's kingdom. The gates of hell "cannot stand" against Christ's church because we are coming against him. Gates don't move. Armies do, and his flimsy gates melt away under the pressure of the one true King and his sons and daughters who have returned to be with him and reign with him. You have so much more power, life and hope than you realize, and today is an invitation for you to receive it and take your rightful place to reign within the already active Kingdom of God!

## NOT (FULLY) YET, BUT SO MUCH ALREADY

The Kingdom of God is a dominant theme in the New Testament, mentioned 116 times. Of these references, 41 come just from the gospel of Matthew, which was written to tell us about the King and his Kingdom. You will quickly see that the Bible describes the Kingdom in a tension — in one sense, it is already here, but in another sense, the Kingdom has not yet reached its fullest incarnation. We've focused quite a bit on the not yet and not nearly enough on the already! We are still at war and not yet in our final home. We are not yet at the day when our King will part the clouds and remove us from the presence of this fallen kingdom. We are not yet at a place with no sickness, grief, tears or pain. But we must see the overwhelming reality of what is already ours today so that we do not lose heart in the not yet. In other words, you already have everything that you need at your disposal to reign victoriously in the midst of what is not yet!

You are already:

- A citizen of a new Kingdom
- Qualified to fully hear the voice of your Father
- A saint and no longer under the slavery of the old corpse, the sin nature
- In possession of all that you need for life and godliness
- The salt of the earth that preserves it and keeps it from rotting
- The light of the world that shines like stars as you hold out the Word of life and
- In possession of all of the power and authority necessary for the Kingdom of God to come on earth as it is in heaven.

These few scriptures drive home the power and authority that is already ours:

"Jesus called his twelve disciples to him and *gave them authority* to drive out impure spirits and to heal every disease and sickness" Matthew 10:1 – Emphasis added.

"Then Jesus came to them and said, "*All authority* in heaven and on earth has been *given to me. Therefore go* and make disciples of all nations, baptizing them in the name of the Father and of the Son and of the Holy Spirit, and teaching them to obey everything I have commanded you. And surely I am with you always, to the very end of the age" Matthew 28:18-20 – Emphasis added.

"The seventy-two returned with joy and said, "Lord, even the demons submit to us in your name." He replied, "I saw Satan fall like lightning from heaven. I have *given you authority* to trample on snakes and scorpions and to overcome all the power of the enemy; nothing will harm you. However, do not rejoice that the spirits submit to you, but rejoice that your names are written in heaven" Luke 10:17-20 – Emphasis added.

"But you *will receive power* when the Holy Spirit comes on you; and you will be my witnesses in Jerusalem, and in all Judea and Samaria, and to the ends of the earth" Acts 1:8 – Emphasis added.

"And so it was with me, brothers and sisters. When I came to you, I did not come with eloquence or human wisdom as I proclaimed to you the testimony about God. For I resolved to know nothing while I was with you except Jesus Christ and him crucified. I came to you in weakness with great fear and trembling. My message and my preaching were not with wise and persuasive words, *but with a demonstration of the Spirit's power, so that your faith might not rest on human wisdom, but on God's power*" 1 Corinthians 2:1-5 – Emphasis added.

"For the *kingdom of God* is not a *matter of* talk but of *power*" 1 Corinthians 4:20 – Emphasis added.

The purpose of power and authority is to remove the places of the tyrant king's rule and to reestablish the Kingdom of God. Accordingly, Jesus says, "If I drive out demons by the Spirit of God, the Kingdom of God has come upon you" (Matthew 12:28). Jesus again offers this right to rule to his children. This is what it means to be "co-heirs" (Romans 8:17, Galatians 3:29) — not just receiving the spoils of the king but restored to reign with him again. Jesus **gave** us power and authority at the same time that he **gave** us his only Son so that we might have eternal life (John 3:16). Believers widely accept the supernatural gift of salvation but get nervous about God giving them the power and authority to see the enemy's enterprise and all that it brought fall today. The New Testament consistently tells us that God has given us power and authority because the Kingdom of God manifests that power to topple satan's fallen kingdom in the here and now.

The power of God to preach, heal and set the captives free is not reserved for the super charismatic or gifted. We have to remove that whole mystical and sensational aura from God's power and authority. Normal Christians — ordinary believers — should see the sick healed and the captives set free by the power of God through them. This fuels our love with more than just words of encouragement or well wishes.

Churches regularly address the believer's right to rule in preaching the Kingdom but oddly neglect the other two pillars of healing and setting the captives free. A big part of that, especially in relation to healing, has to do with our experiences or lack thereof. We prayed for someone who wasn't healed. We saw a revival with exaggerated or even planted healing stories. But we cannot interpret God's Word by our experience. We will either walk by faith or by sight (2 Corinthians 5:7). God has surrounded us with more than we need to taste and see that the Lord is good. Our sight shows us so much of his majesty, but if we walk by sight and by our reasoning, we will fall because when push comes to shove, we will have made a god out of our understanding. Instead of trusting God's Word, we are making our final authority our own opinion.

I don't understand why some people are healed and others aren't. Like many of you, I've known the heartbreak and frustration all too well of praying for healing and not seeing the results I expected. I honestly tell God that I don't understand. I will also tell you, though, that if I read God's Word faithfully, he fully bought the Kingdom, and he's given us power and authority to reign with him. He is the God who heals and speaks and wants to move through sons and daughters who are crazy enough to take him at his word and let him be God through them. So back around the time of Naples, I made a decision that I would walk by what God says and not what my eyes see.

Since then, I have seen the power and authority of God flow through me and my crazy friends as we walk out the Kingdom together. I have witnessed an abundance of testimonies of miraculous physical healings and incredible freedom from the kingdom of darkness to the Kingdom of light right before my eyes. God definitely still heals. He still sets the captives free. And he still wants to do it through us. He didn't just give us words but power, and that power isn't just about a ticket to eternity but about his reign in our body, soul and spirit now. I don't know everything about healing, and I don't need to know it all. I know the Healer, and he's told me that sickness isn't his friend and that he came to destroy it, so when I see sick people, I'm going to put my hands on them and call for his Kingdom to come on earth as it is in heaven! After all, if we want to see healing, we have to pray for sick people, right?

We have been invited again to reign with our King now, not just when we leave this earth. Go into a place of intimacy with your Father and ask him to make the power and authority that he purchased for you evident in your life today! Ask him to stir faith in you and to remove the filters that have made you cynical or caused doubt. If you are wrestling with walking in your power and authority, I encourage you to take that into your intimacy with the Father and use the material in Appendix 3 for further help. Ask him to move you off the bleachers of hesitation to "get into the game" so that the same ministry that flowed through his original disciples flows through you!

## QUESTIONS:

1.  When you think about God calling you to heal the sick or set the captives free, what emotions do you experience? Why? Read Luke 10:1-12, 17-21. What do you think Jesus meant when he said the Father revealed his Kingdom to "little children?" How does this passage comfort you?

2.  We are called to live in this kingdom as "foreigners," "strangers" and "exiles," spending our strength to point people to an eternal Kingdom of hope. Ask the Holy Spirit to reveal any places you are clinging to the treasures of this world as if it were your home. In what practical ways is he calling you to "make the most of your time" as an ambassador of his hope?

3.  The Bible says that Jesus "gave" you power and authority to manifest his Kingdom in the same way that he "gave" you salvation. How is he calling you to walk deeper in your inheritance today? Pray for one another.

## CHAPTER 12

# COMMUNITY:

*Belonging to an Encouraging
and Empowering Family*

---

We've covered a lot of ground in our journey together. We've talked about the following:

- How God came to fully restore your original glory
- How you can hear his voice
- How he **longs** to speak to you every day
- How everything in your life flows from intimacy with your Daddy, a place affectionately called the Overflow and
- How power and authority and the ability to surrender — all of it — is already yours in Christ to receive and release.

I just have one final charge to give you.

Don't go alone.

Alone is scary. Alone is uncertain. To put it bluntly, alone is stupid when together has been purchased. Don't go alone. You weren't meant to go that way.

When I was about 5 years old, my parents took my sisters and me to the Strawberry Festival, a large, local fair. The fair included all of the typical attractions: a carousel, a Ferris wheel, bumper cars and a fun house. They had booths with balloons that kids could throw sharp darts at, and it wasn't only allowed, but they'd cheer and give you a stuffed animal for popping one! Of course, no fair experience is complete without the food: deep-fried Twinkies and onion rings, Polish sausages and funnel cakes, popcorn and cotton candy. My eyes glazed over as I stood in the middle of a row of brightly lit trailers of food for as far as I could see! My parents informed me that the smoke coming out of the trailers was from cooking, but I thought that it was the glory cloud of God's presence. I was in heaven!

Somewhere in the sensory overload of it all, I became separated from my family. I panicked. I was short and didn't hit a "growth spurt" until tenth grade, so all that I could see from my little vantage point was a sea of butts. I don't know if you've ever tried to identify your parents by looking at their butts, but I don't recommend it. I thought that I would need counseling for years! Unbeknownst to me, several yards away, my parents were even more frantically searching for me.

I was completely alone. Fear and uncertainty and hopelessness settled in. Fortunately, a kind security officer took me by the hand, and together, we traversed our way through the sea of butts to the "lost-and-found" station on the opposite side of the fairgrounds. The building looked like a train car. Not just any car, mind you. A **caboose**. Another butt! The air conditioner blasted a cool welcome as I walked through the doors. The friendly workers invited me to join the other "lost kids" who were coloring at a table as they waited for their parents. I felt safe. Minutes later, my worried parents rushed through the door and scooped me up into their arms. I could breathe again. The world was right because I was no longer alone.

The New Testament has 37 "one another" commands. Just a few include love one another, bear with one another, live in harmony with one another and spur one another on. God surrounded us with these commands to do life together because we were never intended to be alone. God himself isn't alone, but exists as a Trinity of relationship. In the first chapter of Genesis, our Creator says, "Let *us* make man in *our* image!" (Genesis 1:26). Before any of this beautiful creation, God walked in perfect relationship as Father, Son and Holy Spirit. We were made for relationship because God himself is relational. Our culture is not truly relational even though we talk a lot about relationships and even obsess about our relational "needs." But most of us do not live relationally as God designed.

Discipleship comes through intimacy, and we need two types of intimacy — "upward" and "outward" — or vertical and horizontal relationships. Upward intimacy means that we are in relationship with our Father. A lot of our growth comes in quiet and even isolated places. We've addressed the need to prioritize time alone with God. Without it, there is no Overflow. Solitude is vital, but it isn't complete without the relational connection that we need as outward beings created for horizontal relationships. Although God walked face to face in the garden with Adam, he still said that it "wasn't good" for him to be alone (Genesis 2:18). Think about that for a minute. God himself said that we needed more than just us and him. We were made to be part of a family. A community. A Body. A Bride.

Jesus told the Apostle Peter that he would build his church and that nothing could stand against it (Matthew 16:18). The word "church" means "gathered ones."[35] Jesus' church is group of committed people gathered together in a common unity, a community. If Jesus birthed a community that would make hell shudder, and if Acts 2 is the birth of that community, we need to learn what type of community they shared and be willing to adjust our own priorities and schedules accordingly. We do not need more campaigns or programs to add to our overly busy lives, but we need to learn how to walk in real community. The book of Acts offers us an exhilarating and inspiring glimpse of what this looks like:

"They devoted themselves to the apostles' teaching and to fellowship, to the breaking of bread and to prayer. Everyone was filled with awe at the many wonders and signs performed by the apostles. All the believers were together and had everything in common. They sold property and possessions to give to anyone who had need. Every day they continued to meet together in the temple courts. They broke bread in their homes and ate together with glad and sincere hearts, praising God and enjoying the favor of all the people. And the Lord added to their number daily those who were being saved" Acts 2:42-47.

Devoted. Sharing their lives. Clearing their schedules to be together. So full of love for each other, they'd give the shirt off their own back to help another dear brother or sister experience Overflow. Enjoying the journey. Walking in favor. In awe of the miraculous power of God in their midst. The church was so contagious that the whole world took notice as crowds kicked down the doors to join them every day. This community looked like what Jesus promised — the whole world knew that they were his disciples by how they loved each other. God wants this for his Church today. We have implemented a lot of church programs and campaigns that are designed to help foster community. Perhaps you've used some of them yourself. If so, you already have a picture in your head about what it looks like for you to "not to go it alone." But our preconceptions might be incomplete and even flat-out wrong. We need to look at the elements of community that we were wired to require — the same elements that thrived within the early church and that stand open as an invitation to us. This will look a little different for every person. Programs change regularly, depending on the seasons for that particular group of people. However, the principles of community never change.

## CORE COMPONENTS OF BIBLICAL COMMUNITY

Seven words typify the type of community that the early church experienced. While this isn't a complete list, you can use it as a launch pad. Implement these seven principles in your family, with an accountability partner, in a mentoring relationship, in a small group at your church or in other settings as God leads.

In the pages ahead, you will have many opportunities to stop and really consider if the relationships in your life look like the type of community you were created for. I urge you to take your time after each section and pray. Ask yourself if you are walking in healthy and intentional biblical community because if you are not, you are walking alone. And alone is no good.

## COMMITMENT

As a teenager, I sometimes ordered 12 CDs for a penny through mail-in clubs designed to make you sign away your life. However, the clubs had just one catch: you had to commit to buy several CDs at their insane prices over time. Even worse, every month they'd send a statement with more offers, extending your commitment even longer. At 15, instant gratification took over common sense, and I bought all the "deals" until commitment kicked in. I started to see just how much the "free" CDs would cost. In addition, I had to tell the company every month that I did not want the "featured selection" — another seriously overpriced CD, usually one that no one wanted.

We have this idea of commitment as a nasty word that means that you "have" to do something in order to enjoy any benefits of membership. We think this way about church. We believe that commitment to the church will "cost" us something in terms of membership classes, the number of weekly worship services we attend and ministry involvement. We substitute busy activities but miss the real heart that drives the activity and think that we are in real community just because we are showing up at all of the events. Beyond that, a new generation is rising up that questions "why" they need to do any of those things. Many are stepping away from church attendance because, though they've been told for years that they "should" attend all these things, they cannot connect the dots as to "why." Instead, they are choosing to fill their time seeking community in other venues.

Commitment doesn't mean what you have to do to be accepted. When I married my wife and committed to love her, I wasn't thinking of all the rules that I had to keep. Instead, I was enraptured with love for her and with wanting to spend every moment of my life with this incredible person. I would have done anything for her well-being and joy. I thought about how, though this beautiful queen of my heart could marry anyone who she desired, she joyously committed to interweaving her story with mine. Commitment isn't some yoke under which we suffer but a gift from a very loving Father. In relationships, "commitment" is the mutually agreed-upon decision between people to do whatever it takes to walk in harmony because where they will go together is so much more enthralling than where they could ever go alone. You are intentionally declaring your unwavering dedication to an identifiable person or group of people as you are called by the Holy Spirit. Another biblical word that goes with this kind of commitment is "devoted:"

"They *devoted* themselves to the apostles' teaching and to fellowship, to the breaking of bread and to prayer" Acts 2:42 – Emphasis added.

The word "devoted" means "to stick to something continually and not come off."[36] When "lovebug" season comes in Florida, every driver knows how "devoted" those bugs are to vehicle windshields! Being *devoted* is like Super Glue: you adhere yourself to specific people with a lasting bond. In addition, *devoted* means "to give continuous and unending care to" and "to persevere with and not faint." You make a priority of the relationship, protect it, nurture and continually pour into it, and do not give up when it gets hard or you face conflict.

The early church was "devoted" to four things: the apostles' teaching, fellowship, the breaking of bread and prayer.

- The apostles' teaching — Every week, churches across the globe gather to learn the apostles' teaching as they open the Word of

God. We were meant to learn how to walk in God's Kingdom together. If you aren't part of a community like that, please ask the Lord to connect you.

- Fellowship — I used to think that "fellowship" was when people from church gathered together to eat food! Actually, the Bible's concept of fellowship goes much deeper and means "to share your life together," an attitude of the heart of giving anything for their well-being and joy.[37]

- Breaking of bread — Third, the believers committed their time to one another, meeting daily in worship and in their homes. We need to have people who we walk with through life with, opening up our schedules to them to provide mutual care to each other.

- Prayer — Prayers in this context isn't referring to private times of intimacy with God but time as a community that makes it a priority to actively pray for one another. Just as my childhood experience at the Strawberry Festival, we become disoriented and forget where we are or where we need to go. Our enemy thrives on isolation, which is why our Daddy tells us to stick together and to call on him for each other as a committed praying community.

Committed relationships cannot happen in a crowd — we must know others by name. Committed relationships cannot happen without agreement — we must be intentional and deliberate. Committed relationships cannot happen without priority — we must make time in our packed schedules.

Take a moment right now with the Holy Spirit as you answer a few questions. Don't be discouraged by this process. But be honest and ask him to lead you to a family where you can commit.

1. Am I committed to any other believers? Who are they? Who does my Daddy want me to commit my heart to?
2. What are my biggest barriers/hindrances to being truly committed to other believers?
3. Does Daddy need to heal me from any wounds in the past from

4.  If you are a part of a local church, ask yourself the following: "Am I making community a priority? What am I allowing to distract me?"

5.  What is my next step to be committed?

## COMMONALITY

Every group that you've probably ever belonged to has shared a common purpose, a core reason for coming together and a common goal they are trying to accomplish. A book club at Starbucks shares the commonality of looking super trendy, drinking expensive coffee and possibly talking about a book! A soccer team shares the commonality of sportsmanship and competition. An army in wartime unites under the commonality of protecting the citizens and rights of their great nation. Whether you're socializing, on a team or fighting a war, commonality plays a major role in turning strangers into partners and partners into family.

Commonality places us on the same battlefield. It puts us in a room full of people with similar hurdles and challenges and more importantly, the same great hope that drives us. Commonality hoists the same trophy of victory that we link arms to lay hold of together. Commonality grafts beautiful individuals into a unit that manifests much more glory than all of their combined solo efforts could ever achieve. The early church became a family empowered by their common love, purpose and goal. Where commitment called them to prioritize relationships with one another, commonality pointed to their target. They met to experience intimacy with God and manifest him everywhere.

The early church was so on fire for the mission that no one even considered their own belongings as theirs. They gave and sold all of their property and possessions to meet the needs of the community. This wasn't a revolution of politics or government that they were trying to set up but a revolution of love. They made a willing choice because these people had already found their treasure in Jesus and knew that they woke up that morning so that they could help others find it, too. Imagine the level of closeness, the trust and the beauty of being in a family like that. Their commonality ran far deeper than waving across the room at the 9:15 service or signing a membership card together.

Admittedly, they lived in a different era. They could walk to each other's homes and had a much less complex schedule than what we face in the age of technology. Maybe that's part of our problem. Maybe all of the scientific breakthroughs designed to make us more productive have only made us busier, chasing our own private dreams. We put our kids in sports and dance and clubs. Our time and finances go toward fine-tuning our hobbies. Work fills our days as we spend more hours there than necessary. We have calendars chock-full of events and lay down in our bed, exhausted while we fall asleep not counting sheep but appointments for the next day. If we're being honest, most of us would admit that we feel too busy to spend private time with God and too busy to build and protect meaningful relationships with others. So we come up with new apps and tools and steps to somehow buy more time. Maybe we really need is an overhaul of priorities. After all, one of Jesus' final prayers was that his Body would be one just as he and the Father are one. As long as you believe that walking in community is an option, you will never have enough time.

Perhaps you don't live close enough to others in your community to regularly have dinner together. The times when you gather for prayer or to more deeply learn how to live in God's Overflow will undoubtedly be distinct. But you can never have that kind of relational intimacy if you do not choose to open the door to your schedule and make intentional space for other believers.

The size of this group will differ. Community might start as small as when "two or three are gathered together" in his name. You might meet with a small group at your church or with a few people for breakfast every week to study God's Word and pray for each other. Don't worry about how it looks. Focus instead on building a true community of commonality!

Ask the Holy Spirit these questions:

1. Who do I want by my side as I grow closer to God?
2. Who am I already spending time with?
3. How can we focus more intentionally on helping each other grow in our faith?

## CONTRAST

I like people who are like me. They laugh at my jokes and understand my perspective. And we don't disagree often because we see the world very similarly. Relationships like this encourage us, but our growth will be limited if we only surround ourselves with people who think exactly like we do. We require contrast. For example, the 12 disciples who Jesus chose to change the world differed greatly from each other. Matthew, a Jewish tax collector, was hired by wealthy Romans to forcibly collect monies from all Jews. Many pious Jewish citizens held a highly unfavorable opinion of this profession. Just look at this scholar's description:

"As a class, tax collectors were hated by their fellow Jews. This was almost inevitable. They represented the foreign domination of Rome. That they often overcharged people and pocketed the surplus is almost certain...they were considered to be renegades who sold their services to the foreign oppressor to make money at the expense of their own countrymen."[38]

While you process how far off his rocker the other disciples must've thought Jesus fell in choosing Matthew, consider the choice of another one of the 12: Simon the Zealot. The Zealots were a Jewish political party that despised any sense of submission to the Roman people as an unforgivable abandonment of true faith, and they were willing to die for what they believed. They refused to pay taxes and fought and even killed leaders and friends of Rome. They would have especially hated anyone who was a Jew by birth but who aided Roman rule in their homeland. Imagine how awkward the moment must have been when Matthew, the tax collector, and Simon the Zealot learned that they were to become a family of so much love that it would reveal to unbelievers how big God is (see John 13:35). Talk about a contrast between two people who could not be more different!

Jesus beautifully handpicked someone — Matthew — who was misunderstood and seen as unclean. He saw something in Matthew that no one else did, and every time that we read Matthew's gospel, we catch a glimpse of the remarkable grace and transformation upon his life. At the same time, Jesus chose someone so driven to remaining pure to God that Simon made those around him nervous that he would go overboard. But Jesus saw past Simon's radical behavior to a heart that passionately desired to know him. Although Matthew and Simon were on different sides of the aisle, they actually needed each other despite their protests to the contrary. They understood unique aspects of walking with God yet had different blind spots and areas of weakness. The Apostle Paul described it:

"Just as a body, though one, has many parts, but all its many parts form one body, so it is with Christ. For we were all baptized by one Spirit so as to form one body—whether Jews or Gentiles, slave or free—and we were all given the one Spirit to drink. Even so the body is not made up of one part but of many. Now if the foot should say, "Because I am not a hand, I do not belong to the body," it would not for that reason stop being part of the body. And if the ear should say, "Because I am not an eye, I do not belong to the body," it would not for that reason stop being part of the body. If the whole body were an eye, where would the sense of hearing be? If the whole body were an ear, where would the sense of smell be? *But in fact God has placed the parts in the body, every one of them, just as he wanted them to be.* If they were all one part, where would the body be? As it is, there are many parts, but one body. *The eye cannot say to the hand, "I don't need you!" And the head cannot say to the feet, "I don't need you!"* 1 Corinthians 12:12-21 – Emphasis added.

If you are going to experience true biblical community and the depths of biblical discipleship, you will need to be in relationships where you differ greatly from others. We have the tendency to surround ourselves with only people who see things the way that we do. We would rather spend time with people with whom we share lots in common, and we feel uncomfortable around people who see the world differently than us. This causes some Christians to build relationships almost exclusively on common personalities, life stages and interests. Do not limit yourself to only letting in people who look like you because all of you will fall into the same ditches with no one to help you out. Our diversity helps us fully manifest what it means to be the Body of Christ. You want people in your life who will broaden your perspective on the beauty of creation and the sometimes confusing journey of life.

Beyond that, we need to build true relational community environments that swing the doors open wide and welcome people to uniquely express worship to their King no matter how they differ from us. We need to be "yes-and" people, not "either-or" people. "Either-or" people limit acceptable expressions of pursuing God by putting them into neat little boxes that fit a particular culture or personality type. They make statements like, "Either you worship with your hands raised, or you're not really surrendering to God."

"Yes-and" people say, "Yes, how I worship God pleases him, and how you worship him pleases him, too!"

This doesn't mean chaos or any type of display that distorts true worship. Instead, we need to make sure that we truly applaud what God applauds. Like a jigsaw puzzle, he made each of us to manifest different expressions of the vast abundance of his glory and when we connect our lives together as puzzle pieces, the whole world enjoys a fuller manifestation of who he is. God wants to display his manifold and multi-faceted wisdom through the church so that all the spiritual forces of darkness are knocked off their high horse (see Ephesians 3:10). You are one piece in a beautiful mosaic displaying God's glory. You need to embrace the other beautiful mosaic pieces, especially those who bring something unique to the table.

Let's enjoy different clothing fashions and musical styles within the church with a "yes-and" attitude. Let's applaud when people worship in loud jubilation and when they sit in reverent reflection. Let's make sure that we aren't always separating people into predetermined life stages but learn to develop deep relationships with others because they offer a distinct perspective of the majesty of our Creator. We need them, and they need us. Let's celebrate the diversity of gifts and recognize that we bring our gifts to the Body and that it wouldn't be complete without us. Let's encourage each other's strengths and support each other in our weaknesses. Perhaps you see an aspect of living for God clearly that others in the church haven't yet grabbed onto. Don't withdraw into quiet judgment against the Bride. **You** see it because God has entrusted you to patiently and lovingly help them see it. You bring contrast to the scene. Realizing that should fill you with gratitude not pride. After all, if you can see something clearly that others cannot, other "voices of contrast" in the Body likely see something that you desperately need in your walk with your Daddy.

Stop and be honest with God about a few questions:

1.  What needs within the Body of Christ do I see that others don't? Am I intentionally making our Body stronger by sharing my unique perspective?
2.  Who in my community approaches life with Jesus differently than me and sharpens me? Am I intentionally in relationship with them?
3.  Who in my community annoys me because of their different approach to God? Do I need to forgive them? Do I need a deeper relationship with them to learn something new?

## CONSTRUCTION

When Jill and I bought our first home, we joyfully purchased in a new subdivision with no other homes. As the third buyers in this community, we chose our lot, picked features for our home and saw the transformation from an overgrown plot of land to the home where we'd welcome our first three kids into the world. We watched them lay the foundation as single blocks came together to form walls powerful enough to weather Florida hurricanes. We observed our roof come into place one beam at a time. We walked through the building, just imagining how the finished product would look as we viewed through walls only framed in wood. We saw in our mind's eye as we carried on conversations like, "I'm calling you from the kitchen right now!"

Jesus uses a similar construction process with us. He already purchased everything that we need and plowed up the fallow ground of our heart. We have built our house upon the rock, and Christ has seated us with him in heavenly places. Yet, every day we walk in an ever-increasing glory as we practically learn how to fully receive and live in the reality that is now ours. One of the biggest reasons that God calls us to embrace biblical community is because we're supposed to "build each other up" and to fully demonstrate the unity of his Body.

The Bible uses the key word, "prophecy," to describe the process of building up one another. Traditionally, we think of prophecy as the revealing of some future event and prophets as oddballs who lived alone and warned of judgment through bizarre pictures. The full picture of prophecy and prophets goes much deeper. We need to demystify and take the weirdness out of these concepts because prophecy is one of the most foundational gifts that our King has given to us so that we could experience our complete construction. To "prophesy" simply means to speak what God wants to say to others. In Greek, the word "prophecy" has three different pictures:

1. To foretell future events, especially pertaining to the Kingdom of God

2. To declare direction about a present circumstance that can only be known by God, such as a word of knowledge, and

3. To teach, refute, reprove, admonish or comfort others as you speak to them what God is saying.

Whether it pertains to something in the future, something that is presently happening or bringing clarity to something that already took place, to "prophesy" is simply to hear encouragement from your Daddy for someone else and to obediently speak to them. We're all supposed to walk in this beautiful gift. Look at how the Apostle Paul challenges us:

"Follow the way of love and eagerly desire gifts of the Spirit, especially *prophecy*...the one who prophesies speaks to people for their strengthening, encouraging and comfort" 1 Corinthians 14:1, 3 – Emphasis added.

God would not call you to "eagerly desire" something that he doesn't want you to have, and he says that he wants you to eagerly desire to prophesy. When you do, you allow him to speak through you to build up the person, according to their needs! Every dad wants his kids to speak encouragement to each other:

"Let no corrupting talk come out of your mouths, but *only* such as is good for building up, as fits the occasion, that it may give grace to those who hear" Ephesians 4:29 (ESV) – Emphasis added.

When we are together, we are to release prophecy: speaking encouragement to one another so that we will impart grace in that situation. Jesus only spoke what the Father was saying (see John 5:19, John 8:28, John 12:49), and we are only to speak what builds up others. It would stand to reason that we need to be people who come together, expectant for God to speak to us and through us.

In your community, he will confirm to you what others have been praying for and give you clear direction and encouragement for your life. In fact, this book wouldn't have been written without the faithfulness of several people in my community who repeatedly told me that God was calling me to write. Thank you, Edgar and Jill, for your obedience and your patient perseverance. I am forever grateful! Your community will also help you hear when you're headed in the wrong direction and can provide specific counsel to redirect you.

You will learn to more clearly hear the voice of God and to understand his Word. You will learn how to walk in deeper freedom and how to minister that freedom to others. You will be surrounded by people who will respond when the Holy Spirit prompts them to teach you truths of his Kingdom and who will speak to remind you of his character or your identity that you've forgotten in the midst of difficult circumstances. God also wants to use **you** to be that voice for others. **You**, not just pastors. In fact, God gave us pastors and the other offices of the church to build **you** up in preparation to do just that:

"He gave the apostles, the prophets, the evangelists, the shepherds and teachers, *to equip the saints for the work of ministry, for building up the body of Christ*, until we all attain to the unity of the faith and of the knowledge of the Son of God, to mature manhood, to the measure of the stature of the fullness of Christ" Ephesians 4:11-13 (ESV) – Emphasis added.

In your community, sometimes you will be the building, and sometimes you will be the voice that the Holy Spirit is using to build up someone else. Don't become nervous and shy away from it. You were born for this and the Holy Spirit wants to Overflow out of you to reveal his love and build up someone else! Raise your gaze and jump into a community that expects God to speak to and through each person for the building up of all!

Ask the Holy Spirit:

1. Who could mentor me in a deeper walk with Jesus?
2. Who can I mentor for their spiritual growth?
3. Am I making intentional space for these people in my life?
4. Am I asking God to speak to me and through me to others? If not, do that right now!

## CARE

Jesus said that the entire world would know that we are his disciples by the way we demonstrate our love to one another. Care means the active manifestation with our hands of the love that is in our hearts. God calls us to be a part of a community that doesn't just say that we love each other but that demonstrates love with our energy, prayer, time and resources. James worded it as follows:

"Suppose a brother or a sister is without clothes and daily food. If one of you says to them, "Go in peace; keep warm and well fed," but does nothing about their physical needs, *what good is it?*" James 2:15-16 – Emphasis added.

Just as it is not good to be alone, it is not good to be in a community that is all talk and no action. Galatians 6:2 says, "Carry each other's burdens, and in this way you will fulfill the law of Christ." The law of Christ means that we love him with all that we are and Overflow in love for others. You fulfill this command by bearing one another's burdens. The word translated as "bear" means, "to take up something that is burdensome with your hands and help carry it!"[39]

We become stressed and overwhelmed, and we do not see God as clearly in an area of our life as we did even one day before. We find ourselves in a tight circumstance with our health, job or family that feels like a weight that is too heavy to bear. Though we live in a culture that tells us to "be your own hero" and to "pull yourself up by your own bootstraps," Jesus called us to walk through life with the support of others beside us.

Sometimes, we will need a shoulder to cry on. Other times, we will be feet ready to help run needed errands. Sometimes, we will be a mouth to offer words of encouragement and direction from heaven to our friend in need. But always, we will be hands that go to the throne of grace in passionate prayer for each other.

Intercession, passionate prayer for loved ones is one of the most powerful ways that we can demonstrate care for them. Many of us relegate prayer to a low position. When we hear about a need, we quickly move, speak, give advice and do everything in our power to solve it without ever stopping and asking God what he wants to do. Then, once we've exhausted all of our options and called everyone we know for help and advice, we say apologetically, "I guess that all we can do now is pray." We are saying that "all" that we can do is go to the God who rules all of creation and who purchased all that we need for life and godliness, the God who says that our friend is his favorite kid and ask him to move. We are leaving a lot of resources on the shelf until the eleventh hour. If we understood the true power of faithful, fervent prayers that refuse to give up on God's promises, we'd soon realize that prayer is the most powerful weapon in our entire arsenal to help our community be victorious in their battle!

My friend, Luckson Ngozo, a pastor in Zambia, recently said that the reason he believes that people don't pray more is that we think too highly of our own abilities when it comes to counseling, advice and our efforts. Teaching from Luke 11, he noted that in the parable of persistent prayer, a man's friend comes to his home at midnight, starving. The first man immediately goes to the home of yet another friend and pounds on the door to meet the need of his famished guest. Luckson noted that prayer is always "a friend going to a Friend for a friend!" He continued that the man was ultimately successful in his request because he didn't quit asking for what he knew was available despite the fact that the door was closed.

However, he started with an admission of his own lack. "I have nothing to give him." Luckson went on, "If we understood that we really have nothing, we'd spend a lot more time in prayer for our loved ones, bringing them before the One who has everything that they need!"

We've been called to bear one another's burdens. Sometimes, the Holy Spirit will immediately point out that he wants to use what is already in your hands to help. Other times, like the man awoken at midnight, you will realize that you "have nothing" to solve the overwhelming circumstance. He then wants to use your empty hands lifted in intercession. If we'd become communities rooted in fervent, stubborn, unrelenting prayer about everything that God has already promised — people who would pray until we see with our eyes what we proclaim with our faith — we'd see a revival that could not be contained.

Ask the Holy Spirit the following questions as you search your heart:

1. Who are the people who "have my back? Who can I count on to be there when I am overwhelmed, the prayer warriors who will keep knocking on my behalf?
2. Who do I offer that kind of support and care to?
3. What is a current need where I need prayer support?

## CONFESSION

Wait. Confession?!? Have I committed some kind of crime, and the police will be interrogating me? We run from and resist confession, a word filled with so many negative connotations in our culture. We don't want other people to see our blemishes, flaws or brokenness. We don't even want to admit them to ourselves. We present "Glamour Shots" and selfies, adding excessive filters, as true representations of who we really are. We desperately need to recapture the true meaning of confession. Before we proceed, let's clarify what confession is not.

We do not need to confess our sins to one another to receive forgiveness.

That has fully addressed at the cross by Jesus' blood alone. We don't need confession as some sort of shaming program to try to embarrass us. Confession doesn't mean airing our dirty laundry and struggles to everyone we know. The type of confession that the New Testament talks about should happen in an intimate community intended to protect your dignity, not run your name through the mud. Although you have already been given a new nature and are completely loved by your Father, you have an enemy who longs to blind you from living like it. We need confession because our enemy's key weapon is deception, which thrives in an environment of isolation. If he isolates you, then he can wear you down, attack areas you do not yet see clearly and bury you in shame. You need confession so that shame will lose its power in your life and so that you can experience wholeness. Look at what James has to say about it:

"Is anyone among you suffering? Let him pray. Is anyone cheerful? Let him sing praise. Is anyone among you sick? Let him call for the elders of the church, and let them pray over him, anointing him with oil in the name of the Lord. And the prayer of faith will save the one who is sick, and the Lord will raise him up. And if he has committed sins, he will be forgiven. *Therefore*, confess your sins to one another and pray for one another, *that you may be healed.* The prayer of a righteous person has great power as it is working" James 5:13-16 (ESV) – Emphasis added.

The phrase, "confess your sins," means "to acknowledge openly and joyfully where you have fallen down and deviated from the truth."[40] No filter. No editing. No excuses. When you confess, the poison dart of shame is removed and as your community seeks the Holy Spirit alongside you, that arrow that you couldn't seem to shake begins to dislodge. Confession is something to embrace joyfully because the community helps you pull down strongholds and experience healing that leads to a new level of wholeness with your King!

Take a minute right now to invite the Holy Spirit to speak to you about these questions:

1. Who am I completely vulnerable with about my deepest struggles?
2. Do I struggle with anything that I have not shared with anyone? If so, you are isolated in that place. Take some time to pray about who you can share with.
3. Where do I regularly trip up in patterns of sin or mindsets that weigh me down?

## CONQUEST

Of all the words that God laid on my heart to describe what real community looks like, this one is my favorite! The word "conquest" means "a kingdom spreading its rule into enemy territory!" [41] That sounds a whole lot like, "I will build my church, and the gates of hell won't be able to stand against it." Jesus likely had conquest in mind when he proclaimed, "The Kingdom of God is forcefully advancing and forceful men lay hold of it" (Matthew 11:12). All of creation has been groaning in anticipation since that moment in Eden when our Daddy promised that one day, he'd send a Rescuer to crush the enemy and restore our call to reign with him. From generation to generation through judges, prophets, priests and kings, the message was "one day, the Kingdom will come." As soon as Jesus' head emerged out of the water at his baptism, the message of hope changed to "the Kingdom has now appeared and is within you!"

Jesus designed his church to be the community to manifest his love, his power and his hope.[42] Jesus said that it would be better for him to go away and send the Holy Spirit into a global collaborative community who manifested his presence every place their feet touched:'

"Awe came upon every soul, and many wonders and signs were being done through the apostles...*and the Lord added to their number day by day those who were being saved*" Acts 2:43, 47 – Emphasis added.

The Church is the hope of the world because we carry the One who himself **is** hope! Some have claimed that we are irrelevant, outdated, unreasonable and invisible. Often, our own action or lack thereof has fueled those feelings, but in reality, we are the Body of Christ, and we have the Spirit of God. We've been sent on a mission to live in such powerful community that people should be kicking down the doors to get in! In our modern, self-help culture, the idea of conquest has often been pushed to the back burner because we've been told that having a perfect image and being universally loved is everything. As a result, many believers, who really love Jesus, completely lack confidence to pray for another person and cannot give a "reason for the hope" they have (see 1 Peter 3:15). Even fewer feel like the same power that rose Jesus from the dead is already alive in them (see Ephesians 1:18-23). Without that understanding, church becomes a place to get us through another week so that we can "improve" as individuals. The church is supposed to be a place where we grow and find encouragement and care, but the only reason that we're here and not in heaven is because we are in an hour when "the Kingdom of God is advancing." Right now. And we're supposed to be the forceful ones who lay hold of it. Not just pastors. Not just public speakers. Not just revivalists. Not just certain denominations. The Spirit of God has breathed upon his Church and commissioned her for conquest.

Our churches — and our cities, states and nations — will change drastically when we see the following happen:

• When we live and breathe commitment to our King and each other
• When we make it our priority to be in intentional communities around the commonality of "loving Jesus with all that we are and overflowing to others everywhere"
• When we allow people in our communities who are contrasting voices to sharpen us
• When we allow God to constantly speak to us and through us to build up others
• When we become communities who demonstrate our care through feet

that move and hands that pray fervently for his will to be done in each other's lives "on earth as it is in heaven"

- When we drop our guard and become vulnerable with each other, confessing our sins to fight for the ever-increasing freedom and glory Christ paid for to come to complete fruition.

When those things happen, we won't be able to keep people out of the church.

Advertising, marketing and creativity have their place, but sometimes, we supersize those things as the "key" to church growth. In reality, the only key is the Spirit of the Living God, pouring out his tangible love, presence and power through his children. These things are fully available to **every** church and community!

That said, two key factors must be present if we are to be families of conquest: hunger and expectation. As I think about my own community, I pray that we pass "the hunger test" with flying colors. The hunger test means that people want to be more like Jesus when they spend time with me. They want to pray more, worship with more abandon, take more risks for the Kingdom and know him with greater purity and fervency.

The second key factor needed for conquest is expectation. We need to again believe that the gospel is not only personally powerful but that it transforms communities and nations! We need to raise our expectations and our prayers as well. Communities of conquest expect God to show up and to revive the families in their church, their city, their state, their nation and the world. They expect to see answers to their prayers and celebrate those answers together. They do not grow content or comfortable because they are on mission to globally overthrow a tyrant king's enterprise. They expect revival because they walk intimately with the Reviver. The early church looked like a conquering and expectant group of heroes, and that kind of expectation to see the Kingdom expand through us needs to fill our churches today!

People sometimes attack large churches, saying that they must be compromising, watering down the gospel or entertaining people, which is why so many people show up. If you've found yourself saying or believing that, please stop. You are judging your dear brothers and sisters in Christ who are working tirelessly for the gospel. When you say that increased attendance equates with compromise, you are dangerously close to believing that the power of God won't draw people or that his Kingdom isn't supposed to expand. Beyond that, you are taking your eyes off the real target. We are surrounded by people in a plentiful harvest field who need the hope of Almighty God. Bless our mega-churches and pray for deeper manifestations of the Holy Spirit daily on their congregations just as you do in your own life and church. Pray for God to bless the work of their hands and continue to expand it. Pray that in all of their activity, requests and even demands that people put on their time that they would never lose the wonder of humbly and joyfully walking as sons and daughters before their radiant King. Encourage them whenever you can.

On the other hand, people judge small churches as if they are second-rate, inferior or somehow less passionate for the gospel. If that's you, please stop. I have been part of a relatively small congregation that yearns for the true gospel and has tirelessly prayed for revival and sought the Holy Spirit to advance his Kingdom. God has changed so many lives through our ministry through his power and anointing, but that hasn't always translated to a full house on a Sunday morning. I'm not making excuses — just challenging us to be faithful and let our King bring the fruit.

Some love the intimacy of relationships in a smaller congregation. But God desires his Kingdom to grow in conquest! If you don't believe that God has called your church to be a mega-church, then ask him to make you a "planting church" — a church that raises up leaders and plants new congregations around your community and the world as yours grows beyond its capacity. Encourage and pray for leaders of small churches. They work so sacrificially and tirelessly for the gospel, often without encouragement, support, recognition, thanks or even pay. Remind them of their great worth. Jesus said that some of the people closest to the throne of God were not as well-known or highly gifted here but shook the heavens and earth through their "Overflow." A number of lay leaders and small church pastors are included in that number. Thank God for each of them.

Whether your church is big or small, God has called **you** to take up your part in a community of conquest! Ask the Holy Spirit to lead you as you answer these questions:

1.  Do I have confidence to pray for others or share the hope within me? Why or why not?
2.  Who in my community stirs a deeper hunger for Jesus in me — so that simply being around them makes me want to love him more?
3.  Do I help the people in my community hunger more for Jesus? Why or why not? How can I grow in this?
4.  Am I expecting revival through me? My family? Our church? Why or why not? How can we be more intentional?

## RESCUED FROM THE "SEA OF BUTTS"

Just as I was rescued at the Strawberry Festival, your King has graciously stepped through the crowd to take you by the hand and lead you out of your lost condition and isolation. He has brought you into his family so that you will no longer walk alone in the crowd but live in real community. Even more, he wants to use **you** and your community just like he used the security guard when I was in the "sea of butts." He wants to give you active eyes and ready feet to see people and take them to the "lost and found" where they can be reunited with their Daddy and become part of a family that is the very hope of the world.

# NO GOING BACK:

*"Don't Wait and See." Go and **Live!***

---

You are breathing right now at this very moment for **this**: To love your God with every fiber of your being and then to "Overflow" from that place. Maybe you're a planner, and as you're finishing this book, you're looking for a few tools to add to your spiritual tool belt. However, the heart of the whole journey that we've taken together isn't about nuts and bolts but about how Jesus already purchased everything that you need for life and godliness and made it all available to you. **Right now.** Overflow is about his Kingdom pouring out of you, not as the result of accumulating more tools but as the natural byproduct of true intimacy with him as you see clearly who he is, who you are, who the people around you are and the amazing power and hope that he's put at your disposal. God gives his Kingdom not to experts but to kids. The Kingdom is yearning and screaming to pour out of you right now.

You might wonder where to go from here. Make **everything** about sitting at his feet and knowing him. Keep your heart both fully open to him and fully belonging to him. When our intimacy is unshakeable, revival is inevitable because revival is simply a group of people coming into agreement with what Jesus already offers. We aren't waiting for further payment. His work really is finished, and Christ in you really is the hope of glory! So just be with him every moment. Reorder your priorities to protect whatever it looks like for you to sit at his feet. Be willing to say "no" to other activities, even really good ones. Listen to your Daddy and do what he says. Slow down. Don't be in such a hurry to get places. Your mission is the countless sons and daughters that you cross paths with every day. If we'll slow down, we will see opportunities to manifest the Kingdom everywhere! Ask God to speak to you about people and be ready to share whatever he says to you.

We cannot hesitate to pray for people. If you and I want to see the King of Glory heal his kids and break chains off their lives, we have to pray and declare what we're hearing. You might worry, "What if it doesn't work?"

To that, I respond, "But what if it does?" Beyond that, we are coming before our King who always hears us, so it always works! The timeline might be different from what you expect or the answer might not be clear to you. Walk by faith, not sight, because though God has given us a billion ways to see his glory with our eyes, our physical eyes will let us down. Trust and don't overthink it! When you feel discouraged, remember that his love for you never moves or shifts and isn't based on your performance, but on his unchanging grace and completed sacrifice. When you find yourself clinging to something that doesn't look like who you are anymore, don't settle. Know in that moment, he wants to bless you more than you can imagine, but you have to let go of what's in your hands! You have more power and glory in you than you can possibly imagine.

As you go all in for Jesus, some people, even Christians, might not respond the way you expected. They might become defensive or try to caution you from going overboard as one "those" Christians. They might even tell you that they are "really happy for you…but" that you shouldn't expect such zeal from others. What they're usually saying is that they're not happy for you at all. While their intentions are good, they might feel threatened. They, too, have tried many things to walk in Jesus' favor and seeing your passion might be tough for them. Don't get upset or judge them. Pray for them.

Encourage them that this life of Overflow is available to all.

Right now, you are being stirred and held by a Daddy who has longed for this moment. A line has been drawn on the carpet for you, too. Your Daddy is asking, "Are **you** ready to cross the line, son? Are you ready to cross the line, daughter? Are you ready to stop guarding your reputation and instead recognize your identity? Are you ready to lay down everything to just **know** me and live in Overflow?" He has a mailbox there with your name on it. Are you ready to change your home address? Take a minute right now just like I did in that hotel room in Naples and tell your King that you are ready to do just that. Cross the line.

This is my prayer for you:

"Daddy, you are incredible! When I think about all you've offered us, it is beyond amazing, beyond our understanding, beyond good news. We are astounded by you and the beautiful place of Overflow where you invite us to live. I pray for these amazing sons and daughters of yours. You know them each by name and have dreamed of them and this moment since before the foundation of the world. As they come to you with pure and sincere hearts, baptize their whole being with the fire of your Spirit. Right now, burn away everything that is not of you. Show them that their old nature is dead so that they can leave it in their past. Take that fire and kindle a passion that burns in their bones for you. Anoint them now and release new gifts. May they hear your voice just as you always intended. May they see people with your eyes and be surrounded with opportunities to pour out your Kingdom every day to others around them. May their very life become your message. Consume them fully! Fill them with joy inexpressible. It is truly finished! And may they see people come into your Kingdom, the sick healed and the captives set free, not from a distance, but with their very eyes as you do it through them. Take over fully now! Amen!"

I would love to hear from you as you live your own "Life in the Overflow." If you have questions or your own praise reports, please share them with me. I want to celebrate with you and help you live out this life. You can reach me directly at pastorchuckammons@gmail.com. Also, be sure to check out www.theoverflowbook.com, where you'll find free teaching videos, small group guides, a children's curriculum and more. I look forward to connecting with you!

## DON'T "WAIT AND SEE." GO AND LIVE!

# APPENDIX 1

## "A SPARK OF LOVE"
### *by Josiah Ammons*

### Introduction:
You might have read my dad's book, "Life in the Overflow." Well, I'm his son, Josiah, and this book will show you how a 9-year old boy can hear and talk to God.

### Chapter 1: Joy!
When I was 8, my dad had just come home from a trip, and he told me and my older brother, Bradley, all about his amazing trip. Now, at this point, I could not hear God's voice, but I just was not listening because God really speaks to us every day, even if it's not in words. Now, back to the story. I wanted to hear God's voice, but I thought that I was not good enough. That's not true. You don't have to be a pastor to hear God's voice. So, my dad prayed, and then, I heard this amazing voice say, "**Joy!**" Then, I found out someone was coming over to our house that night, and my dad called her "Joy!" Then, I heard the word, "empower," and my dad told me this **epic** verse: Romans 15:13 - "May the God who gives you hope fill you with great joy. May you have perfect peace as you trust in Him. May the Holy Spirit fill you with hope."

### Chapter 2: The Overflow
I'm not copying my dad's amazing book, which you should read if you have not. By the way, I'm 9 now, so it's been a year. A new service started at my church called "The Overflow." Since my dad was teaching, I went to the big service since there was no class for older kids. I was bored, and the next day I had to wake up at 6 a.m. for school. I thought that I should listen and pay attention, and I started getting visions!

## Chapter 3: A Spark of Love Can Start a Fire

One day, I was doing some homework when I had a vision and heard some words: "A spark of love can start a fire." I think that we can start that fire: tell the world about Jesus. Tell them about the cross. The world needs to know, and we're going to tell them.

# ╺╾ APPENDIX 2 ╼╸

## Q & A: HOW DO I LIVE OUT "LIFE IN THE OVERFLOW?"

### Questions About Hearing God Speak

**Q:** *I don't think that I can hear God speak. How can I know if I can hear him?*

**A:** The amazing news is that God has been speaking to you since before you were born when he breathed his image into you. He desires to speak to you and rejoices to do so. A lot of people, me included, know all too well the shame of feeling like they are "failing" to hear God. You cannot fail if you want to hear him. He promised that every hungry heart would be filled! He **is** speaking to you. You just need to learn to recognize his voice. God speaks differently to people, depending on their sensitivity and personality. I have never heard his audible voice but feel strong promptings within my spirit. The more that I realized that this was God, the more that I listened. As I was learning, I made sure to ask people around me their opinion about what I thought God might be saying to me. They helped me to not be afraid that I'd hear wrong. Learning to hear God's voice is an art. Give yourself grace. Take heart: God is speaking to you, and you will learn to hear him regularly!

**Q:** *How can I tell when something I sense is 'God' or not?*

**A:** If you think that you've heard or sensed God saying something to you, you might wonder how you will know if it's him, your own feelings or just some bad pizza that you ate. The following tips should help:

1.  *Does it line up with the Bible?* God said that his Word is the word of prophecy made "more certain" (2 Peter 1:19). God will never tell you something that contradicts his own Word. The more time that you spend in his Word, the more clearly you will hear his voice. You will continually grow in your ability to hear, so don't get discouraged!

2.  *What do people I trust who regularly hear from God think?* Don't be embarrassed or fear that you'll get it wrong. Ask questions. Lots of them. No question is dumb when it comes from a hungry heart! Ask people who walk with God if they think that this is what God is saying.

3.  *Don't trust your feelings.* Feelings are a beautiful gift from God but don't trust them further than you can throw them. Feelings change and are influenced by various factors, such as how much rest you've had, how busy life is, your own sometimes flawed or incomplete perceptions and more. Some people base their decisions on what they think that God is saying by how they "feel." People sometimes say that they believe that God is telling them to quit something because it was hard and stressful or that they should continue in a sinful behavior because it made them feel good. These things contradict the Word of God, so they are clearly not God speaking. You can only afford to have one God, and your feelings cannot be it! However, you can apply one final tip that relates to your feelings. Search your heart and ask if you are honestly willing to follow wherever God wants to lead you. If the answer is "yes," ask him to increase his peace upon your heart if this is from him and to warn you if it is not.

**Q:** *How can I grow in my ability to hear God speak to me?*

**A:** Hearing God is like a muscle; it grows the more you exercise it. Apply the following tips to exercise the muscle:

1.  *Spend time in God's Word:* If you want to know what someone sounds

like, surround yourself with what they've already said. When my wife writes something, I recognize it as her personality because I've spent so much time talking to her and reading her letters. If you want to know what God is saying, immerse yourself in what he's already said.

2. *Make a priority of stillness:* We live in a culture of instant responses. Learn to regularly be patient and quiet before the Lord. Ask him what he wants to say to you and wait. Don't rush. He might give you a phrase, a word or even a picture. He might give you direction about a specific situation. You might want to write it down or ask someone you trust who hears God if they think that you are hearing correctly.

3. *Get in biblical community:* Connect with people who hear God speak to them. Ask questions. Ask them to pray over you and pray with you.

**Q:** *I felt like God wanted me to say something to someone, but it seemed weird. What should I do?*

**A:** Join the club! I cannot tell you how many things God has laid on my heart that seemed weird, unhelpful or off-the-wall. The more I have come to know his voice, though, the more I have been willing to step out and just share what I am sensing. I typically preface it with, "I know this might seem weird, but as I was praying for you, I felt like God said _____. Does that make sense to you?" You'd be shocked at the number of times it is exactly what they needed to hear. Sometimes, though, it doesn't make immediate sense to them, either. That's ok. I was at Chipotle once when I walked past a guy and immediately felt God tell me to tell him that he should take the job. I wanted to run. The man was a complete stranger. But I obeyed. He didn't know of any job but was so thankful that I cared enough to share. But who knows if his wife called about a job offer when he left or if a job popped up the next week and he would've been uncertain about what to do? If I have to choose between possibly looking weird and sitting safely on the sidelines without risk or reward or being part of something supernatural, I will take the risk! Share what you are sensing. And don't state more than you heard. You don't have to make it sound super spiritual or do mental gymnastics so that it makes sense. Just listen, repeat what you hear and watch God be God!

## Questions About Prayer

**Q:** *I hear other people pray so eloquently and feel like I must not be doing it right. How do I learn how to pray?*

**A:** People sometimes use flowery words that seem difficult to follow, but prayer is simply talking to a friend who you trust. You already know how to do that! Pray from an attitude of vulnerability; go to God with what you feel and desire and what is on your heart. Don't try to sound holy — he made you sound like you for a reason. Use your words and your personality. Do not try to lock yourself into a pattern or pray beyond how the Holy Spirit leads you. Your goal is that Jesus will become your closest friend, so talk to him about everything: your victories, your defeats, your fears and your concerns. Prayer doesn't need to follow a specific "method." You were made to talk to him, and if you have given your life to him, his Spirit is already in you. Don't be intimidated. Be **you**!

## Questions About Bible Study

**Q:** *What kind of Bible should I use?*

**A:** One that you will read! Seriously, find one that you can understand and that will meet your needs. The best Bible in the world sitting on the shelf does little good! However, we have various types of Bibles from which to choose. Don't be intimidated. Consider the following:

- *Find the right version for you.* Our modern Bibles have been translated from the original languages of Hebrew, Aramaic and Greek, and are quite impressive in their scholarship. Choose a version that balances readability with faithfulness to the original text. I study from a lot of versions, but faithfully use several: The English Standard Version (ESV) Bible, The New International Version (NIV) and the Passion Translation by Brian Simmons. The first two offer excellent readability and faithfulness to the original text. The Passion Translation is a labor of beauty. In it, Simmons pulls out literary creativity and the depth of the original languages into English. It also has study notes about the nuances of the original words. I use the three versions together.

- *Consider a study Bible.* If you are new to the Bible or feel lost in the story, a study Bible provides notes concerning the historical background and cross references to related passages of scriptures to help you understand the context. You have many options in study Bibles, but I prefer the Life Application Study Bible, which comes in a variety of versions.

**Q:** *I don't "get" the Bible. How can I learn to understand it?*

**A:** I can relate to your struggles. I loved God, but couldn't understand his story. Don't confuse difficulty understanding the Bible today with never understanding it in the future. The Bible was written in the common language of the day, and anyone, no matter their age, can access its treasure. However, the events take place in a much different time with much different social, religious and political customs than ours. The following tips should help:

- *Be patient.* Too many people try to read for a few days and then quit, throwing up their hands in frustration. You can understand his Word, but you need to give yourself some grace and time as you make it a priority.
- *Start well.* If the Bible is new to you, Leviticus might not be the best starting point! Ask the Holy Spirit where to begin. Consider going to the gospel of John, the book of Romans, or Galatians or Ephesians. Or start in the Psalms.

- *Ask questions.* Being in community with people who have fallen in love with God's Word is vital! Don't be ashamed to ask tons of questions. I **love** it when people text or email me Bible questions! Ask, ask, ask!
- *Learn to read in context.* This is **huge**! The Bible is one book and won't contradict itself. People come up with strange theology when they isolate verses to fit their views. Look at what is being said in light of everything around it. For difficult passages, start with established and certain truths about God in the Bible. For instance, if you are wrestling with Job, start with the fact that the Bible is overwhelmingly clear about the love and holiness of God and that he will never do wrong to mankind. So, whatever is going on there, you know that God isn't hurting Job.

**Q:** *Are there any resources to help me better study my Bible?*

**A:** Absolutely! I have lots of books in my library not because I am super smart but because I have lots of questions! God has placed us in the midst of a global "cloud of witnesses" that have walked with him on every continent and in every era. We should take advantage of the opportunity to connect with the **many** resources available to the Body of Christ. This practical counsel will help you:

- *Pay attention to the source.* In the age of the internet and mass publishing, a lot of information out there about God and his Word circulates freely, much of which simply isn't true. Some who do not believe the Bible to be his Word want to explain how to understand it. People regularly share their opinions without faithful study of the Word. Find quality resources, which are readily available. Look for people who walk in the power of God and in intimacy with him.
- *Use internet Bible Tools:* The internet offers free and accessible tools to study God's Word. Bible Gateway is an online search engine to help you find Bible topics, passages and cross references. The

Blue Letter Bible, one of my personal favorites, gives the Hebrew or Greek meaning for every verse of the Bible. You simply select a passage and hit the button for "concordance" to research the context.

- *Go to the Christian book store.* Lifeway and Family Christian Stores provide great resources that are designed to help you. If you don't have either of these stores in your area, Google "Christian bookstores" to find one near you.
- *Ask the Holy Spirit.* Without becoming super spiritual, **he** is the anointing who came to teach you all things. Get quiet before him and ask him to reveal what his Word means. Then, confirm it with someone who walks with God!

## Questions About Identity

**Q:** *I know what God says about me, but sometimes feel like a disappointment to him. What can I do?*

**A:** Again, I can relate and still have those feelings try to take root some days. These suggestions can help you walk in victory:

- *Don't trust your feelings.* As noted above, we can't depend on our feelings to speak truth. While we should acknowledge them, we instead need to rely on the Word of God to guide us.
- *Speak truth over yourself.* Go to God's Word. Find out what he says about you and declare it out loud over yourself. "I renounce the lie that I am a failure and declare the truth that I am the beloved of my Daddy!" To help with this, we've published a companion guide, "Devotions for Life in the Overflow," with 50 daily declarations about your identity.
- *Disarm the enemy.* We've been told to take every thought captive and to make it obedient to Christ. Speak directly against the lie that is attacking you and the accompanying negative feelings and command them to go.

- *Find support from your community.* If you are dealing with regular feelings of shame, failure, disappointment or others, you likely need to remove a stronghold. Start with Appendix 4 and 5 in this section. Go to your community of faith and find someone who knows their authority in Christ and get the freedom you need!

## Questions About Healing

**Q:** *What do you do when you pray for someone and nothing seems to change?*

**A:** This happens regularly to me and to nearly everyone I know, even those who "successfully" pray for healing for others. Keep the following key points in mind:

- *Don't allow your experience or lack thereof to interpret the Bible.* People often base their faith on their experience when they don't see results. Before they know it, they are praying weak and vague prayers that sound more like Hallmark cards than declarations of war from victorious princes and princesses. In the parable of persistent prayer in Luke 11, Jesus tells us to boldly and unapologetically to "keep asking, keep seeking and keep knocking" even when the door is shut. If God said that he wants to do it, he will accomplish it! Sickness is a result of the enemy's kingdom, and God came to demolish it. He healed people everywhere that he went and told us to go in his authority and do the same.
- *Be still and ask the Holy Spirit.* Too many times, I have retreated in haste when I haven't seen the immediate fruit of victory, but they call it a battle for a reason. If you are praying for something that Jesus purchased for you, and if you are not seeing results, don't worry. Don't run and hide or think that you are the "worst intercessor of the century." Stop and ask him what you need to do next. Don't rush or become intimidated.
- *Don't elevate your logic and don't give up.* Many people get stuck in healing because they want a formula that works like clockwork and when

that doesn't happen, they back away. Jesus never healed a person twice in the same way. One of the keys to healing is understanding that God came to heal, that he wants to use ordinary, messy sons and daughters and that **all** that he wants you to do is slow down and trust him. Don't worry about not getting it right. Most people who regularly walk in healing report that they prayed for countless people before they saw anything but finally determined, "I am not backing away from healing. God purchased it, and I won't be intimidated or deterred by what my eyes don't see." Take his Word at face value and don't ever give up!

**Q:** *Are there any resources that you can recommend to learn more about healing?*

**A:** Yes, you can find many great resources. Some of my favorites are: "The Essential Guide to Healing: Equipping All Christians to Pray for the Sick" by Bill Johnson and Randy Clark and "Lord, Heal Me" by my good friend, Richard Mull.

**Q:** *Like the man who came to Jesus, I really want to believe in healing but sometimes feel, "I believe, help my unbelief." What should I do?*

**A:** Do not walk in condemnation — I applaud your hunger! The following advice should encourage you:

- *Pray.* Pray for the Holy Spirit to settle the reality of his healing deep into your spirit.
- *Spend time with people who walk in healing.* Listen to their stories. Ask questions. Follow them around and pray with them for healing. Have them pray over you — receive the laying on of hands from them and power through impartation.
- *Obtain resources that deepen your faith in healing.* In addition to the previously mentioned books above, check out an amazing DVD series by Wanderlust Productions (www.wpfilm.com) that follows ordinary believers and stories of healing all around the world. You

will be encouraged by their beautiful and amazing testimonies. The DVDs are: "Finger of God," "Furious Love," "Father of Lights," "Holy Ghost," and "Holy Ghost Reborn" and as of the printing of this book, are available on Netflix.

- *Attend a Power and Love Conference.* You read my testimony in the previous pages. This incredible conference takes place at international locations. Check out the schedule at www.powerandlove.org.

## Questions About Deliverance

**Q:** *How do I know if the enemy has a stronghold in my life?*

**A:** Our enemy is a defeated foe, so we don't need to walk around, acting like a demon hides behind every bush. Satan would like nothing more than for us to obsess over him and fill our conversations about where he is or what he is doing. Don't give him that attention. Every moment of every day, lift your eyes to your King! Even so, the enemy hates us and uses deception, fear and isolation to try to torment and ensnare us. You can see a stronghold at work in the following situations:

- *Is there a pattern of behavior or a regular mindset in your life that doesn't line up with God's Word?* If you keep repeatedly trying to break an addiction or a mindset and feel exhausted but aren't experiencing freedom, a stronghold that the enemy has set up in your mind likely needs to be torn down.
- *If the answer is yes in any area, take it to your Daddy in times of intimacy.* Ask the Holy Spirit to reveal truth and to bind the enemy. If you are still struggling, go to a friend who understands their authority and pray specifically to break it. Appendices 4 and 5 have some great tools to help you!

**Q:** *I'm just an ordinary Christian. How can I lead others to freedom?*

**A:** Simply put, that's what ordinary Christians do! Jesus gave the 12 and the 72 — and us — this awesome responsibility. It isn't about your experience or giftedness but about "Christ in you, the hope of glory." Spend time with people who understand their authority and learn from them. Ask the Lord to open your understanding and pray over anyone he brings in your path for his freedom to reign in them!

## Questions About Community

**Q:** *I don't go to church. Is there another way to find real community? Isn't it enough to just spend time with my Christian friends?*

**A:** I understand the struggle. I used to hate church and only went because I didn't want God to be mad at me. Then, I realized that church isn't a chore — it's a family, a community, an army, a Body, a Bride. The Church is Christ's gift to us so that we don't have to walk alone. While you can receive encouragement from YouTube videos and books and Bible reading apps, these cannot replace the intimacy that God intends to take place in the regular coming together of the local bodies of Christ. You need to look people in the eye and let them into your heart. For many, that type of intimacy is uncomfortable, but as long as you think that connecting with others is an "option" for "one day," you won't move. He called his Church to be the hope of the whole world! Do not give up your search, but look for a church that preaches freedom and abundant life in Jesus. Look for a church that recognizes the Christian life is a joy! Even more, be vulnerable and quiet before the Holy Spirit and ask him where he wants you to go. I bless you in your journey!

# APPENDIX 3

## SCRIPTURES ABOUT YOUR POWER AND AUTHORITY IN THE KINGDOM OF GOD

"Jesus called his twelve disciples to him and gave them authority to drive out impure spirits and to heal every disease and sickness" Matthew 10:1 – Emphasis added.

## NOTES:

"**Gave**" – In Greek, the word "didomi" means "to give someone something that belongs to you for their advantage;" "to freely supply all necessary means;" and "to give a person something you want them to administer."[43] Something "given" is not based on merit and cannot be earned. Jesus "gave" the disciples "all the necessary means" for overcoming the enemy "for their advantage." He told them that it was "for our good" when he went away and sent the Holy Spirit (see John 16:7). He "gave" the disciples the authority that belonged to him because he wanted them to administer it. He gave them his power and dominion over the Kingdom just as he did in the Garden of Eden.

"**Authority**" – The word "exousia" means "the freedom to do as one chooses" and "the power of rule or government."[44] In the Kingdom of God, "authority" is God reestablishing his rule over the kingdom that the enemy set up on the earth. The enemy's reign is sin, sickness and separation from God, a rule of torment and brokenness. Jesus came with "authority" — the right to do as he wished and rule victoriously, removing all power of the enemy's kingdom. "Authority" is the power of God flowing through three specific activities: preaching the Kingdom, healing the sick, and setting the captives free. The people saw that Jesus preached the Kingdom of God with authority (See Matthew 7:29). The leaders saw that Jesus' authority made unclean spirits lose their right to stay (See Mark 1:27). Jesus gave the disciples authority to heal the sick (See Mark 3:15). These three activities are the core work of Jesus' ministry (Luke 4:18), the Kingdom of God and of a disciple. The Apostle Paul's mission was to "open their eyes from darkness to light, from the authority of the devil to God" (Acts 26:18). Authority and power move people from the enemy's reign over their body, soul or spirit to God's reign. Jesus "gave" this authority to the 12, the 72 and then to us! Authority disarms the enemy's rule and establishes God's rule in its place. All authority belongs to Jesus as he purchased it at the cross.

"Then Jesus came to them and said, "All authority in heaven and on earth has been given to me. Therefore go and make disciples of all nations, baptizing them in the name of the Father and of the Son and of the Holy Spirit, and teaching them to obey everything I have commanded you. And surely I am with you always, to the very end of the age" Matthew 28:18-20 – Emphasis added.

## NOTES:

"**Therefore, Go**" – When you see the word "therefore," find out what it's "there for." "Therefore" points to the rightful conclusion in light of what has been shared.[45] Jesus has all authority over the enemy, which was given to him by his Father. Therefore, **we** are to go make disciples because just as he was "given" authority, he has "given" authority to us (see Luke 10:19). Without access to his authority, it doesn't make any sense for him to send us out. In the Great Commission, he promised that he and his authority would be with us always. In John 14:16-18, he said: "I will ask the Father, and he will give you another advocate to help you and *be with you forever—* the Spirit of truth. The world cannot accept him, because it neither sees him nor knows him. But you know him, for *he lives with you and will be in you. I will not leave you as orphans; I will come to you*" (Emphasis added). He is "with us" because he is "in us," and his authority is "in us."

"**Make disciples**" – This passage, the "Great Commission," is the Great Mission that God has given us authority to complete. Just as Adam and Eve ruled over the dominion of creation in the garden, we are to rule within the Kingdom of God, bringing people from the reign of the enemy in their body, soul and spirit to complete restoration under the reign of their Father. We are not just on earth to "be" disciples but to "make" disciples. We have to shed the erroneous idea that disciple-making is just for pastors or well-trained ministry leaders. Every believer has this responsibility and privilege! It isn't based on our giftedness, our personality, our intellect or our social skills. Discipleship takes place when someone comes into agreement with what God offers. It isn't a "training class" full of steps; it is the authority and voice of God from heaven touching his children, often through a willing vessel like you. A "disciple" is someone "baptized" in the Father, Son and Holy Spirit. The word "baptize" means to "completely submerge" or "to dip under" so that they will be cleansed. It also means "to overwhelm."[46] We have appropriately made a big deal out of believer's baptism and that a person has been washed clean when they make a public profession of their faith. The real picture goes much deeper. A true disciple is someone "fully submerged" and overwhelmed by the love of their Father in heaven, by the cleansing that makes them acceptable to God and the complete empowering of the Holy Spirit in their whole being. To be "baptized" in the Father, Son and Holy Spirit is to be completely lost in his presence so that he overtakes you and flows through you. Disciples should learn to obey and fully give their lives to the full counsel of God: "everything" that he taught. This includes the Kingdom of God flowing through us in preaching, healing and setting the captives free.

"He appointed twelve that they might be with him and that he might send them out to preach and to have authority to drive out demons" Mark 3:14-15 – Emphasis added.

## NOTES:

These verses probably sum up the total picture of a disciple's life better than any. Jesus calls us first and predominantly to "be with Him!" As Jesus emphasized to Martha, everything flows from intimacy with God. In the place of intimacy, he breathes life, love, freedom and infinite joy upon us and then fills us to overflowing and sends us out. The word "send" is "apostello" and means "to send something to its appointed place."[47] We were created to reign with God, which was fully restored to us at the cross. From the place of intimacy, Jesus is ready to "send you to your appointed place" so that people will find life! The list of preaching and casting out demons did not exclude the ministry of healing. Just as the Old Testament referred to as "the law and the prophets" or "the law, the writings and the prophets," this ministry of preaching, healing and setting the captives free was usually listed together. However, sometimes only two of them were listed together. Since all sickness ultimately comes from the kingdom our enemy set up, this simplified statement refers to the entire ministry.

"Then Jesus went around teaching from village to village. Calling the twelve to him, he began to send them out two by two and gave them authority over impure spirits. These were his instructions: "Take nothing for the journey except a staff—no bread, no bag, no money in your belts. Wear sandals but not an extra shirt. Whenever you enter a house, stay there until you leave that town. And if any place will not welcome you or listen to you, leave that place and shake the dust off your feet as a testimony against them." They went out and preached that people should repent. They drove out many demons and anointed many sick people with oil and healed them" Mark 6:6-13 – Emphasis added.

## NOTES:

As he prepared to send his disciples out in authority, this short paragraph is the only recorded training that Jesus gave them. In a culture obsessed with learning, processing and study, we, as believers, have all too often leaned on the crutch of "I'm not ready yet." We cannot train to do the impossible. The sick are healed because the God of healing heals them through you. People are set free from the enemy because the Purchaser of their freedom flows through willing conduits like you and me. We can answer like Peter did in Acts when someone was healed: "Why do you look at us as if by our own power or godliness we made him well?" (See Acts 3:12). It isn't our power, godliness or training but the authority of God flowing through you. What we need more than training is to be vessels hungry for all of his Kingdom, love and power to operate in our lives. We need to be like the first disciples: fully dependent on God's presence and not on our knowledge.

"But about that day or hour no one knows, not even the angels in heaven, nor the Son, but only the Father. Be on guard! Be alert! You do not know when that time will come. It's like a man going away: He leaves his house and puts gives authority to his servants, each with their assigned task, and tells the one at the door to keep watch. Therefore keep watch because you do not know when the owner of the house will come back—whether in the evening, or at midnight, or when the rooster crows, or at dawn" Mark 13:32-35 – Emphasis added.

## NOTES:

Jesus shared a parable about the Kingdom of God and his return. Notice what he says: The Kingdom is like a man going away for a time. This man refers to Jesus when he left after the resurrection who promised to return for us (See John 14:2-3, Acts 1:11). When he left for heaven, he gave authority to his servants (see Acts 1:8), and gives us each an assigned task. Remember that "authority" usually refers to the three key activities. Those with authority will keep working at their appointed tasks until he comes back. This parable is a call for his servants to "keep watch" or give focused attention to something and be aware of "their assigned task" so that they can be found faithful. We are servants who have been given authority and called to give focused attention to our assigned task!

"The seventy-two returned with joy and said, "Lord, even the demons submit to us in your name." He replied, "I saw Satan fall like lightning from heaven. I have given you authority to trample on snakes and scorpions and to overcome all the power of the enemy; nothing will harm you. However, do not rejoice that the spirits submit to you, but rejoice that your names are written in heaven" Luke 10:17-20 – Emphasis added.

## NOTES:

"**Submit**" – This word "hypotasso" means to "to be put under the control of another" or "to obey."[48] These 72 unnamed disciples were shocked because the enemy had to obey the authority that Jesus had given them. When we walk in Overflow with our Father and respond to what he says, the enemy has to submit.

"**Fall**" – The word "pipto" means to "descend from a standing position to laying facedown."[49] The enemy had to "cease and desist" at the authority of Jesus through ordinary people, just like he does today!

"**Trample**" – The word "pateo" means to "crush under your feet."[50] This was what God the Father promised the enemy that the Messiah would do in Genesis 3:15. Now, Jesus gave that *same* authority to these 72, opening the ministry of ordinary people reigning over the enemy in His name.

One final note: As exciting as our right to reign is, Jesus tells us that our real reason for rejoicing comes not from our authority but from intimacy with our Father. We rejoice because we are his. From that position, he gives us authority for others to find the same joy!

"He told them, "This is what is written: The Messiah will suffer and rise from the dead on the third day, and repentance for the forgiveness of sins will be preached in his name to all nations, beginning at Jerusalem. You are witnesses of these things. I am going to send you what my Father has promised; but stay in the city until you have been clothed with power from on high" Luke 24:46-49 - Emphasis added.

## NOTES:

"**Clothed**" – The word "endyo" refers to the putting on of a shirt or garment.[51] Other scriptures use the same word to tell believers to "put on the new man" (See Ephesians 4:24, Colossians 3:10). This refers to something that is fully yours for the taking that you simply put on. We have now been "clothed" with the Holy Spirit.

"**Power**" – The word used here for "power" is "dynamis" from which we get the word "dynamite," which means "strength, power or ability, especially for performing miracles."[52] We need "power" to preach because the Kingdom of God is not merely a matter of talk or about the cohesiveness or persuasiveness of our presentation. It is fully about the power of God that flows from the intimacy with our Father (See 1 Corinthians 4:20). The Holy Spirit brings power when he comes upon our lives. We need "power" to be witnesses who help people come in to the Kingdom.

"But you will receive power when the Holy Spirit comes on you; and you will be my witnesses in Jerusalem, and in all Judea and Samaria, and to the ends of the earth" Acts 1:8 – Emphasis added.

## NOTES:

"**Receive**" – The word, "lambano" means to "grasp with the hand" and is the picture of something being offered to you that you reach out and take.[53] *Power is not earned.* It is something we simply "receive."

"For Christ did not send me to baptize, but to preach the gospel—

not with wisdom and eloquence, lest the cross of Christ be emptied of its power. For the message of the cross is foolishness to those who are perishing, but to us who are being saved it is the power of God" 1 Corinthians 1:17-18 – Emphasis added.

## NOTES:

The gospel or "good news" is a message of power not human information. Many of our methods focus on our positioning and presentation. While these might be practical, no method or tool can release "power," which comes only from God. We need to be conduits for the Holy Spirit to pour his power through us to bring others to him. Sustained power for the gospel comes only from sustained intimacy with God!

"And so it was with me, brothers and sisters. When I came to you, I did not come with eloquence or human wisdom as I proclaimed to you the testimony about God. For I resolved to know nothing while I was with you except Jesus Christ and him crucified. I came to you in weakness with great fear and trembling. My message and my preaching were not with wise and persuasive words, but with a demonstration of the Spirit's power, so that your faith might not rest on human wisdom, but on God's power" 1 Corinthians 2:1-5 – Emphasis added.

## NOTES:

Paul's full confidence in his ministry did not come from human eloquence, literally "excellence" or wisdom. His confidence came from the Overflow of knowing Jesus and a demonstration of the Holy Spirit's power, literally "making his dynamis fully manifest."

"For the kingdom of God is not a matter of talk but of power" 1 Corinthians 4:20 – Emphasis added.

## NOTES:

The Kingdom itself, the work that we have been called to do, is not a matter of talk or "speeches, discourses, reason or teaching." Our hard work to study and convince others that our position is correct is entirely fruitless apart from the Spirit's power. The Holy Spirit might very well call you to deeper study or understanding but only as we walk in intimacy with him so that his power flows through us!

"For though we live in the world, we do not wage war as the world does. The weapons we fight with are not the weapons of the world. On the contrary, they have divine power to demolish strongholds. We demolish arguments and every pretension that sets itself up against the knowledge of God, and we take captive every thought to make it obedient to Christ" 2 Corinthians 10:3-5 – Emphasis added.

## NOTES:

"**Wage war**" – We get our word "strategy" from the word "strateuo," which means to "lead soldiers to a military expedition" or to "fight."[54] The life of a disciple is described as a war between the enemy and mankind and not a casual encounter but a war in which we've been called as commanders in the army to reign victoriously under our King.

"**Weapons of divine power**" – Our weapons are not the instruments used in human warfare. Rather, they are instruments to equip believers with the very power of God. The purpose of this power is to disarm the enemy and dismantle his lies.

"**Demolish strongholds**" – We have been given power to "demolish and destroy" strongholds. The word translated "strongholds" is "ochyrma" and has a dual meaning — "a castle or fortress" and also "an argument or reasoning that fortifies itself in your mind so you rely upon it."[55] A stronghold is a lie that the enemy has forged so deeply that we have come to believe and lean or rely upon it. We live as though it were true even though it is false. Someone under a stronghold can recognize that their belief or behavior defies logic, and counsel does not help them. Instead, they need the power of God to break it. This ministry has been given to every redeemed son and daughter of God. We must understand the power that our Father has entrusted to us!

"I keep asking that the God of our Lord Jesus Christ, the glorious Father, may give you the Spirit of wisdom and revelation, so that you may know him better. I pray that the eyes of your heart may be enlightened in order that you may know the hope to which he has called you, the riches of his glorious inheritance in his holy people, and his incomparably great power for us who believe. That power is the same as the mighty strength he exerted when he raised Christ from the dead and seated him at his right hand in the heavenly realms, far above all rule and authority, power and dominion, and every name that is invoked, not only in the present age but also in the one to come. And God placed all things under his feet and appointed him to be head over everything for the church, which is his body, the fullness of him who fills everything in every way" Ephesians 1:17-23 – Emphasis added.

## NOTES:

**"Spirit of wisdom and revelation"** – Different from "book smarts," this knowledge doesn't come from diligent effort or study or understanding because you had a high SAT score. "Wisdom" is the word "sophia" and means "a broad knowledge about diverse matters."[56] God gives "wisdom" in interpreting dreams, giving sound counsel or advice or understanding how to impart and apply truth in your own life or the life of another. "Revelation" comes from the word "apocalypsis" and means "the manifestation of truth, especially things previously unknown."[57] Wisdom occurs when we are able to tell someone what to do regarding a situation. Revelation is when we see something that previously wasn't clear to us. Both flow from the God of all truth as keys to help us and others draw near to him.

**"So that you may know Him better"** – "So that" phrases in the Bible give you the intended goal of the statement. When God says that he is offering the Holy Spirit to breathe wisdom and revelation into your life, he is aiming at a specific target in your life; a specific goal that he desires to accomplish. God doesn't give his wisdom and revelation just for the sake of amassing knowledge. He doesn't want you to simply troubleshoot how to "do life better" or more efficiently. He is offering limitless knowledge that our minds cannot learn **so that** we will know our Daddy better. Everything in our lives flows from our intimacy with our Father, and he gives us supernatural wisdom and revelation so that we can see him more clearly.

**"Incomparably great power"** – The word "incomparably" or hyperballo means to "throw beyond the mark" or to "transcend or surpass" something.[58] A visual image of this word is hitting a baseball out of the ballpark and out of sight so that it travels much further than necessary. To have something given to you that is "hyperballo" is to be given more than you need to reach the goal. The word "great" is "megethos," which means something that is "great, abundant, intense and overwhelming."[59] The power that God gives to **you** as his child today is far greater, more abundant, more intense and more overwhelming than any situation that you will face for his Kingdom — so much more power than you need or know! He defines it as the same power that raised Jesus from the dead, which now lives in us! He said it far exceeds any power of any enemy. The Apostle John put it like this: "Greater is the one who lives in you than the one who lives in the world" (1 John 4:4). We plus the Holy Spirit is always a majority! We've been "given" greater power than the enemy so that we can use it as Jesus intended: to destroy the works of the devil (1 John 3:8)!

# ⟶ APPENDIX 4 ⟵

## TOOLS TO LEAD YOURSELF OR OTHERS IN SURRENDER
*by Len Harper and Chuck Ammons*

Your great Daddy and King has commissioned you to make disciples of all nations, teaching them to obey everything that Jesus commanded and to be fully baptized or immersed into the Kingdom of the Father, Son and Spirit. One of the most beautiful ways that we reign with our King is by helping another person recognize and remove strongholds of their enemy so that they can walk in freedom and fully receive all that their Daddy offers. This ministry isn't just for pastors but for sons and daughters, so don't be overwhelmed. You were born for this! Use this prayer guide to bring each area before the Holy Spirit. You can use it for your own walk, too. In everything, take your time, be still and listen to him. The Spirit of God is the best teacher! May the kingdom of the enemy flee, and may you see "Christ in you, the hope of glory" (Colossians 1:27)!

These questions are designed to prepare people to uncover any open doors in their life. Encourage them to spend personal time before the Holy Spirit with the Open Doors List (see Appendix 5). Ask them, "What do you want God to do in your life today?"

## Questions to determine source of strongholds:

### 1. Unconfessed sin against God:

Ask, "Did you allow God to search your heart for any and all unconfessed sin, such as sexual sin, occult activity, false religions and generational sins? Have you forgiven yourself? What do you fear most that someone will find out about your past?"

Confess the sin to God, and cast out any spirits that came in through that open door. Then, seal it shut with the blood of Jesus!

## 2. Unresolved father/mother issues:

Ask, "How would you describe your relationship with your father? What do you need most to forgive him of? How would you describe your relationship with your mother? What do you need most to forgive her of?"

Lead them through forgiving father/mother. Break ungodly soul ties with your father/mother and cast out any spirits that came in through that access point and close it off!

## 3. Unforgiven judgments or words against others:

Ask, "Did you complete your forgiveness list? Who was the most difficult for you to forgive? (Usually, this is the person who hurt them the deepest.) Who was next? What patterns of conflict do you see in your life?"

Break ungodly soul ties with the person that they forgave and cast out any spirits that came in through that access point and close it off!

## 4. Unfulfilled vows/covenants/agreements:

Ask, "Have you asked God and others to forgive you of broken promises and vows? Have you forgiven others for breaking promises and vows to you?"

Break ungodly soul ties related to those broken vows and cast out any spirits that came in through that access point and close it off!

## 5. Unresolved traumatic events:

Ask, "What do you fear most? What is the most traumatic thing that has happened to you? What would be next?"

Forgive the people that caused the trauma and cast out any spirits that came in through that access point with the blood of Jesus!

Evidences of emotional strongholds rooted in trauma:

a)  Inability to trust others/make deep friendships/trust God
b)  Anger/rage
c)  Depression
d)  Hopelessness
e)  Loneliness, feelings of abandonment
f)  Stoic, showing little or no emotions
g)  No passion/drive
h)  Obsessive/compulsive behavior.
i)  Addictions, such as eating, gambling, pornography, etc.
j)  Boring, unfulfilled life

# APPENDIX 5

## WALKING IN FREEDOM: OPEN DOORS LIST

Jesus came to set us completely free from every fruit of the enemy's kingdom. Satan's power in our lives comes from our agreement with his lies as we open doors to allow his kingdom in, either knowingly or unknowingly. Get in a quiet place and ask the Holy Spirit to speak clearly to you about any area in your life where the enemy's power and influence needs to be broken. Be vulnerable. Be honest. Don't rush. Your Daddy loves you. He bought it all and waits to meet you in the place of intimacy.

As the Holy Spirit reveals areas that he wants to heal, you might find that you need someone in your biblical community who understands their authority to help you walk out freedom. Admitting that you need help doesn't show weakness — our Daddy made us part of a family of encouragement and empowerment so that we could walk out these areas together!

### OCCULT:
Our enemy is obsessed with trying to counterfeit God's power through offering secret knowledge that actually leads to slavery (see Deuteronomy 18:9-12).

List all dealings you have had with the occult. Examples include: Ouija, séance, horoscope, new age, superstition, witchcraft, oaths, Santeria, palm reader, roots, etc.

### Prayer Declaration (Occult):
*Lord Jesus, I confess seeking counterfeit information and power from satan and his kingdom that should have come from God Almighty. I confess as sin (<u>name all occult sins from your list</u>) and even those I do not remember. Lord, I repent and renounce these*

*sins and ask you to forgive me. In the name of Jesus, I now close the door to all occult practices. Satan, I rebuke you, in the name of Jesus, and I command all spirits to leave me now.*

## ADDICTIONS:

We were made to give our entire allegiance to our King as "all that we need." Addictions are counterfeits that substitute to fill a void in our heart or to numb a pain, but our King longs to fill that space instead.

List any addiction or compulsive behaviors. List any activities that are holding you in bondage or that you turn to for comfort or fulfillment, such as alcohol, drugs, nicotine, pornography, sex, gambling, approval, etc.

### Prayer Declaration (Addictions):

*Lord, I repent for (list every addiction) and the way I trusted it to bring me fulfillment, satisfaction or used it to numb pain in my life. I repent for any joy that I found in this counterfeit savior. I renounce it and break all compulsion to continue in this activity. I look to you alone as my joy and will not chase fulfillment in my circumstances. I command every spirit of addiction to be entirely removed from me and for truth to wash over me. Thank you for your amazing grace!*

## FEARS /PHOBIAS:

Our enemy thrives on fear and seeks to keep us in bondage through chronic worry, anxiety and stress. He uses these major entry points for his kingdom, but you can be completely free because you've been loved by the One who didn't give you a spirit of fear (2 Timothy 1:7). In fact, his perfect love casts it out (1 John 4:18).

List any situations about which you find yourself regularly worrying, such as fear of failure, fear of rejection, finances, health, relationships, future, etc. List any places of chronic stress or anxiety. List any particular phobias that torment or terrify you.

## Prayer Declaration (Fears/Phobias):

*Daddy, you haven't given me a spirit of fear. I acknowledge that fear is from my enemy, and I renounce my agreement with (list every fear and phobia). I repent for not trusting you to give me all that I need and that you are sufficient to hold my life fully and firmly in your hands. I give you every emotion tied to fear and declare that they are not mine to have. I command every enemy and every spirit of fear to flee from me in Jesus' Name.*

## ABUSE, HURTS AND REJECTION:

One of the most heartbreaking 'open doors' is through trauma at the hands of another person, especially someone who you trusted. This often occurs during childhood. Though our enemy relentlessly attacks us, our great God is the Healer of all and already took every wound. He wants you to bring these hurts to him.

List all memories that the Holy Spirit brings to mind when you have endured abuse — physical, emotional or sexual — or any traumatic bullying, hurts, rejection or neglect, either real or perceived.

### Prayer Declaration (Abuse, Hurts, and Rejection):

*Jesus, I bring you my brokenness. As strange as it sounds to say, I forgive you, Lord. I know that you never do wrong, but I forgive any feeling in my heart that you weren't there for me or that you didn't prevent this from happening. I choose to trust you with my life. I break the trauma off my emotions. I silence the enemy from telling me that I cannot trust you. I choose to forgive (list every person involved in your abuse or rejection) and in Jesus' Name, I command every spirit that has tormented me to leave now.*

## BROKEN COVENANTS, VOWS AND CURSES:

We serve the God who is a God of his Word. He calls us to make our "yes, yes" and our "no, no," but when we make commitments that we don't fulfill, these broken commitments can hold us in bondage.

List all broken covenants and vows of the past, such as marriages, church membership, failing to pay bills or curses spoken over your life.

## Prayer Declaration (Broken Covenants):

*Lord Jesus, I confess that I have broken covenant/vows with you. I recognize this as sin, and I ask you, Lord, to forgive me now for breaking these between you and (name each relationship and situation out loud). I now use my authority in Jesus Christ and break any curses that this has brought upon me and order every spirit in satan's kingdom to leave me now.*

## DEATH (including miscarriages and abortions):

Death was never supposed to take place. We were designed to live forever, so a ruthless enemy wants to bring trauma or convince us to make wrong agreements through the heartbreaking loss of a loved one when we are most vulnerable.

List the death of any loved ones to whom you were especially close.

## Prayer Declaration (Death):

*Daddy in heaven, I bring you my pain and heartbreak. Thank you for the gift of (list each person) in my life and the joy that they brought me. I break any trauma regarding learning about their passing and all of the emotions that accompany my grief. I ask you to completely heal me, and I choose to trust you regarding their eternity. I command all torment to be silent and for every spirit of the enemy to flee.*

For abortions: *Lord, I repent for my part in ending this life that you began. I cannot bear this great grief that has filled my heart. Thank you for your endless and beautiful forgiveness that washes away every stain, and thank you that you hold my child. I break every agreement with abortion and command every tormenting spirit to be silent and to leave me now, in Jesus' Name. Fill me with your peace!*

## UNFORGIVENESS:

Just as God forgives us, he calls us to trust him to be the only judge of others and to release those who've wronged us to him (see Matthew 6:14-15).

List all people from childhood to the present, dead or alive, who God brings to mind that you hold resentment against or need to forgive.

## Prayer Declaration (Unforgiveness):

*Lord, I confess that I have not loved but have resented (list each person individually) and have held unforgiveness in my heart for (list the specific offense - be real). I know that my enemy is never flesh and blood and that this person is made in your image and that you have great dreams for them. God, you saw what happened, and you promise that you will deal with it righteously. I thank you that I am not a pawn to be stolen from, but that you will meet **all** of my needs, according to your riches of your glory. As I need grace and freedom, please work in my life and theirs, freeing us from every scheme of the enemy. I choose to forgive and release all judgments against (person). Now, I forgive and accept myself in the name of Jesus.*

## SEXUAL SIN:

God intended sexuality to be expressed only within the loving, committed marriage relationship between one man and one woman and even calls lust "adultery of the heart." He wants us to have completely pure marriages (see Matthew 5:27-30, Hebrews 13:4).

List all people who you have been sexually involved with outside of marriage. Examples include: premarital sex, extramarital sex, rape, molestation, incest, homosexuality/lesbianism, bestiality and even your spouse if you came together sexually prior to marriage. List any sexual sins you have participated in, such as pornography, lust, masturbation, impure thoughts, emotional adultery, or flirting with someone other than your spouse.

## Prayer Declaration (Sexual Sin):

*Thank you, Jesus, for making me intentionally with a beautiful plan for my sexuality. I invite you to be the Lord of all my life, especially my sexuality. I repent for every place where I have traded the distinct and pure beauty that you planned for me with sexual sins. I ask you to set me free of all sexual sin and from any spirit associated with them (list any sins in which you have participated, repenting even for the temporary thrill they brought). I ask you to free me from ungodly soul ties to everyone with whom I have had an ungodly sexual relationship. (List every person you have been sexually involved with outside of marriage). I recognize that this is sin, and I do not want to continue in these relationships. I invite you to speak truth over me about my full sexuality. May I see it like you do. Any spirit in satan's kingdom that has entered me through any of these sexual sins, I order you to leave me now by the authority that I have in Jesus Christ and declare that you have no further right in my spirit, soul and body. In the Name of Jesus.*

## SOUL TIES:

A "soul tie" is simply a connection between you and another person that "ties" the two of you together. There can be godly ties of love and ungodly ties, such as control and manipulation.

List all people, dead or alive, who have had an ungodly control over you or with whom you have had an ungodly dependence, such as parents, bosses, teachers, coaches, siblings, church leaders, etc. This includes anyone with whom you have had a sexual relationship (see above.)

## Prayer Declaration (Soul Ties):

*Lord, I know that my life is to be under only your control and that I do not have room for two masters. I repent for every ungodly soul tie and come to you to sever all control, manipulation and dysfunction. (List each person, repenting for the specific wrong agreement. Forgive them and yourself). I now use the authority that I have in Jesus Christ and break and renounce these ungodly soul ties and command any demonic spirits that tormented me through these relationships to leave me now.*

# BIBLIOGRAPHY

### Come Away
*Brock Human*
2007. Capitol CMG Genesis
(Admin. by Capitol CMG Publishing)

### The Zondervan Pictorial Encyclopedia of the Bible
*Ralph Earle*
1975. Grand Rapids: Zondervan

### Epic: The Story God is Telling
*John Eldredge*
2004. Nashville: Thomas Nelson Publishers

### Waking the Dead: The Glory of a Heart Fully Alive
*John Eldredge*
2006. Nashville: Thomas Nelson Publishers

### Love Does: Discover a Secretly Incredible Life in an Ordinary World
*Bob Goff*
2012. Nashville: Nelson Books

### The Weight of Glory
*C.S. Lewis*
1949. New York: HarperOne, 2001

### Running Just to Catch Myself
*Mark Schultz*
2003. Crazy Romaine Music
(Admin. by the Loving Company)

# RESOURCES

## The Drama of Scripture
*Craig G. Bartholomew and Michael W. Goheen*

## Epic: The Story God is Telling
*John Eldredge*

## Love Does
*Bob Goff*

## The Essential Guide to Healing
*Bill Johnson and Randy Clark*

## Lord, Heal Me
*Richard Mull*

## The Jesus Training Manual
*Richard Mull*

## The Passion Translation Bible
*Brian Simmons*

## Life Application Study Bible
*Tyndale Publishers*

## Wanderlust Productions Films
A beautiful and amazing journey that follows ordinary believers all around the world in stories of healing. The individual DVDs are "Finger of God," "Furious Love," "Father of Lights," "Holy Ghost" and "Holy Ghost Reborn." (www.wpfilm.com)

# ENDNOTES

1   http://www.azlyrics.com/lyrics/hillsongunited/oceanswherefeetmayfail.html. Accessed July 21, 2016.

2   http://www.azlyrics.com/lyrics/jesusculture/comeawayletmein.html. Accessed June 10, 2016.

3   https://www.blueletterbible.org/lang/lexicon/lexicon.cfm?strongs=G3306&t=KJV

4   C.S. Lewis, The Weight of Glory. p26 https://books.google.cat/booksid=WNTT_8NW_ qwC&printsec=front-cover&dq=cs+lewis+the+weight+of+glory&hl=en&sa=X&ved=0ahUKEwim7t6o7aPNAhUG1mMKHTXMC-CkQ6AEIlzAA#v=onepage&q= Accessed June 12, 2016

5   https://www.blueletterbible.org/lang/lexicon/lexicon.cfm?strongs=G5046&t=NIV

6   https://www.blueletterbible.org/lang/lexicon/lexicon.cfm?strongs=G3089&t=NIV

7   https://www.blueletterbible.org/lang/lexicon/lexicon.cfm?strongs=G2041&t=NIV

8   https://www.blueletterbible.org/lang/lexicon/lexicon.cfm?strongs=G2641&t=NIV

9   https://www.blueletterbible.org/lang/lexicon/lexicon.cfm?strongs=G4878&t=NIV

10   https://www.blueletterbible.org/lang/lexicon/lexicon.cfm?strongs=G5182&t=NIV

11   https://www.blueletterbible.org/lang/lexicon/lexicon.cfm?strongs=G4657&t=NIV

12   https://www.blueletterbible.org/lang/lexicon/lexicon.cfm?strongs=G3126&t=NIV

13   "I Have Decided to Follow Jesus," attributed to S. Sundar Singh. Public Domain. Accessed June 15, 2016. http://library.timelesstruths.org/music/I_Have_Decided_to_Follow_Jesus/

14   https://www.google.com/?gws_rd=ssl#q=define+consumer. Accessed July 21, 2016.

15   http://www.churchleaders.com/pastors/pastor-articles/139575-7-startling-facts-an-up-close-look-at-church-attendance-in-america.html. Accessed July 21, 2016.

16   https://www.blueletterbible.org/lang/lexicon/lexicon.cfm?strongs=G4137&t=NIV

17   https://www.blueletterbible.org/lang/lexicon/lexicon.cfm?strongs=G3875&t=NIV

18   https://www.blueletterbible.org/lang/lexicon/lexicon.cfm?strongs=G5545&t=NIV

19   http://library.timelesstruths.org/music/Jesus_Loves_Me/. Accessed Aug. 3, 2016

20   https://www.blueletterbible.org/lang/lexicon/lexicon.cfm?strongs=G949&t=NIV

21   http://religionnews.com/2013/04/04/poll-americans-love-the-bible-but-dont-read-it-much/ Accessed July 21, 2016.

22   John Eldredge, "Epic." Nelson Books. P. 7 and 8

23   Accessed June 20, 2016. http://www.azlyrics.com/lyrics/markschultz/runningjusttocatchmyself.html

24   John Eldredge, "Waking the Dead." Nelson Books. P. 14

25   https://www.blueletterbible.org/lang/lexicon/lexicon.cfm?strongs=H3045&t=NIV

26   https://www.blueletterbible.org/lang/lexicon/lexicon.cfm?strongs=G4161&t=NIV

27   https://www.blueletterbible.org/lang/lexicon/lexicon.cfm?Strongs=G40&t=KJV

28   https://www.blueletterbible.org/lang/lexicon/lexicon.cfm?Strongs=G3364&t=KJV

29   https://www.blueletterbible.org/lang/lexicon/lexicon.cfm?Strongs=G27&t=KJV

30   Bob Goff, "Love Does," Thomas Nelson, p. 194

31   https://www.blueletterbible.org/lang/lexicon/lexicon.cfm?Strongs=G266&t=KJV

32   https://www.blueletterbible.org/lang/lexicon/lexicon.cfm?Strongs=G4137&t=KJV

33   https://www.blueletterbible.org/lang/lexicon/lexicon.cfm?Strongs=H1616&t=NIV

34   https://www.blueletterbible.org/lang/lexicon/lexicon.cfm?Strongs=G3581&t=NIV

35   https://www.blueletterbible.org/lang/lexicon/lexicon.cfm?Strongs=G3941&t=NIV

36   https://www.blueletterbible.org/lang/lexicon/lexicon.cfm?Strongs=G1577&t=NIV

37   https://www.blueletterbible.org/lang/lexicon/lexicon.cfm?Strongs=G4342&t=NIV

38   https://www.blueletterbible.org/lang/lexicon/lexicon.cfm?Strongs=G2842&t=NIV

39   Ralph Earle, "The Zondervan Pictorial Encyclopedia of the Bible," Zondervan, p. 606

40   https://www.blueletterbible.org/lang/lexicon/lexicon.cfm?Strongs=G941&t=NIV

41   https://www.blueletterbible.org/lang/lexicon/lexicon.cfm?Strongs=G1843&t=NIV

42   https://www.google.com/#q=definition+conquest

43   https://www.blueletterbible.org/lang/lexicon/lexicon.cfm?Strongs=G1325&t=NIV

44   https://www.blueletterbible.org/lang/lexicon/lexicon.cfm?Strongs=G1849&t=KJV

45   https://www.blueletterbible.org/lang/lexicon/lexicon.cfm?Strongs=G3767&t=NIV

46   https://www.blueletterbible.org/lang/lexicon/lexicon.cfm?Strongs=G907&t=NIV

47   https://www.blueletterbible.org/lang/lexicon/lexicon.cfm?Strongs=G649&t=NIV

48   https://www.blueletterbible.org/lang/lexicon/lexicon.cfm?Strongs=G5293&t=NIV

49   https://www.blueletterbible.org/lang/lexicon/lexicon.cfm?Strongs=G4098&t=NIV

50   https://www.blueletterbible.org/lang/lexicon/lexicon.cfm?Strongs=G3961&t=NIV

51   https://www.blueletterbible.org/lang/lexicon/lexicon.cfm?Strongs=G1746&t=NIV

52   https://www.blueletterbible.org/lang/lexicon/lexicon.cfm?Strongs=G1411&t=NIV

53   https://www.blueletterbible.org/lang/lexicon/lexicon.cfm?Strongs=G2983&t=NIV

54   https://www.blueletterbible.org/lang/lexicon/lexicon.cfm?Strongs=G4754&t=NIV

55   https://www.blueletterbible.org/lang/lexicon/lexicon.cfm?Strongs=G3794&t=NIV

56   https://www.blueletterbible.org/lang/lexicon/lexicon.cfm?Strongs=G4678&t=NIV

57   https://www.blueletterbible.org/lang/lexicon/lexicon.cfm?Strongs=G602&t=NIV

58   https://www.blueletterbible.org/lang/lexicon/lexicon.cfm?Strongs=G5235&t=NIV

59   https://www.blueletterbible.org/lang/lexicon/lexicon.cfm?Strongs=G3174&t=NIV

Made in the USA
Lexington, KY
23 September 2018